TREATING PATIENTS WITH ALCOHOL AND OTHER DRUG PROBLEMS

Psychologists in Independent Practice

Leon VandeCreek, Series Editor

TREATING PATIENTS
WITH ALCOHOL AND
OTHER DRUG PROBLEMS:
AN INTEGRATED APPROACH

ROBERT D. MARGOLIS
AND
JOAN E. ZWEBEN

AMERICAN PSYCHOLOGICAL ASSOCIATION
WASHINGTON, DC

Published by the
American Psychological Association
750 First Street, NE
Washington, DC 20002

Copies may be ordered from
American Psychological Association
APA Order Department
P.O. Box 92984
Washington, DC 20090-2984

In the UK and Europe, copies may be ordered from
American Psychological Association
3 Henrietta Street
Covent Garden, London
WC2E 8LU England

Typeset in Palatino by EPS Group Inc., Easton, MD

Printer: Capital City Press, Montpelier, VT
Cover designer: Minker Design, Bethesda, MD
Technical / Production editor: Tanya Y. Alexander

Library of Congress Cataloging-in-Publication Data
Margolis, Robert D.
   Treating patients with alcohol and other drug problems : an integrated approach / by Robert D. Margolis, Joan E. Zweben.
      p.   cm.
   Includes bibliographical references.
   ISBN 1-55798-518-9 (pbk.)
   1. Substance Abuse—Treatment.   I. Zweben, Joan E.   II. Title.
   [DNLM: 1. Substance Abuse—therapy.   2. Alcoholism—therapy.
3. Psychotherapy—methods.   WM 270 M329t 1998]
RC564.M29   1998
616.86'06—DC21   97-42378
DNLM/DLC
for Library of Congress   CIP

British Library Cataloguing-in-Publication Data
A CIP record is available from the British Library

Printed in the United States of America
First edition

To Karen Margolis
and to our parents,
Ely and Marjorie Margolis
and
Benjamin and Ruth Zweben

Contents

Acknowledgments

I (Robert Margolis) would like to thank my colleagues at Ridgeview Institute for the opportunity to develop and direct a treatment program for adolescents for the past 10 years. I also would like to thank my friends and colleagues who are in recovery from alcohol and drug problems. They have taught me more about the disorder than anyone else. Norma Simon first encouraged me to write this book. Most important, I would like to thank my wife, Karen. Her contribution to this book has been enormous. Editing, rewriting, searching for references, and typing are some of the tasks she performed. I have no doubt that this book would have been less informative and certainly less readable without Karen's help. Joan Zweben and I express our profound gratitude for this unselfish effort.

Since 1979, I (Joan Zweben) have had the pleasure of working with colleagues in building a comprehensive alcohol and drug treatment program in which I had the resources to develop specialized services. The superb leadership of these affiliated organizations by Susan Wengrofsky, Marta Obuchowsky, and Bruce Jack, as well as their management teams and staff, created an environment in which all of us grew, along with our patients. It is this kind of sustained experience that deepened my understanding as a clinician and contributed much of what I have to offer in this book.

We would also like to thank several people who worked specifically on the manuscript. Stephanie Brown and George De Leon gave us comprehensive and thoughtful reviews prior to the last revision. These commentaries strengthened our book, although Brown and De Leon are in no way responsible for its shortcomings. Mary Walther, Julie Kahn, Suzanne Conklin, Emily Worthington, Al Roth, and Robert Zimmerman provided various forms of technical assistance that improved and facilitated completion of the book.

TREATING PATIENTS
WITH ALCOHOL AND
OTHER DRUG PROBLEMS

Introduction

This book was written for clinicians as well as those who are preparing to become practitioners in the field of mental health and substance abuse problems. We have believed for a long time that there is a need for a text that introduces the student to the field of alcohol and other drug (AOD) problems and that focuses on theory, assessment, and treatment from a variety of different perspectives. In presenting different theoretical models and approaches to assessment and treatment, we have attempted to point out commonalities as well as controversial issues that inevitably arise from the intersection of different perspectives. We believe that a knowledge of these issues is especially important today because of the increased demand by professionals, third-party payers, and consumers for demonstrated evidence of proficiency in these areas. The certificate of proficiency offered by the American Psychological Association's College of Professional Psychology is a prime example of the recent focus on documented proficiency.

This book also is written for a range of practitioners, from clinicians in a variety of treatment settings to those in specialty addiction treatment settings. For several decades epidemiological studies have demonstrated that alcohol and drug use are so widespread in clinical populations that practitioners cannot assume that it is not an issue even in the absence of warning signs. Instead, alcohol and drug use need to be ruled out, not in. Yet the more experienced the clinician, the less likelihood he or she has any systematic training in addressing these problems. Mild-to-moderate problems with alcohol and drugs can and should be handled by the therapist who has the patient in treatment for other presenting problems. For many of these patients, a little attention to the problem goes a long way because the therapist is in a prime position to do early intervention. It is especially important for those in supervisory roles to update their knowledge to ensure that those in training will be adequately prepared for the clinical populations they will face.

For patients with severe problems (who often minimize the effect of their alcohol and drug use when they present to psychotherapists in the community), effective referral requires knowledge of the treating agency to whom the therapist is directing the patient. Even in situations where referral to a specialized treatment center is indicated, the therapist can continue to play a vital role in the treatment process. This role may involve serving as primary or family therapist or monitoring care as the patient moves through the continuum of treatment. In any case, the therapist who is knowledgeable about addiction treatment is better prepared to support patients and family members through this difficult process. In this book the authors describe the major addiction treatment modalities and the types of patients appropriate for them. They also describe the basic assumptions and operating principles of treatment modalities in an effort to minimize the miscommunication that occurs when professionals from different "cultures" attempt to collaborate on the patient's care.

We hope that the book will broaden the perspective of psychologists already working in addiction treatment settings. It is typical even for practitioners in the field to be unfamiliar with major modalities other than those with whom they regularly interact, particularly if the populations served, basic assumptions, and clinical practices are different from their own. For example, it is common for those working in hospital-based inpatient settings treating insured patients to be unfamiliar with methadone maintenance despite the fact that it is one of the major treatment modalities for opiate use. Such lack of familiarity can result in inappropriate recommendations, and at best it makes it less likely that the patient will actually connect with and engage with an appropriate treatment modality. Broader knowledge of the available resources will assist the therapist to help the patient become more "treatment ready," even as the therapist becomes more skilled at dealing with alcohol and drug issues in ongoing therapy.

Addiction treatment settings are designed for those with severe problems who arrive relatively willing to acknowledge they have a problem and to begin to address it. Although patients are usually ambivalent, addiction treatment settings start from the premise that focus on AOD use is appropriate. In other settings (e.g., private therapists' offices, mental health programs, homeless shelters, criminal justice settings, social services), patients arrive with minimal awareness of the relationship between alcohol and drug use and their other problems or with some awareness and resistance to focusing on it. Alcohol and drug use influences feeling states and behavior long before people meet criteria for addiction. When patients have a coexisting disorder, the impact is often magnified. Therapists are often unaware of the potential influence on premature dropout and failure to progress in treatment. When they do become aware that alcohol and drug use might be a problem, they seek to refer the patient to self-help meetings, specialty treatment settings, or both. Many clinicians resist the idea of learning to address such problems themselves, striving instead to increase their effectiveness at referral. Although referral is certainly appropriate for some, we hope that this book will enhance the confidence and skill of the psychotherapist in addressing alcohol and drug use in the context of their ongoing work.

Therapeutic Orientations: Abstinence and Harm Reduction

It is important to clarify some of our basic positions and biases on controversial issues. We believe that AOD disorders are best understood from a biopsychosocial model. There are a variety of factors from genetic vulnerabilities to traumatic life events to family and social dynamics that can help to propel the individual into a drug-using lifestyle (see chap. 2 in this book). Furthermore, we believe that AOD disorders can correctly be considered as existing along a continuum ranging from use to dependence characterized by increasing loss of control and increasing functional impairment. We also believe, however, that once individuals reach a certain stage in their chemical abuse they move beyond a point at which their consumption of AOD is voluntary, or at least potentially under their control, to a point at which their consumption of AOD is involuntary and beyond their control. This is the point that the fourth edition of the *Diagnostic and Statistical Manual of Mental Disorders* (American Psychiatric Association, 1994) defines as dependence (see chap. 3 in this book), the point that others might label as addiction or alcoholism, and the point that Alcoholics Anonymous (AA) refers to as "crossing the wall."

We agree with Alan Leshner, the director of the National Institute on Drug Abuse (NIDA), when he stated that the clinical condition of addiction is a "biobehavioral phenomenon" (Leshner, 1997) characterized by a movement from a state in which AOD use is at least under some degree of voluntary control to a state in which AOD use is both compulsive and uncontrollable. Leshner characterized addiction as a "different state" from that of abuse. In describing the difference between addiction and abuse, Leshner pointed out that he was not describing the difference between physical and psychological dependence. He saw that difference as not being a meaningful distinction from a clinical perspective. Drugs such as cocaine and methamphetamine produce little or no physical dependence, but they are among the most highly addictive drugs for humans and animals. Rather, the distinction is based on the breakdown of "physical control systems, motivational control systems, and associative memory systems" (Leshner, 1997) that characterize the behavior and experience of the addicted individual. The involuntary, out-of-control nature of drug addiction is a function of fundamental brain changes brought on by the drug use itself (Leshner, 1997). In support of this view, Leshner referred to the latest brain imaging research: "People use drugs and then, at different rates for different individuals, it's as if a switch flipped in their brains and they moved from one state to another state" (Leshner, 1997), a state of some voluntary control to a state of uncontrollable compulsive use.

The fundamental point, in our opinion, is not whether addiction is caused by brain changes, psychosocial factors, or a combination of factors but that addiction is a primary disorder, different from abuse. This primary disorder is characterized by a loss of control and increasing use despite negative consequences. Our position results both from our understanding of the scientific evidence and from our extensive clinical experience with these individuals. It has profound implications for our work with patients with AOD problems.

In most of what we do, we operate from an abstinence-based model. Our recommendation to patients who meet the criteria for dependence is complete abstention from alcohol and illicit drugs and use of psychoactive medications only as prescribed by physicians familiar with the patient's history and knowledgeable about addiction. This does not mean that we terminate those who cannot or will not become or remain abstinent but that we endorse abstinence as the goal offering the widest margin of safety and potential benefit.

This emphasis grows out of our work in specialty addiction treatment, in which most of our patients have spent a significant portion of their life conducting a personal experiment on controlled alcohol and drug use to the detriment of school and work performance, relationships, and health. Encouraging patients to prolong this experiment serves no useful purpose and may place the therapist at some risk for liability. However, even with patients whose history is less clear-cut and whose use appears to be mild to moderate, the abstinence model allows the therapist to bypass many ambiguities. Are patients minimizing their drinking or drug use? Is moderate alcohol consumption exacerbating their depression? Is patients' difficulty accessing feelings related to their weekly marijuana consumption? Is the intractable marital bickering related to the moderate but nonetheless disinhibiting amount of wine the couple consumes when they reunite after work and begin to try to talk?

Given the individual variability in responses to alcohol and drugs, these are questions that have no unequivocal answer. At minimum, complete abstinence (even for a relatively brief period) provides an opportunity for patient and therapist to understand the impact of alcohol and drug use more clearly. Certainly, many will object to this suggestion, even for the short term. However, it appears to us that those patients most highly invested in some form of controlled use are precisely those with attachments and vulnerabilities that make it unlikely that they will succeed in moderating their consumption.

Harm reduction models are increasingly in the spotlight, with good reason. Harm reduction is a public health approach intended to reduce the harm done to alcohol and drug users, their loved ones, and communities. It acknowledges that there are many people who are unwilling to give up their alcohol and drug use or unable to access addiction treatment, and there is merit to helping them reduce the damage caused to themselves and others. Joan Zweben offers harm reduction activities oriented to these public health goals: methadone maintenance not only for patients who are committed to full recovery but also for those merely seeking to reduce some of the negative consequences of their use; a harm reduction center for street drug users unable or unwilling to access treatment; and outreach and education (e.g., clean needles, safer sex) to reduce HIV transmission. In this context, abstinence is seen as the highest form of harm reduction, but not the only form.

Abstinence-oriented addiction treatment, with all its failings, has been well documented to reduce or eliminate illicit drug use and associated crime and to improve health status (including psychiatric status), employment, and family functioning. These improvements occur despite the fact that many do not achieve long-term continuous abstinence but instead have lapses and relapses, perhaps for years. It is accomplishing harm reduction goals even when it does not achieve the gold standard of continuous abstinence. In this sense, harm reduction coexists naturally within an abstinence-oriented approach, particularly when clinicians appreciate that improvement is fostered by retaining the patient in treatment, not terminating him or her prematurely. It is not possible to blend these philosophies within all settings. Staff in residential treatment have the responsibility to maintain safety in the facility, and allowing active drug users to remain in residence has a contagion effect that is unacceptable. Outpatient treatment, however, offers greater flexibility to move the patient in and out of activities, thus continuing treatment for the individual while reducing the negative impact of a serious relapse on others.

Debate about harm reduction is increasing in visibility, with proponents often polarized, insisting one approach is superior to the other. We do not wish to participate in that process. However, we do view abstinence as the preferred goal, not only for those with severe problems but also for those with lesser problems. This does not mean that we take a punitive approach toward those who continue their alcohol and drug use, but neither do we suggest that moderation goals can achieve the same benefits. Moderation management approaches for alcohol are enjoying a resurgence of interest, but they have not been the subject of extensive, long-term, careful study by criteria that allow comparison with abstinence-oriented approaches. It also is relevant that the amounts of alcohol usually designated as "moderate" are usually well above those considered to be devoid of negative health and psychosocial consequences. Other harm reduction approaches, such as HIV education and counseling, are valid in their own right, but we prefer to offer them with encouragement to become fully abstinent and access to resources to assist in doing so.

Terminology

We have used a number of different terms in discussing the spectrum of AOD abuse disorders. In addition to AOD abuse disorders, we have used the following terms: substance abuse, substance-related disorders, substance dependence, chemical dependence, addiction, alcoholism, alcohol and drug abuse, and alcohol and drug dependence. Some points should help to clarify the meaning of these terms. The term *abuse* is a broad term that refers to any maladaptive use of a psychoactive substance. The term *substance abuse* encompasses dependence. The term *dependence* refers to a more severe form of abuse characterized by a habitual use of a substance that is taken more frequently and in larger amounts over time, leading to increasingly negative consequences. The line between abuse and dependence is often difficult to discern, but an individual is generally considered to be dependent on a substance when attempts to quit or cut back have been unsuccessful even in the face of increasingly negative consequences. This is explained in more detail in chapter 3, along with the associated information from the fourth edition of the *Diagnostic and Statistical Manual of Mental Disorders*. The terms *alcoholic, addict, alcoholism,* and *addiction* refer to individuals or conditions related to dependence. Thus, an alcoholic is, by definition, substance dependent. In deciding which terms to use in which context, we have tried to be consistent with the terminology that is most commonly used in a given context. For example, when discussing private treatment centers, we do not refer to AOD abuse treatment centers but to addiction treatment centers. When discussing public-sector or psychological treatment approaches, we are more likely to use terms such as AOD abuse or substance abuse.

Both of us are clinicians who are continuously engaged in teaching and writing. As such, we have endeavored to address complex clinical issues by drawing on whatever research is available, offering clinical opinions on which there is widespread consensus when possible, and offering our own personal views on matters that are controversial or on which there appears to be no prevailing consensus. We have attempted to distinguish these sources in our writing.

The research base in many areas of the addiction field is enormous and in other areas it is sparse. For example, it would be difficult to exhaustively report the work done on the genetics of alcoholism, efficacy and safety of methadone maintenance, or the biomedical factors involved in cocaine dependence. These topics have been extensively studied over a long period of time. Other factors are more difficult to study rigorously. What produces successful recovery? We know a great deal about specific interventions that are effective in the short term, but what are the essential ingredients of that complex process by which some succeed and others do not? Research money is always limited, and the emphasis on psychosocial factors has varied over time. Clinicians, as always, must often make decisions on the basis of the information they have available and their clinical instincts honed by experience.

Overview of Contents

Although we had psychologists in mind when writing this material, we also believe that our integrated approach will appeal to psychiatrists, medical professionals, social workers, community substance abuse counselors, and those working in social services, juvenile services, and the criminal justice system. We hope our content choice can be of service to the entire treatment community.

In chapter 1 we discuss our view of the lack of participation of psychologists in mainstream addiction treatment and describe how fulfilling this type of work can be for the individual therapist. We then review, in chapter 2, five models or theories of addiction. We believe that effective treatment for patients with AOD problems requires an integrated biopsychosocial approach so that the therapist can maintain great flexibility in dealing with AOD problems.

In chapter 3 we discuss in detail the process of assessment of AOD problems and disorders, and in chapter 4 we describe the treatment modalities and continuum of care available for substance abusers (summarizing research data on efficacy when available). Models and approaches for both residential and outpatient treatment are described. We then offer, in chapter 5, a variety of ways to determine appropriate treatment, ranging from the problem–service matching approach to the Patient Placement Criteria developed by the

American Society of Addiction Medicine to select levels of care. This chapter also looks at treatment associated with the criminal justice system, a rapidly expanding arena of treatment activity.

In chapter 6 we aim primarily to introduce therapists to a recovery-oriented model, in which treatment is modified to address the changing tasks of the patient. These efforts can be integrated into ongoing psychotherapy provided that the therapist is willing to shift the nature of his or her activity to best achieve the recovery task of the patient.

In chapter 7 we write about family therapy, which is an essential component of treatment. We review the reasons for its popularity and the tasks of a family therapist as they apply specifically to AOD problems. Group activities form the cornerstone of addiction treatment, and in chapter 8 we describe a variety of these structures. Professionally led groups include motivational enhancement groups, recovery groups, network therapy, and harm reduction group activities. We describe the characteristics and distinctive issues of recovery groups in some detail. Self-help groups, particularly 12-step groups descended from AA, constitute a powerful resource with no financial barriers; hence, we give special attention to how therapists can facilitate their use.

Relapse prevention is embedded in good treatment; however, the variety of approaches and issues merit separate consideration, particularly because these have a strong research base. In chapter 9 we describe common relapse precipitants and effective strategies for addressing them. We also discuss medications, both as tools and as relapse hazards. Addiction treatment at its best is multidisciplinary, and it is important that all practitioners have some comfort with these medical aspects of treatment.

Conclusion

New research and treatment methods are constantly evolving in this field. We have tried to be comprehensive. At a certain point the decision had to be made to stop writing even though much remains to be covered and new information is developing. We hope that this book will help readers think innovatively about their treatment approaches, work more effectively with the AOD abuse treatment system, and relate more compassionately with individuals suffering with these problems.

1

Psychologists in the Substance Abuse Field

Alcohol and other drug (AOD) abuse is a major public health problem in the United States. There are more than 120,000 deaths annually related to excessive alcohol consumption (McGinnis, 1993). Between 1992 and 1995 there were more than 1 million substance abuse–related clinic admissions per year (Substance Abuse and Mental Health Services Office of Applied Statistics, 1997): "Alcohol and other drug use has been implicated as a factor in many of this country's most serious and expensive problems, including violence, injury, child and spousal abuse, HIV/AIDS and other sexually transmitted diseases, teen pregnancy, school failure, car crashes, escalating health care costs, low worker productivity, and homelessness" (National Clearinghouse for Alcohol and Drug Information, 1995, p. 1).

As the understanding of AOD problems has evolved, the treatment field also has undergone dramatic changes. In the 19th and early 20th centuries, AOD problems were dealt with as a moral or spiritual condition best handled by religious organizations. Alcoholics and drug users were considered sinners who needed to exercise willpower in choosing not to consume their drug of choice. In the early 20th century, alternative views of addiction began to emerge. The psychiatric community began to offer psychodynamic explanations of addiction. An example is the early psychoanalytic view of alcoholism as a regressive phenomenon or a return to infantile fixations such as oral dependency needs (Frances, Franklin, & Borg, 1994, p. 239). The psychiatric approach to addiction dominated treatment centers until the 1970s. In 1935 Bill Wilson began the Alcoholics Anonymous (AA) movement after his treatment needs were unmet by the professional community and his own efforts at sobriety failed. The AA program taught that alcoholics had a disease in which their responses to alcohol were different from other people's responses. The AA program is based on the belief that the alcoholic must abstain from mood-altering chemicals and develop a connection to a power greater than oneself. AA believes that stopping drinking is a first step to recovery. Developing a sober state of mind or serenity, however, is what separates an individual who is merely "dry" from one who is in recovery. To aid the alcoholic, AA has developed a series of 12 steps based on spiritual and behavioral principles. Applying these 12 steps in all of the individual's daily affairs is the core of a good recovery program (Alcoholics Anonymous, 1976). The program became very popular as alcoholics found supportive, understanding help and learned coping skills for living without alcohol. In the 1960s treatment centers based on the principles of AA were established. The centers were often deliberately located away from major metropolitan areas in places such as Center City, Minnesota (Hazelden), and Statesboro, Georgia (Willingway), in an attempt to avoid pressure from the psychiatric community. Eventually, mainstream psychiatric treatment centers began to adopt the AA program. AA programs were more understandable to the average person, the disease concept seemed to alleviate the moral stigma, and the programs provided practical solutions for the problems that recovering individuals faced. This model still prevails in the majority of treatment centers today.

Psychologists have questioned this view of addiction in part because scientific research was not available to support its efficacy. They developed other approaches to addiction such as cognitive–behavioral modalities, relapse prevention, and motivational enhancement. These approaches are sup-

CARF

ported by efficacy research. In response to pressure from funding agencies, public and private, for increased accountability in regard to outcomes, treatment centers are now beginning to incorporate these new strategies into their treatment protocols.

Lack of Participation by Psychologists

Despite the fact that psychologists developed these new effective strategies, there are a relatively small number of psychologists specializing in the field of addiction. Both of us have noted a lack of participation by psychologists in mainstream addiction conferences. Zweben and Clark (1991) noted that there were less than 12 articles published in the *American Psychologist* that dealt with substance abuse in 1989. It was not until 1993 that the American Psychological Association (APA) approved a division of addictions. This lack of attention to a major health care problem, although perplexing at first glance, is understandable in light of certain obstacles or barriers for psychologists in the field.

In this chapter we examine these obstacles and the problems they may create for clinicians. The obstacles as we see them include a lack of education and training in substance abuse disorders, a sense of hopelessness about treating and managing addictions, the rift between the psychological community and mainstream addiction treatment field, and the conflict between some aspects of traditional psychotherapy training and addiction treatment. These barriers need to be dealt with by the profession as a whole and by individual psychologists pursuing careers in the addiction field. Until these issues are addressed, psychologists may continue to operate on the fringes of the addiction treatment field and to make clinical misjudgments leading to untoward consequences for their patients. We not only describe the barriers but also suggest ways of overcoming them and provide reasons why clinicians should want to work with this difficult population.

Lack of Education and Training

A major factor in perpetuating ineffective practices is that the knowledge and skills needed to address alcohol and drug problems is almost never included in basic clinical training and is at best available as an elective or a course mandated by state licensing boards. Recently trained graduates are more likely to have had some exposure, but cross-trained practitioners are rare. The data suggest that addiction problems are not dealt with in a comprehensive way in most training programs. Selen and Svanum (1981) surveyed 107 APA-approved clinical training programs and received feedback from 74 program directors. The survey was designed to assess the degree to which research, clinical course work, and training were offered or required in graduate programs. The results showed a modest level of research activity on addiction and a minimal level of training and evaluation, treatment, and prevention (Zweben & Clark, 1991). Selen and Svanum comment that psychologists' investment in these areas is indifferent and sparse.

Schlesinger (1984), in a survey of 436 graduate psychology training programs, noted that 34% of the programs offered little or no exposure to the area of substance misuse, approximately 25% required it, and the remainder offered some exposure through elective courses or experiences. Schlesinger (1984) noted that

> psychology as a profession views misuse as similar to, rather than different from, other behavioral disorders and, as such, believes that no specific competency should be required of students beyond the competencies and assessment of treatment for which students are now trained. (p. 136)

Lubin, Brady, Woodward, and Thames (1986) replicated Schlesinger's study and found similar results. The finding that substance abuse is not viewed as a distinct disorder or entity and thus requires no special competency is particularly significant because this is exactly the opposite view taken by the vast majority of mainstream treatment providers.

In a paper presented at the APA convention in 1994, it was reported that approximately 90% of graduate students indicated that they had had no formal course work in the area of substance abuse. As a result of the lack of education and training, "many therapists today find themselves in the remarkable position of having no systematic understanding of how to identify, treat, or appropriately refer alcohol and drug problems, despite the fact that we are in the middle of an epidemic of chemical use of unprecedented proportions" (Zweben & Clark, 1991, p. 1434). Zweben and Clark noted that attending AA meetings is almost sure to produce horror stories in which alcoholic individuals commonly share how they have been mistreated by a psychologist or other mental health professional. Their addiction was allowed to progress unnoticed and unchecked and was not addressed until it became a crisis. Our clinical observations suggest that it is not uncommon for an alcoholic or drug addict to progress to the late stages of the disorder before it is detected. Unfortunately, it is sometimes the case that the patient appears in the emergency room with an overdose and the psychologist or other mental health professional is not even aware that the problem exists.

Even for those psychologists who do not wish to specialize in the field of addiction, a thorough knowledge of the signs and symptoms is essential because all psychologists with direct patient contact will be confronted with incidences of alcohol and drug dependence. Substance abuse disorders can and do mimic virtually every other psychiatric diagnosis (Zweben & Clark, 1991). Not knowing the signs and symptoms of the substance abuse disorder can lead not only to misdiagnosis and poor outcomes but also to legal vulnerabilities for those therapists who miss the signs and incorrectly diagnose the problem (Zweben & Clark, 1991).

In outpatient therapy settings, it is important that therapists become capable of addressing mild-to-moderate cases of alcohol and drug use in the context of ongoing work, especially when there is an existing therapeutic alliance. In the case of more severe problems, therapists need to facilitate recognition of the problem and enhance motivation to address it, thus cultivating patient readiness to engage in specialized addiction treatment when needed. There are, however, large numbers of cases in which the AOD use is manageable by a clinician with some specialized training who is not an addiction specialist. Such training would be similar to that defined by the APA College of Professional Psychology in its substance abuse proficiency. The knowledge-base objectives consist of elements considered necessary for the clinician in general, not specialist practice. Managed care organizations are increasingly aware that untreated substance abuse is costly in health terms alone and are requiring documentation of proficiency by their licensed professionals. There is a consensus that basic professional training does not prepare the clinician to address alcohol and drug use, and other preparation is needed.

Sense of Hopelessness About Addiction

The second barrier that psychologists face is a sense of hopelessness about addiction and, more specifically, about addicts and alcoholics. Some psychologists believe that addicts and alcoholics are incorrigible. Some psychologists see all addicts as character impaired and thus untreatable or as treatable with a poor prognosis at best. One of us attended a seminar on addiction at a psychological conference several years ago. During the seminar, the presenter began with a blanket statement that addicts are motivated by a desire to act out. To understand addicts, one had to understand the concept of acting out, according to the presenter. Although addicts frequently engage in acting-out behaviors, it is an overgeneralization to explain addictive behavior in terms of the addict's predilection to act out. Rather, most addiction professionals view acting-out behaviors as the addict's attempt to come to terms with an overwhelming need to satisfy addictive cravings that are, at this point, beyond control.

In a similar vein, Imhof, Hirsch, and Terenzi (1983) stated that "it has been the author's experience that with regard to diagnostic considerations, the majority of these patients (addicts) fall into the categories of narcissistic and borderline personality disorders" (p. 499). Imhof et al. then explained how addicts use the defense mechanisms of splitting and projective identification and that these defense mechanisms in turn can evoke strong countertransferential reactions from therapists.

Many addiction professionals, on the other hand, are likely to see the personality dynamics as a consequence of the substance abuse rather than as a preexisting etiological factor. Zweben and Clark (1991) examined the diagnostic criteria for borderline personality disorder (as defined in the revised third edition of the *Diagnostic and Statistical Manual of Mental Disorders*, American Psychiatric Association, 1987) and concluded that too little emphasis has been placed on the differential diagnosis between borderline personality disorder and addiction. As a result, many psychotherapists observe behaviors that technically meet the criteria for borderline personality disorder but may in fact reflect an underlying addictive disorder masquerading as a characterological impairment.

Zweben and Clark (1991) pointed out that many of the symptoms of borderline personality disorder such as unstable interpersonal relationships, impulsivity, affective instability, anger control problems, suicidal behavior, identity disturbance, and feelings of emptiness or boredom also are characteristic of substance-abusing patients. These symptoms often disappear or markedly lessen after the cessation of substance abuse, suggesting that they are secondary to the addictive process and not symptomatic of underlying character pathology. "Those who work with patients for long periods during their recovery observe a gradual shift in many behavioral patterns once abstinence is solidly established, an impression which is supported in the empirical literature (Vaillant, 1981, 1983)" (Zweben & Clark, 1991, p. 1439).

The importance of this differential diagnosis is twofold. First, to the degree that one views addictive disorders as being a reflection of impaired character pathology, the treatment will necessarily focus on those underlying intrapsychic conflicts that produce the character pathology rather than on a cessation of the alcohol and drug use itself. Yet, this pathology frequently tends to lessen or disappear as the individual remains abstinent from mood-altering chemicals. Without a focus on abstinence, however, the practitioner is likely to feel frustrated because the same set of maladaptive behavior patterns will continue.

Second, the view that addiction is a reflection of underlying character pathology is significant because such disorders are considered less amenable to psychotherapeutic interventions. Whether it is the antisocial character pathology alluded to by the presenter at the addiction seminar or the borderline-narcissistic features suggested by Imhof et al. (1983), it is generally regarded that ingrained character pathology is more difficult to treat and thus more likely to evoke negative or countertransferential reactions from the therapist (Imhof et al., 1983).

Imhof et al. (1983) described some of the countertransferential reactions that the therapist may have in treating drug-addicted patients. The therapist may assume the role of the "good parent rescuing the bad impulsive child" (Imhof et al., 1983, p. 503). The overinvolvement of the therapist initially is an attempt to rescue the addict, but it may lead later to disappointment and resentment when the addict continues to act out despite the therapist's best efforts. "The therapist often then becomes both furious and hurt at this betrayal, labels the drug addict as resistant and acting out' and may proceed with plans to discharge the patient as un-treatable on an outpatient basis" (Imhof, 1983, p. 503).

Amodeo (1995) summarized some of the frustrations that all therapists feel in treating this most difficult population when she wrote about power struggles between addicted individuals and their therapists:

Because alcoholism and drug dependence are conditions characterized by impulsive and compulsive behavior, therapists are repeatedly confronted with control related issues. Clients may come to sessions high or intoxicated and fail to respond to the therapist's limit setting. They may report drinking and drug use between sessions or describe behavior such as violence against family members, unprotected sex with strangers, taking tranquilizers

and alcohol together or using dirty needles. These experiences are likely to stimulate the therapist's anxiety
and feelings of being out of control, especially for those
therapists for whom control was a difficult early life issue. Common therapist responses to this behavior which
can undermine the relationship and potential success are
rigid limits, emotional distancing, feelings of betrayal
and adopting a moralistic attitude. (p. 110)

A familiar scenario is a young and idealistic therapist who
secures a position at an addiction treatment center with
dreams of helping those who are truly in need. Over time,
the therapist becomes frustrated when the addicted patients
tell lies, relapse on a regular basis, and manipulate therapy sessions. The therapist may feel like a failure and a bad
therapist. These feelings are expressed as frustration, anger,
and eventually burnout. The once-eager psychotherapist
develops

a self-protecting, narcissistic distancing which manifests
itself as indifference, tiredness, boredom and in general,
separation from the therapeutic interaction. Such burnout features are not uncommon when considering the
consistent and intense demands that the patient makes
and the recidivistic and chronically relapsing manifestations of the addictive disorders. (Imhof et al., 1983, p.
504)

These burnout reactions closely parallel society's moralistic
and pejorative view of alcohol and drug abuse. Addicts are
often viewed as weak-willed or even as sinners. Although
this moralistic stance is not often overtly found among psychologists, it is common in the larger society. To the extent
that the psychologist moves from idealism to boredom and
burnout, the attitude is perceived by the addiction patient as
being judgmental and rejecting. As the psychologist moves
from a posture of rescue into a posture of anger, resentment,
and burnout, he or she may begin to chastise patients for not
being able to achieve sobriety or, even worse, for not being

able to control their drinking. This behavior only reinforces addicts' sense of shame and self-loathing, further increasing the chances that they will continue to drink and use drugs to medicate these feelings. Addicts and alcoholics are intensely sensitive to shaming messages of condemnation because they have received these types of messages for many years.

By contrast, the more experienced therapist will view this same behavior in a different light. For some patients, the desire to use has become so compelling from both the physiological and psychological standpoint that not using, in the early days of abstinence, appears to be overwhelming. Abstinence is the major goal of early-stage, recovery-oriented psychotherapy. Experienced therapists will acknowledge that relapses are a frequent, if not inevitable, component of this disorder. They will be less likely to view these frequent relapses as an expression of addicts' hostility, but rather will see them as a reflection of the loss of control that addicts experience, which is driven by the overwhelming physiological and psychological demands of the drug dependency itself.

In this way, more experienced therapists can join with addicts in acknowledging their sincere if not always successful attempts to achieve sobriety. They can offer specific motivational and behavioral techniques to help patients achieve and maintain sobriety and abstinence. They will make this struggle the major focus of early-stage recovery. In so doing, they can achieve an alliance with patients that is more compassionate and more effective in helping patients to achieve their desired goals.

Undoubtedly, working with this group can be extremely frustrating. Disappointments and relapses are common. The therapist must be prepared to deal with the reality that the disorder is truly life threatening and that not all patients can be helped. One of the most humbling aspects of working with this population is the increasing realization that one has virtually no control over whether patients choose to drink or use drugs abusively. However, we both have found great rewards in working with this group and describe them at the end of the chapter.

Rift Between Psychologists and Mainstream Addiction Treatment Field

For many years there has been a philosophical and practical rift between the psychological community and the mainstream addiction treatment community. The philosophical divide results from differing beliefs over the nature of addiction. The majority of addiction treatment centers subscribe to the disease model of addiction (see chap. 2 in this book). Briefly, this model states that addiction is a biochemical disorder in which individuals cannot consistently control their alcohol- and drug-using behavior outside of total abstinence. The disorder is not curable because they will never escape the biochemical condition, but they can live a normal, rewarding life without the use of alcohol or drugs if they accept their powerlessness over the alcohol or drugs; strive for abstinence; and adopt the support, values, and methods of a new social group, AA (Wallace, 1996, pp. 15–21).

The prevailing view within the psychological community is that of a learning or behavior model in which alcohol or drug use is learned as other behaviors are learned through positive and negative rewards (Marlatt, 1985; McCrady, 1994; W. R. Miller & Hester, 1995, p. 5). Because the behavior has been learned, it also can be unlearned, changed, or controlled through these same methods. Each person needs an individualized treatment plan, and the treatment goals may differ from one person to another. In other words, some people may need total abstinence and some may not. Improvement in the disorder results from increasing individuals' self-efficacy and self-control.

The philosophical rift has been accompanied by general ill-will and negative personal attacks as well as several unfortunate consequences detrimental to everyone in the field including the patients (Wallace, 1989, pp. 267–306). First, the mainstream addiction community downplayed the psychosocial factors of addiction and ignored some of the advances that psychologists have made in techniques to help these patients. Major advances such as Marlatt's (1985) relapse prevention techniques, Sisson and Azrin's (1993) community reinforcement approach, or O'Farrell's (1993) behavioral marital therapy, are underused in the mainstream treatment community. The patient populations of these institutions suffer because these advances are efficacious for the treatment of substance-related disorders and have been validated by controlled outcome studies.

Second, psychologists have downplayed the biochemical aspects of addiction. Psychology textbooks tend to understate the contribution of biochemical forces in the shaping of addictive disorders. For example, Thombs (1994) stated that, "simply put, the disease model is not well supported by empirical data. In fact, most of its major hypotheses are disputed by research findings" (p. 44). (See chap. 2 for a review of the abundant research data supporting the disease model and the biochemical basis of some addictions.) Because psychologists have tended to downplay this aspect, they have lost credibility in the treatment community.

Third, psychologists' beliefs that addiction is a learned behavior and can be unlearned, changed, or controlled through conditioning and skills training has led some to investigate controlled drinking as a proper goal for alcoholics. This factor may have caused psychologists the greatest damage in the mainstream treatment community. For many years prominent learning theorists did research trying to support that alcoholics can learn to drink in a controlled social fashion (Sobell & Sobell, 1978, 1993). The mainstream community, however, after many years of clinical experience, concluded that alcoholics cannot drink or use drugs in any kind of controlled fashion. "In the United States, the predominant (90%) form of addiction treatment is abstinence based" (Flaherty & Kim, 1997, p. 402). Many substance-dependent individuals try their own efforts at controlled alcohol and drug use for many years before they enter treatment (Schuckit, 1989b; Vaillant, 1983). They make their own rules for drinking or using on certain days or certain hours or certain situations. Typically, they find that "rules can be bent, intake escalates, and a crisis develops" (Schuckit, 1994, p. 4). Even though substance-dependent individuals may have temporary periods of controlled use, the overall trend in their life is typically toward greater loss of control and escalation of use. Research is now supporting the treatment community's position that controlled drinking is an inappropriate goal for substance-dependent alcoholics (Goldsmith, 1997, p. 393; Schuckit, 1994, p. 4; Wallace, 1989, 1996).

At this time many psychologists who formerly supported controlled drinking have recognized that it does not work for most substance-dependent individuals (Hester, 1995; Sobell & Sobell, 1993). However, the controversy continues. Some learning theorists do not acknowledge the database that suggests that a controlled drinking strategy is both ineffective and dangerous with alcohol- and drug-dependent individuals (Wallace, 1989, 1996). Others include alcohol abusers as appropriate candidates for controlled drinking strategies but do not draw a clear line of demarcation between dependence and abuse. Sobell and Sobell (1993) stated that only "chronic alcoholics" (p. 4) are inappropriate for moderate drinking approaches. They then defined chronic alcoholics as individuals whose life is

> centered around procuring and consuming alcohol and who, upon stopping drinking, suffer severe withdrawal symptoms .... Some chronic alcoholics will experience significant brain and other end organ damage ... usually [there are] few meaningful relationships with family members, vocational problems, and a history of alcohol related arrests. (Sobell & Sobell, 1993, p. 4)

They summarized the description of the chronic alcoholic as follows: "We mean the stereotypical image of the alcoholic, the image often portrayed in the media" (Sobell & Sobell, 1993, p. 4).

This issue continues to divide psychologists, especially those who seek to expand the limits of controlled drinking experiments, from the larger mainstream addiction community. More important, however, controlled drinking procedures that use broad definitions of terms, such as *problem drinker*, may be placing patients at risk. These strategies rely heavily on self-report data, which are not consistently reliable

(National Institute on Alcohol Abuse and Alcoholism, 1993, p. 327). They also fail to take into account that, for a sizable subgroup of individuals, this disorder is progressive and what is defined as problem drinking today could well be alcoholism in a few months. For example, women have a telescoped course and typically suffer damage far more quickly and at lower levels of consumption than men (Blume, 1992). Controlled drinking discussions also do not address the data indicating progressive physical and social harms once relatively small amounts of alcohol levels are exceeded (Ashley, 1996). Finally, a variety of researchers have examined the literature and have not found support for controlled drinking interventions with patients who meet the criteria for dependence (Goldsmith, 1997, p. 393).

For individuals who have not progressed to the point of substance dependence, moderate drinking may be a viable treatment goal as indicated by a number of controlled outcome studies (Hester, 1994). Schuckit (1994) stated that moderate drinking strategies have shown "promising results" (p. 4) for patients who do not meet dependence criteria but that "abstinence is accepted as the only clinically relevant goal for treatment programs that focus on those who meet criteria for dependence on any substance [including] tobacco use and for the intake of illegal drugs" (p. 4). The controversy is still not over, and the issue continues to be divisive.

From the psychologists' view, the mainstream treatment community has been using a model and methods that have not been tested or proved to be effective in treating addiction. In addition, they have been using these methods for everyone without regard to individual differences. Controlled trials studying the different methods of treatment have not shown *to their satisfaction* the effectiveness of the disease model. On the other hand, controlled trials have shown *to their satisfaction* that methods based on learning and behavioral models are effective in treating addiction. They believe that controlled drinking may be a satisfactory goal of treatment for some substance abusers. They believe that the 12-step approach does not work for everyone (Sobell & Sobell, 1993). Some patients do not mesh with the 12-step approach, and these people need other treatment methods that are not found in mainstream treatment centers. They believe in enhancing self-efficacy and self-control rather than admitting powerlessness over the substance use.

A practical rift between the two communities occurred because the mainstream addiction treatment field is dominated by physicians, and they have not been receptive to psychologists' work in the field. For many years treatment centers did not allow psychologists to be primary therapists, and the physicians did not welcome them to the environment. As a result, many psychologists have attempted to treat substance-dependent individuals on their own without the support of a structured treatment environment.

Both sides have been entrenched and unyielding in their viewpoints, but each is beginning to recognize that the other side has something of value to offer. Addiction is a complex multivariate disorder. Simple reductionistic theories on either side do not work. The addiction treatment community is gradually adopting the psychologists' learning and behavioral techniques for changing behavior. Psychologists are gradually coming to understand the biochemical and genetic basis for the disorder. Treatment centers now facilitate psychologists working as primary and family therapists. Continued progress at rapprochement is necessary, and we hope that this book will contribute to the process.

Conflict Between Insight Psychotherapy and Standard Addiction Treatment

In some ways, training in traditional psychodynamic psychotherapy runs counter to techniques and approaches necessary during the early stages of recovery. This conflict provides yet another barrier for psychologists entering the addiction treatment field because some of the therapy techniques learned in graduate training must be unlearned before one is able to successfully treat substance-related disorders. Many therapists are trained to search for the underlying or "root" causes of psychological and behavioral problems. Under ideal circumstances, as the therapist and client work col-

laboratively to explore and uncover these dynamics, pathological and dysfunctional patterns of relating and behaving
are replaced with healthier patterns. Attitudes and thinking
are restructured to accommodate these new patterns and to
reinforce the patient's sense of self-esteem, integrity, and serenity. Psychodynamic psychotherapy can be appropriate
during later stages of recovery when abstinence is more secure, but during the early stages it can create difficulties.

First, to spend time searching for root causes of alcoholic
drinking in the early stages of recovery might be compared
to a paramedic rushing to the scene of an accident, finding
victims lying on the ground bleeding and taking time out to
examine why this accident occurred in the first place (e.g.,
faulty brakes, speeding, wet roads) before attending to the
injured victims. Thus, to focus on the root causes of drinking
or drug-using behavior may lead to minimizing the overwhelming physiological and psychological imperatives that
propel this disorder into a full-blown syndrome and that account for much of the uncontrollable cravings and erratic behavior of alcoholic and drug-addicted patients. Psychodynamically trained therapists sometimes find it difficult to
shift their focus from why a person drinks to how to stop. It
is difficult for them to accept that assisting a person to learn
how to stop drinking requires surprisingly little understanding about why he or she drinks.

Second, insight-oriented psychotherapy sometimes inadvertently supports the complex set of defense mechanisms
such as denial, projection, and rationalization that addicts use
to explain and maintain their drinking and drug-using behavior. Several writers (Levy, 1987; Vaillant, 1981) have
pointed out that for an alcoholic who is drinking, any excuse
can be considered an adequate reason to drink. Thus, the
alcoholic often comes to therapy stating, "I drink because my
wife nags me" or "I drink because my boss won't get off my
back." These rationalizations often obscure the reciprocal nature of the interaction: His wife nags him and his boss will
not get off his back because he drinks, and this feeds the
cycle. As Vaillant (1981) stated,

my thesis is that the patient who tells us that he drinks because he is depressed and anxious may in fact be depressed or anxious because he drinks. He may draw attention from the fact that it is painful for him to give up alcohol. The alcoholic's denial may be simultaneously at a conscious, unconscious, and cellular level. In no other mental illness is the deficit state so clearly a product of disordered chemistry and yet the secondary conflicts and association so dynamically fascinating to psychiatrists. The greatest danger of this is wasteful, painful psychotherapy that bears analogy to someone trying to shoot a fish in a pool. No matter how carefully he aims, the refracted image always renders the shot wide of its mark. (p. 49)

Searching for the root causes through psychotherapy may lead to a misconception that once the causes are addressed and dealt with therapeutically, the drinking or using will stop and that it cannot be expected to cease before these underlying issues are resolved. Substance-dependent patients desperately want to be told that their drinking or drug-using behavior is not as bad as it appears. They want to believe that at some point in the future they can drink or use chemicals moderately. If only they could find the real causes of why they abuse, they could perhaps return to a state of normal drinking or social use of chemicals just like everyone else. An inexperienced therapist may come to believe that through the strength of the transference relationship and the working-through of the unconscious conflicts that led to the drinking in the first place, responsible or controlled use of alcohol and other substances may be possible for the patient.

This line of thinking on the part of patient and therapist is a recipe for therapeutic failure for the patient and frustration, anger, and ultimately burnout for the therapist. Many alcoholic and drug-addicted patients continue with one-to-one psychotherapy precisely because it supports their denial and rationalizations. Alcoholic and drug-addicted patients are often adept at concocting reasons for their drinking and drug-use behavior. Either consciously or unconsciously, addicted individuals may begin to seduce the therapist into the belief that they are "really getting somewhere" when in fact they are becoming increasingly mired in rationalizations as the denial system becomes stronger and stronger. If the patient returns to drinking or drug using, the therapist then becomes angry or frustrated and may view the relapse personally as a rejection of the strength of the therapeutic bond, which the therapist believed was strong enough to keep the patient from drinking or using.

The dysfunctional circle is now complete. The therapist is now locked in a power struggle over control of the patient's drinking. Inevitably, he or she is on the losing end of this power struggle. The therapist feels anger and frustration, which is often directed at the patient. Patients feel ashamed, believing that they have once again disappointed a significant other in their lives and their self-image as a failure is reinforced.

By contrast, the therapist who is familiar with addiction dynamics will view loss of control as the central problem, not as a symptom of underlying psychopathology. Whether the loss of control is biochemical or psychosocial or some combination of these factors is of secondary importance. The loss of control that the alcoholic or addict experiences can be compared to the diabetic's inability to regulate blood sugar levels. Diabetics are not blamed because they cannot keep their blood sugar within the normal range after eating a doughnut. The loss of control for both the diabetic and the substance-dependent individual is viewed as both expected and irreversible. In both cases, therapeutic efforts are directed at helping individuals acclimate to this condition. In both cases a variety of psychopathological and dysfunctional responses may occur in reaction to the disorders. These conditions, however, are rarely seen as etiologically significant but as a consequence of the condition itself. As S. Brown (1995) noted,

> many clinicians with a psychoanalytic perspective still see out of control drinking as a symptom of an underlying problem. A symptom that should automatically self-correct when the deeper issues are addressed. This

theory relegates alcoholism or a "drinking problem" to secondary diagnostic status, whose etiology is seen as a consequence of another major disturbance: people drink to cope with other difficulties. Although loss of control might be acknowledged, it is still not viewed as permanent and treatment will not focus on abstinence. As a diagnosis of secondary status, there is often no direct treatment focus at all. (p. 13)

Psychodynamically oriented psychotherapy should be delayed in the early stages of recovery because the uncovering of deep-seated affective material too early in the therapeutic process may trigger a relapse for substance-dependent individuals (S. Brown, 1995). Most substance-dependent clients have been abusing substances for several years. They experience the loss of their chemical coping pattern as extremely traumatic. Much like famished people crave food, their daily thoughts are dominated by strong desires and urges to return to chemical use. Even at night, it is common for patients in early-stage recovery to awaken in a cold sweat, having dreamed that they had relapsed and wondering if in fact this was so. Such is the nature of reality for the early-stage recovering individual.

At the early abstinence stage, the emergence of highly charged affective material threatens to overwhelm their shaky sense of self and their precarious commitment to abstinence. Feelings that have been medicated and numbed for years by alcohol and drugs may begin to emerge once abstinence is established. For example, it is not uncommon for patients to recollect early childhood trauma and experience powerful emotions related to it. In addition, profound feelings of shame and guilt about years of using behavior and the sequelae of these behaviors (e.g., legal problems; personal, family, and vocational failures) also begin to emerge. A deep sense of mourning or grief over the loss of alcohol and drugs, often described as being equivalent to losing a family member or one's best friend, also contributes to the affective and emotional instability of the patient. During this time of inner turmoil, it is best to delay the additional stress of psychodynamically oriented psychotherapy. Insight-oriented explorations focused tightly on behavior changes needed to establish and maintain abstinence can be productive. Strong feelings can be acknowledged and discussed from the perspective of how they can be expressed or contained while the patient is building the foundation that will make deeper work possible.

How Psychotherapists Can Work With Addicts

If uncovering affective material, exploring "root problems," and developing a positive transference relationship is not the appropriate role for the psychotherapist in treating early recovering patients, then what is the role of the psychotherapist at this stage of treatment? S. Brown (1985) answered this question as follows:

> So what is the place for psychotherapy in the treatment of alcoholism? There is no relevant place unless the therapist can alter basic beliefs. Therapists must recognize loss of control for the alcoholic and must accept their own total lack of control in being able to make the patient change. Therapists who recognize their own limits can then begin to help the alcoholic accept the diagnosis of alcoholism, the lack of control that goes with it, and the abstinence required. The therapist can help the patient learn how to stay abstinent. (p. 15)

That some aspects of traditional psychotherapy training work against the grain in the treatment of addicts and alcoholics should not be interpreted to mean that all aspects of traditional psychological training are unhelpful in the treatment of this population. To the contrary, research data suggest that certain therapist characteristics such as empathy and the ability to form a positive therapeutic relationship with the patient are significant factors in the treatment of AOD disorders, just as they are in treatment of other psychological disorders (Luborsky, McLellan, Woody, O'Brien, & Auerbach, 1985; McLellan, Woody, Luborsky, & Goehl, 1988). Luborsky et al. (1985) reported that the therapist's ability to form a "helping alliance" (p. 610) is correlated with a positive outcome for patients with an addictive disorder. They stated that "we believe that the therapist's ability to form an alliance is possibly the most crucial determinant of his effectiveness" (Luborsky et al., 1985, p. 610). They went on to assert that "the therapist's qualities required for treating these patients have much in common with those required for treating many other types of patients" (Luborsky et al., 1985, p. 610).

McLellan et al. (1988) identified "consistent and professional patient management practices" (p. 429) as being related to more positive outcomes. These patient management practices include consistently enforcing program rules, making better use of program resources, completing better chart documentation, and increasing the frequency of patient–therapist contact. They noted that the use of basic psychotherapy techniques such as "anticipating problems in the patient and discussing strategy to deal with the anticipated situations, thereby focusing the rehabilitation on the development of new behaviors and new ways of thinking by the patient" (McLellan et al., 1988, p. 429) also were associated with more positive outcomes. In general, the data from this research suggest that certain aspects of traditional psychotherapeutic training such as the ability to form an alliance with the patient on the basis of empathy, efficient patient management techniques, and the introduction of behavioral coping strategies are important elements of successful intervention with addicts and alcoholics, much as they are with patients who suffer from other psychological and emotional disorders.

What are some specific ways in which traditional psychotherapy skills can be useful in working with substance-dependent clients? To a certain extent, the answer depends on the stage of recovery the individual is in. These stages are more fully described in chapter 3, and psychotherapy is covered in chapter 6. At this point, suffice it to say that there are specific tasks with which therapists can aid people who are in the early stages of recovery. For the person who is still using alcohol or drugs, the therapist can maintain a firm but gentle focus on the role of the chemicals in the increasing loss of control and negative consequences in the person's life:

> In the drinking stage, it is the task of the therapist to point out, challenge, and eventually reveal the realities of behavior and belief that maintain an individual's drinking "system." This is the art of establishing a therapeutic alliance in which the client and the therapist are working toward dismantling, slowly but surely, the defenses that maintain the pathology. (S. Brown, 1995, p. 32)

For the person at a later stage who is struggling with early abstinence issues, the therapist can aid in learning nonchemical coping strategies as well as managing and containing negative affective material. It is at this stage that uncovering of affect too quickly may trigger a relapse. "We must not interfere with this new learning process by introducing new material for uncovering exploration unless the person is having difficulty. When behavioral and cognitive abstinence is secure, the client will move to uncovering work" (S. Brown, 1995, p. 44).

The therapist's tools for accomplishing these tasks are exactly those learned in psychologists' training: support, empathy, reflective listening, and cognitive–behavioral coping strategies. Psychodynamically oriented psychotherapy, although not appropriate early in treatment, does come into play and becomes valuable at a later stage when abstinence is more secure. At this later stage, therapy with substance-dependent people begins to more closely resemble therapy with other types of people.

Why Psychotherapists Should Work With These Patients

In this chapter we have examined some of the barriers to the treatment of alcoholics and addicts. These barriers include a lack of formal education and training in the treatment of this disorder; a sense of hopelessness about treating alcoholics and addicts; the practical and philosophical rifts between the psychological community and the mainstream addiction treatment community; and the ways in which traditional psychotherapeutic training is sometimes counterproductive in the treatment of substance-dependent individuals. In the presence of such seemingly overwhelming barriers, one might legitimately ask the question, Why do any psychologists specialize in the treatment of addictive disorders?

As people recover to a sober lifestyle, they experience enormous life-giving changes. It is an exhilarating experience to participate in their rebirth as they emerge from their drug- and alcohol-addicted lifestyle to sobriety. Patients report that these changes touch not only behavior and attitude but every aspect of their life. Physical health, family relations, vocational matters, social relations, and spiritual life can be dramatically improved with recovery. Many go on to make outstanding contributions once they regain command of their positive resources. The therapist who invests the effort, patience, and time to learn about the experience of addiction from the inside finds that empathy and a positive therapeutic alliance with these patients becomes much easier to attain. These are the rewards that make it all worthwhile.

The heartening news is that many problems are not intractable and that some yield to relatively modest intervention. The literature has documented that advice giving is effective for many patients. Clinicians are often pleasantly surprised by how therapeutic strategies such as motivational interviewing yield rapid results in some patients. Successfully addressing alcohol and drug use enhances the effectiveness of all other clinical interventions. The following case example illustrates this point:

> Sam came to treatment with a general malaise and dissatisfaction with his marriage. His wife Nancy was frustrated by his emotional inaccessibility, avoidance of conflict, and felt she was beginning to outgrow him. Feeling disadvantaged by her greater articulateness in cou-

ples' therapy, he refused to participate further but was willing to try individual work with his own therapist. During the initial meetings, the therapist elicited the fact that Sam had been smoking marijuana since he was 15, like others in his middle-class suburban community. He did not view it as a problem. He reported being bored at work, and it emerged he was vaguely dysphoric most of the time. He felt discouraged in his efforts to stand up to his wife and was frustrated by the important deadends in his life. Without asking him to alter his behavior, the therapist raised questions about his marijuana use. During the first 3 months of the treatment, she commented on how his marijuana use may be affecting his symptoms. The dysphoria and malaise he described are accompaniments of marijuana use for many, but not all, people. Its deadening effects lead both to loss of vitality and to conflict avoidance in relationships. The amotivational syndrome often produces a sense of boredom at work, and a lack of capacity for initiative exacerbates the boredom. Because the effects of this drug are more subtle, most people underestimate its negative potential, but abstinence reveals negative consequences more clearly.

To the therapist's surprise, Sam agreed rather readily to her suggestion of an "experiment with abstinence," and over the next 6 months changes began to unfold. His apathy dissipated, bringing irritability and insomnia initially, then renewed interest in work. His comfort level decreased as he became more in touch with his feelings. These changes rendered his therapy much more productive. His dissatisfaction with his marriage came more into the foreground, and he began to respond more assertively to his wife's criticisms. After several months of work with his individual therapist, he expressed willingness to tackle couples' therapy again.

This case illustrates a common dilemma of the therapist. There is often no way to precisely determine the effect of alcohol and drug use until it is eliminated. Individuals vary a great deal in their response to the drugs, so relatively small amounts can have large effects. Alcohol and drug use imitates every other entity found in clinical practice. Anxiety and depression are often exacerbated. The disinhibiting effects of even small amounts of alcohol can escalate marital bickering. Thus, the clinician who is comfortable raising and addressing alcohol and drug use is in a much better position to ultimately assist the patient in making meaningful changes.

Conclusion

Addictive disorders are complex, and we believe that they cannot be reduced to simplistic theories based on biological or psychosocial imperatives alone. We believe that only by integrating these factors can one truly understand the totality of this disorder. Therapists who allow themselves to become locked into a reductionistic view of addictive disorders and to operate from a narrow frame of reference are not likely to be effective in working with this population. On the other hand, those who can remain flexible and open to new ideas are likely to be the most effective in helping addicts move from abusive drinking and drug using into sober lifestyles.

To the extent that our patients will allow us, we can participate in the liberating struggle of their recovery. At times, the role closely resembles that of a parent who is willing to both nurture and set limits. At other times, we are more like a coach offering advice and support, encouraging the patient to try new cognitive and behavioral strategies. At other times, we are more like guides, helping patients explore the inner world of their thoughts and emotions as they struggle with the answer to deeper questions such as "How could my behavior have gotten so out of control?" Like other mental health professionals, we are privileged to observe this process of behavior change and self-exploration. A significant differentiating factor is that with addicted populations, the rate of change is so rapid and the nature of the change so profound. This transformation motivates us to overcome the enormous barriers and sustains us to keep working with addicted individuals.

2

Models and Theories of Addiction

Understanding alcohol and other drug (AOD) abuse disorders can be complex and confusing. Addicted individuals compulsively consume alcohol and drugs despite increasingly negative consequences. Unlike alcoholics, the majority of drinkers are able to regulate their intake of alcohol without loss of control. Alcoholics, on the other hand, like passive spectators watching their lives careen out of control, seem helpless to alter the course of this downward spiral.

What would motivate individuals to act in such a seemingly self-destructive manner? Is it perhaps a genetic susceptibility? Is it a disorder of self caused by early childhood trauma? Is it an attempt to restore homeostasis to a dysfunctional family system? Is it a learned behavior caused by dysfunctional thoughts and behaviors that need to be reprogrammed?

As one might expect, a variety of theoretical models have arisen that try to explain the complexity and the paradoxical nature of addictive behavior. These models fall within a framework of four different paradigms: the disease model, the learning theory model, the psychoanalytic model, and the family systems model.

A fifth approach is to conceptualize addiction as a biopsychosocial disorder that integrates contributions from all four of the major models. There appears to be an inherited biological component to addictive disorders, but this component alone does not explain the complexity of the disorder. Psychological, sociological, cultural, and spiritual factors play a significant role in the cause, course, and outcome of the disorder. Although no one model encompasses the complexity of the disorder, all four models contribute important insights into the nature of addiction. The biopsychosocial model attempts to integrate these insights into a unified theory of addictive disorders.

The Disease Model

The disease model is significant because it has been the dominant influence in treatment approaches since the 1970s. In simple terms, the disease model states that addiction is a primary disorder, independent of other conditions, with a biologically inherited susceptibility to the effects of alcohol and drugs. The disease model views addiction as being similar to other diseases, such as essential hypertension, that have an inherited biochemical component combined with environmental exposure factors. The key characteristics of addiction, according to this model, are loss of control over alcohol or drugs, denial, continued use despite negative consequences, and a pattern of relapsing (N. S. Miller, 1995, pp. 84–85).

Criteria for Disease

A disease may be defined as "a condition of the body that impairs the performance of a vital function" (N. S. Miller & Chappell, 1991, p. 196). Lewis (1991), in an article on the disease model as applied to alcoholism, delineated more specific criteria for the definition of a disease, including (a) a clear biological basis, (b) a set of unique identifiable signs and symptoms, (c) a predictable course and outcome, and (d) a lack of intentional causation. With regard to these factors, Lewis compared alcoholism with eight other diseases, including coronary heart disease, essential hypertension, diabetes mellitus, gout, cancer, syphilis, rheumatoid arthritis, and schizophrenia.

Biological basis and symptoms. The first consideration is the presence of a clear biological basis. Lewis (1991) found the weight of evidence supporting a biological basis for alcoholism to be compelling. (This important and significant research is reviewed in detail later.) For Lewis, the research is sufficient to conclude that "alcoholism can be viewed as a biologically based disease in which genetic predisposition is activated by environmental factors" (Lewis, 1991, p. 259). Second, Lewis found that there are unique and identifiable signs and symptoms of alcoholism. Once again, although there is not a single fixed definition of alcoholism, this situation is similar to the situation prevailing with other diseases. Even though alcoholism is heterogeneous and only the severest forms of drinking can be considered, this situation is not unlike schizophrenia and cancer. Both schizophrenia and cancer, for example, can be viewed as existing along a pathological continuum much like alcoholism.

Predictable course and outcome. Lewis's (1991) third consideration is whether there is a predictable course and outcome of the disease if it is left untreated. Although it is possible to plot a course of alcoholism from early abusive drinking to end-stage disease, he pointed out that many drinkers apparently do not suffer the most severe consequences. This variety of outcomes is by no means unusual, however, and is similar to other diseases, such as coronary heart disease, rheumatoid arthritis, gout, diabetes mellitus, and syphilis.

Intentional causation. Lewis's (1991) last criterion is intentional causation. If the etiology and course of a disease appear to be primarily under the control of the individual, then the condition is thought to be a behavioral problem. If the etiology and course are not under the individual's control, then it is more appropriately considered a disease. The lack of control over drinking (i.e., lack of volitional control) is a central feature of all addictions. Although there are times when the alcoholic may have temporary control over his or her drinking, the "lack of control is characterized by the continued appetite for alcohol in spite of negative consequences and frequent relapse to heavy drinking following periods of abstinence" (Lewis, 1991, p. 261). He pointed to a 1976 definition by the National Council on Alcoholism, which suggested that the individual cannot consistently predict the duration of the episode or the quantity that will be consumed. As another writer, Wallace (1996), explained, "from this point of view, people who cannot consistently predict and control when, where, and how much they drink and drug and/or cannot guarantee their actions once they start to drink or use drugs are perceived as powerless over alcohol or some other chemical" (pp. 21–22). Lewis indicated that learning to gain control over drinking and control of certain factors that precipitate or exacerbate the disease make alcoholism similar to coronary heart disease, hypertension, and diabetes, in which various forms of behavioral control are necessary to effectively manage the disease.

AOD disorders. Lewis (1991) concluded that there is at least as much evidence for alcoholism to be considered a disease as there is for these other conditions to be considered diseases. He indicated that "few diseases fit the model of being purely biological, discreet entities with steadily progressive courses and that show no evidence of volitional influence in their etiology or manifestations" (Lewis, 1991, p. 262). He suggested that many diseases, including alcoholism, are better understood through a biopsychosocial model, which proposes that etiologies can be comprehended by the interaction of biological, psychological, and sociocultural risk factors. Although Lewis dealt only with alcoholism, most disease model theorists believe that a biochemical genetic substrate underlies addiction to other drugs of abuse as well as to alcohol (N. S. Miller & Gold, 1991; Wallace, 1996).

Evidence for Biochemical Genetic Basis

Central to the disease model is the considerable body of research that points toward a biochemical or genetic basis for addictive behavior. For a number of reasons, most of the research on the biochemical basis of addiction has focused on alcoholism. First, alcoholism has been perceived as being the most significant addiction problem, at least in years past. Second, the availability of large sample sizes of alcoholic participants as opposed to other drug-addicted participants has contributed to this discrepancy. In our discussion we have noted the studies that apply to alcohol and those that apply to other drugs.

The importance of this research is twofold. First, it sheds light on the etiology of addictive disorders. Second, if certain individuals are differentially affected by alcohol or other drugs of abuse, then this may explain why alcoholics and addicts are unable to return to moderate levels of drinking or using. Because this research is not commonly reviewed in psychological texts, we review it here in some detail. There are several lines of research: adoption studies, twin studies, sons of alcoholic fathers, and animal studies. Although no single study offers conclusive evidence of the genetic factors in alcoholism, when the results of the many studies are viewed as a whole, they "provide a powerful demonstration of the influence of genetic factors on the risk of alcoholism" (Hesselbrock, 1995, p. 33). (See Begleiter & Kissin, 1995, Goedde & Agarwal, 1989, and the National Institute on Alcohol Abuse and Alcoholism [NIAAA], 1993, for additional details beyond the discussion here.)

Adoption studies. Adoption studies deal with children who were reared apart from their biological parents. The assumption is that genetic traits will appear more frequently in adoptees regardless of the environmental conditions of the adoptive parents. Many children were adopted out in Europe as a result of the family disruptions of World War II. In three studies, Goodwin et al. (Goodwin, Schulsinger, Hermansen, Guze, & Winokur, 1973; Goodwin, Schulsinger, Knopp, Mednick, & Guze, 1977; Goodwin, Schulsinger, Moller, Hermansen, Winokur, & Guze, 1974) examined the development of alcoholism in adopted children in Denmark. In the 1973 study, they compared adopted sons with a biological alcoholic parent against a control group of adopted sons without a biological alcoholic parent. In the 1974 study, they also looked at the nonadopted siblings of the participants in the experimental group compared with the nonadopted siblings and those in the control group. Finally, Goodwin et al. looked at adopted daughters who had an alcoholic parent. Although the last study did not show similar results, the first two studies of the sons did show that sons of alcoholic biological parents were more likely to develop alcoholism than the participants without an alcoholic biological parent.

In the Stockholm Adoption Study, Bohman (1978) looked at 2,324 Swedish adoptees who were adopted at an early age between 1930 and 1949. Bohman's original analysis and data confirmed genetic influences in the development of alcoholism. Later, Cloninger (1983; Cloninger, Bohman, & Sigvardsson, 1981) examined a subset of 862 men adopted out before the age of 3. This subset became the basis for Cloninger's distinction between Type I and Type II alcoholics. Type I alcoholism occurred in both men and women, tended to be less severe than Type II, and had a late age of onset (after age 25). Type II alcoholism occurred only in men, tended to be more severe, and had an early age of onset (before age 25). Type I was called *milieu-limited alcoholism* because it appeared to involve both a genetic predisposition and an environmental provocation. Given the genetic predisposition, this type of alcoholism could be significantly altered in its severity by the presence or absence of certain environmental factors. Type II, on the other hand, appeared to be highly genetically influenced, was not susceptible to environmental influences, and was associated with a higher incidence of criminality (Dinwiddie & Cloninger, 1989, p. 269).

Two other studies by Gilligan, Reich, and Cloninger and by von Knorring, Bohman, von Knorring, and Oreland (cited in Dinwiddie & Cloninger, 1989) confirmed Cloninger's analytic distinction between Type I and Type II alcoholism. In 1996, Sigvardsson, Bohman, and Cloninger (1996) replicated the original Stockholm study and confirmed the existence and heritability of the two forms of alcoholism.

In the United States, Cadoret and Gath (cited in Hesselbrock, 1995) conducted a smaller study of adoption in Iowa. They also found a higher rate of alcoholism in those adopted-

out children with one or more alcoholic parents. Their findings were substantiated by a subsequent study (cited in Hesselbrock, 1995).

As with any discussion of genetic versus environmental
effects, these studies have not been without controversy. Crit-
ics point to the possible biases introduced by adoption
agency practices, the lack of a standard definition of alcoholism, and possible differences between those who place
children for adoption and those who do not (NIAAA, 1990,
p. 46). Another criticism is the possible presence of comorbid
psychiatric disorders that could result in cases that are
judged to be alcoholism but that are in fact major depressive
disorder (Hesselbrock, 1995, p. 31).

The data from adoption studies point to an inherited susceptibility to alcoholism, but they do not elucidate the precise
mode of the genetic transmission or the pattern of heritability.
Nevertheless, the influence of biological parents as a contributing factor in the development of alcoholism appears consistently across the studies in this area. Cloninger's research
indicates that in the majority of cases, there is a genetic and
environmental interaction that affects both the development
and progression of alcoholism in men and women.

Twin studies. The second line of research includes data
from studies of twins. Twin studies typically compare the
rate of alcoholism among monozygotic (MZ) and dizygotic
(DZ) twins. Because MZ twins are genetically identical, differences between them should be environmental. Differences
between DZ twins, however, could be either environmental
or hereditary. If genetics play a role in the development of
alcoholism, then the rate of concordance should be higher
among MZ than DZ twins. Cadoret, in his 1990 review of 13
studies, concluded that there was "a greater concordance for
drinking behavior in alcoholism among identical twins than
among fraternal twins" (NIAAA, 1993, p. 63). These results
suggest that genetic factors play a significant role in determining vulnerability to alcoholism.

In a more recent study, Pickens et al. (1991) attempted to
determine the strength of this genetic influence. Pickens
et al. studied twin pairs in whom one had been treated for

alcohol abuse or dependence. Pickens et al. analyzed the results acording to gender as well as diagnosis (abuse vs. dependence). The findings suggested that genetic factors play a more important role in vulnerability to alcohol dependence than alcohol abuse and that the susceptibility is greater in men than in women.

McGue, Pickens, and Svikis (1992) continued the research begun by Pickens et al. (1991) by looking at the effects of gender and age on the inheritance of alcohol problems among twin pairs. The findings indicated that genetic factors play a significant role in early-onset alcoholism among men: "Consistent with the Pickens et al. study, significant concordance was found for the male twins (MZ males, 77%; DZ males, 54%), but not for the female twin pairs (MZ females, 39%; DZ females, 42%)" (Hesselbrock, 1995, p. 21). Genetic factors play a more modest role in the development of alcohol problems in women and the development of late-onset alcoholism in men. Heath, Meyer, Eaves, and Martin (1991) and Heath, Meyer, Jardine, and Martin (1991) studied the drinking behavior of 3,810 Australian twin pairs. Heath et al. estimated the heritability of drinking frequency to be .66 for women and .42–.75 for men. Heritability of drinking quantity was estimated to be .57 for women and .24–.61 for men.

Kendler, Heath, Neale, Kessler, and Eaves (1992) attempted to determine whether genetic factors would play a significant role in the etiology of alcoholism for women. They interviewed more than 1,000 female twin pairs, of whom 185 met the criteria for alcohol dependence and 357 met the somewhat broader criteria for alcoholism. Kendler et al. noted that the concordance was consistently higher in identical than in fraternal twin pairs. They estimated that genetic influences account for 50%–60% of the total risk for alcoholism in women.

Several researchers have examined the drinking habits of normal (i.e., nonalcoholic) twin participants. These researchers (Jardine & Martin; Kaprio, Sarna, Koskenvuo, & Rantasalo; Partanen, Bruun, & Markkanen; cited in Marshall & Murray, 1989) used sophisticated biometric techniques to estimate proportions of the variance attributable to genetic versus environmental factors. All of these studies indicate that genetic factors do play a role in the development of alcoholism. These factors, however, seem to decrease in importance as the person gets older.

Other researchers (Clifford, Fulker, Gurling, Murray; Clifford, Fulker, & Murray; Fulker, Eysenck, & Zuckerman; Kaprio, Koskenvuo, & Langinvainio; cited in Marshall & Murray, 1989) have found that both genetic and environmental factors play a role in the drinking patterns of normal twins. In some cases, heavy alcohol consumption in one DZ twin seemed to negatively influence alcohol consumption in the other twin (Marshall & Murray, 1989). The drinking patterns of both MZ and DZ twins were more closely paralleled when they were living together than when they lived apart (Clifford et al.; Kaprio et al.; cited in Marshall & Murray, 1989). Both Kaprio and Heath found strong genetic influences in large twin studies (Marshall & Murray, 1989). Heath and Martin (1988) found genetic influences in psychomotor performance and pulse rate among twin pairs after alcohol intake.

In summary, twin studies provide a line of evidence suggesting that alcoholism problems are to some degree inherited: "Like adoption studies, twin studies have provided consistent evidence for a heritable vulnerability to alcoholism" (NIAAA, 1993, p. 63). Remember, however, that other factors besides heredity may influence the concordance rate for alcoholism in fraternal twins. For example, maternal drinking during pregnancy might account for part of the high concordance rate for alcoholism in identical twins. Despite these possible confounding effects, the studies do provide evidence supporting a genetic effect on both the development of alcoholism as well as many aspects of normal drinking patterns between identical twins. In addition, the studies support a genetic environmental interaction in some cases. Most of the studies seem to suggest that there is a greater environmental influence with increasing age and that environmental influences can affect the progression or severity of the disorder throughout the life span.

Animal studies. Animal studies have demonstrated that it is possible to breed alcohol-preferring rats. Li, Lumeng,

McBride, and Waller (1981) were able to selectively breed strains of mice and rats that differ in alcohol-related behaviors. These alcohol-preferring rats meet the criteria for an animal model of alcoholism: They seek it out, ingest it orally, engage in efforts to obtain the drug, develop a tolerance, and become physically dependent (Lumeng, Murphy, McBride, & Li, 1995). In short, Li et al. were able to develop, through genetic breeding and selection techniques, rats that are strikingly similar to human alcoholic participants.

Neurochemical differences before any alcohol exposure between preferring and nonpreferring rats also have been found (Lumeng et al., 1995, p. 182). In the brains of alcohol-preferring rats, studies have indicated that there are lower levels of the neurotransmitter serotonin, a neurotransmitter involved in mood, sleep, and consummatory behavior (McBride et al., cited in Lumeng et al., 1995). In addition, the administration of high doses of alcohol appears to increase serotonin activity (McBride et al., cited in NIAAA, 1993). Researchers have been able to affect drinking levels in alcohol-preferring rats by increasing serotonin and dopamine levels (NIAAA, 1990, p. 47). Another neurotransmitter, dopamine, has been implicated in the etiology of alcoholism (Wise, 1988). Dopamine is experienced as intrinsically rewarding. The activation of dopamine systems within the brain is experienced as a sensation of euphoria, expansiveness, and enhanced power and energy: "Overall, the results support the notion that an innate abnormality in one or more neurotransmitter systems is a major neurobiological factor involved in excessive alcohol drinking behavior" (Lumeng et al., 1995, p. 187).

Results of a variety of studies (NIAAA, 1993) suggest that strains of rats can be genetically bred that are differentially susceptible to the anesthetic or sedating effects of alcohol. For those rats that are most susceptible to the anesthetic effects of alcohol, the inhibitory neurotransmitter gamma-aminobutyric acid (GABA) is potentiated by the effects of alcohol. Alcohol, like benzodiazipines and barbiturates, affects the receptor for the inhibitory neurotransmitter GABA. The actions of alcohol at the GABA receptor augment the flux of chloride ions through channels regulated by GABA, thus reducing the ability of neurons to fire (NIAAA, 1993, p. 68).

Molecular biology has been used to explore the genetic mechanisms that explain the action of alcohol in different strains of rodents. Goldman et al. (cited in NIAAA, 1993) determined that a variation in the gene responsible for the synthesis of the LTW-4 protein is associated with increased alcohol consumption in both preferring and nonpreferring mouse strains.

In addition, strains of mice have been genetically bred that are differentially susceptible to seizures after withdrawal from chronic alcohol intake. The withdrawal seizure-prone (WSP) mice were compared with another group of mice that were withdrawal seizure resistant (WSR). The seizure susceptibility in the WSP mice was 10 times greater than in the WSR mice despite the fact that both groups had identical blood alcohol levels. This research demonstrates that alcohol dependence may have a genetic component because withdrawal symptoms are one of the signs of alcohol dependence (Kosobud & Crabbe; Phillips et al.; cited in NIAAA, 1993).

In addition, the WSP mice display the same sensitivity to the effects of other drugs such as barbiturates, other alcohols, benzodiazipines, and nitrous oxide, suggesting that this inherited vulnerability also may be common to other drug dependencies (Belknape et al.; Crabbe et al.; cited in NIAAA, 1993). Likewise, research demonstrates that tolerance levels are genetically different in different strains of mice (Gatto et al.; Keir & Deitrich; cited in NIAAA, 1993). These studies further underscore the likelihood that alcohol dependence may have a genetic substrate.

Sons of alcoholic fathers.   Research involving the sons of alcoholic fathers has been extremely fruitful in differentiating between environmental and genetic aspects of alcoholism. The majority of this research has been conducted by Schuckit (1985a, 1985b, 1985c, 1986). Schuckit noted that under both high and low doses of alcohol, participants with a positive family history for alcoholism displayed a lower intensity of reaction to ethanol based on a variety of measures. Those individuals with a positive family history rated themselves as being significantly less intoxicated and demonstrated significantly better performance on psychomotor tasks. These individuals also had a different hormonal response to alcohol, suggesting different biochemical reactions. Schuckit speculated that individuals who display a decreased awareness of intoxication and who respond with less physical impairment as a result of intoxication might be handicapped in terms of their ability to distinguish appropriate alcohol intake (Shuckit, 1995, p. 86). These individuals may lack an internal warning system, and, as a result, they may be unable to monitor their levels of intoxication. Despite their inability to monitor their levels of intoxication, their alcohol intake is nonetheless damaging physically and psychologically.

Porjesz and Begleiter as well as other researchers (Begleiter; Begleiter et al.; Porjesz & Begleiter, 1983; Workman-Daniels & Hesselbrook; Schuckit et al.; cited in Schuckit, 1989a) also found differences between those with positive family histories for alcoholism and those with negative family histories for alcoholism. These differences included electrophysiological brain reactions, neuropsychological tests, and learning problems in school. Finally, Goedde et al. (cited in Schuckit, 1989a) and Harada et al. (cited in Schuckit, 1989a) both noted that within Asian groups, the absence of a particular enzyme resulted in elevated levels of acetaldehyde, which resulted in physiological discomfort after drinking. Perhaps as a result, certain subgroups of Asians have significantly lower rates of alcoholism.

Other Research Avenues

A variety of other studies have pointed to different neurotransmitter and neuropeptide systems within the brain as having etiological factors in the craving that alcoholics experience when they begin to drink. N. S. Miller and Gold (1991) suggested that these neurotransmitter systems located within the limbic system appear "to act as a final common pathway for the loss of control over alcohol and drugs of addiction" (p. 285). In fact, evidence shows that drive states such as hunger, thirst, and sex are similar to drugs and alcohol in that they can trigger intense craving for the substance, which can be sufficient to overwhelm volitional control. In this way, N. S. Miller and Gold (1991) speculated that addiction is similar to an acquired drive state in that it "creates a tension that must be reduced" (p. 285). They went on to state that hunger, thirst, and sex activate many of the same neurochemical substrates that are activated by drugs of addiction. In a sense, the drive states entertain the drug and alcohol use as autonomous and unconscious primary acquired drive states. In a similar fashion, N. S. Miller and Chappell (1991) stated the following:

> The loss of control may represent an acquired drive state similar to eating, drinking and sex. Many studies link alcohol/drug actions to regions in the brain where these instincts are located. After stimulation by alcohol and drugs these drive states appear to entertain drug and alcohol use with the same autonomous, spontaneous, and persistent expression as the instincts. (p. 197)

The evidence of a biological genetic basis for addiction is continuing to emerge, and there are numerous studies that have not been discussed in this chapter. For a more thorough discussion, see the excellent reviews of the literature in this area by Goedde and Agarwal (1989), Begleiter and Kissin (1995), and the NIAAA (1993), from which this report was summarized. Most researchers agree, however, that psychosocial factors must be combined with biological factors for the nature and progression of alcoholism to be fully understood. In addition, there may be more than one type of alcoholism with genetic factors differentially influencing the development and progression of alcoholism in different types.

Some of the more fruitful research seems to involve studies that attempt to integrate gene–environment interactions such as that done by Cloninger (1983). Wallace (1996) referred to Cloninger's typology as a "mixed genetic determination/influence model" (p. 21). In this model, different types of alcoholism and other types of addiction exist and different etiological theories are necessary to explain each type (Wallace, 1996, p. 21). Finally, evidence that cultural or societal factors play a strong role in the development of alcoholism is indicated in research by Reich, Cloninger, van Eerdewegh, Rice, and Mullaney (1988). Those investigators found that the frequency of alcoholism, especially in alcoholism-prone families, has been increasing and that the average age of its onset has been decreasing in recent decades. This trend seems to suggest that broad social factors other than just genetics are influencing the risks of alcoholism across the general population.

Conclusion of Disease Model and Genetic Basis

In summary, the disease model is supported by a vast amount of research, only some of which has been reviewed here. Clearly, there seems to be some biochemical basis or inherited susceptibility to addictive disorders. Although much of the research has been conducted on alcohol, there is evidence that some of the other drugs also are involved in this susceptibility. Pharmacologically, there is little reason to suspect that alcohol would be the only psychoactive drug to be influenced by the susceptibility. Many of the same neurotransmitter systems such as serotonin and dopamine implicated in the studies of alcoholism also are affected by other drugs of abuse such as cocaine and benzodiazepines.

The disease model does not specifically address the issue of how environmental and genetic factors interact. In addition, even if there is an inherited biological susceptibility among some alcoholics and drug addicts, does the susceptibility pertain to all who suffer from this disorder? It is not clear, for example, whether there may be a subpopulation of addicts and alcoholics who have developed this disorder as a result of intense unmet psychological needs, family needs, or simply conditioned responses that produced the same disorder. In fact, is it not possible that these individuals may have damaged neurotransmitter or neuropeptide systems through years of a chemical assault on their brains such that their disorder is now indistinguishable from those who were born with an inherited susceptibility? Wallace (1996) described the situation as follows:

> The addict is caught in a vicious cycle: initial positive reinforcement with mutual drug use, which leads to abnormal changes in brain chemistry with chronic use which, in turn, lead to negative mood, affective, and cognitive states. These negative psychological states motivate further drug seeking behavior because the addict remembers the highly reinforcing, positive psychological states associated with neurotransmitter release and enhancement upon initial use. (p. 16)

These questions need to be explored and deserve further careful research.

②Learning Theory Models

Learning theory models derive from and encompass several different schools of thought regarding learned or conditioned behavior. These schools include classical conditioning, operant conditioning, modeling theories, as well as cognitive–behavioral or social learning theories. These theories are based on the understanding that all human behavior is learned rather than determined by genetic factors. Problem behaviors including thoughts, feelings, and physiological changes can be modified by the same learning processes that created the behaviors in the first place (Rotgers, 1996, pp. 175–176). In simple terms, these theories subscribe to the notion that "addictive behaviors represent a category of bad habits including such behaviors as problem drinking, smoking, substance abuse, overeating, compulsive gambling and so forth" (Marlatt & Gordon, 1985, p. 9). These habits are subject to change and thus can be analyzed and modified by applying learning theory principles.

These models also view addictive behaviors as a continuum of behavior ranging from responsible or social use to addictive, compulsive use. Learning theorists contrast their models with the disease model, which they believe uses fixed categories implying the presence or absence of a disease. They view all points along the continuum of use and abuse as being governed by the same set of learning processes. The difference in the place on the continuum is that certain individuals, as a result of conditioning, have adopted dysfunctional or maladaptive patterns of abuse, whereas others are able to use these substances responsibly and moderately.

Although learning theorists acknowledge that compulsive or excessive use of alcohol and drugs can lead to certain disease states (e.g., cirrhosis of the liver), they either minimize or deny the role of genetics and biochemistry in the initiation and maintenance of addictive disorders: "Behavioral theories tend to minimize the causal role of genetic factors while placing a heavier emphasis in the interacting influences of an individual's environment, innate biological makeup or temperament, and learning processes" (Rotgers, 1996, p. 187).

As proof of these learning processes, learning theorists point to studies on alcohol expectancies. Marlatt and Gordon (1985) cited a series of studies (Marlatt & Rohsenow, 1980) that suggest that expectancies can be a more powerful determinant of drug effects than the actual physiological properties of the drug itself. This line of research uses a "balanced placebo design" (Monti, Rohsenow, Abrams, & Binkoff, 1988, p. 142) in which the expectancy of the amount of alcohol being administered is viewed independently of the actual amount of alcohol being administered. Participants' expectations of the potency of the drink and likely effect of the alcohol (i.e., tension reduction, euphoria, etc.) was a greater factor in patient ratings on the potency of the drink than was the actual alcohol content of the drink. In this research, those who were erroneously told that they were receiving a high-potency drink generally tended to expect a significant alcohol effect (tension reduction, euphoria, etc.) and said that they had received a large alcohol effect regardless of the potency of the drink (Monti et al., 1988, pp. 142–143). As a result of this research, Marlatt and Gordon (1985) suggested that these learned behaviors, mediated by factors such as expectation and attribution, are subject to change through learning theory and should provide the focus of attention rather than "relatively fixed physiological processes" (p. 11).

Learning theorists believe that "the same processes by which behavior develops can be harnessed in helping a person change unwanted or undesirable behavior (Krasner, 1982)" (Rotgers, 1996, p. 176). They focus on the environmental and contextual determinants of addictive disorders to try to modify and shape them through these same learning principles. Thus, learning theorists and practitioners require a thorough assessment of each patient, including "situational and environmental antecedents, beliefs and expectations, and the individual's family history and prior learning experiences with the substance or activity" (Marlatt & Gordon, 1985, p. 9). In addition, they analyze the consequences of the drug use behavior to determine effects that may be reinforcing as well as factors that may inhibit future drug use. A careful analysis of these variables leads to a treatment plan that focuses on altering the environment (e.g., Marlatt & Gordon's relapse prevention training) or that may seek to alter the patient's response to these environmental factors (e.g., social skills training, anger management, or assertiveness training protocols).

Other learning theorists focus on cognitive factors that contribute to the initiation and maintenance of substance use such as irrational thoughts that must be modified. The degree to which individual learning theories emphasize changing the environment versus changing the individual's reaction to the environment provides the basis for differentiating one learning theory model from another. These differentiations are as follows: classical conditioning, operant conditioning, modeling, and cognitive mediation of behavior (Rotgers, 1996, p. 178).

Classical Conditioning

Classically conditioned learned responses can help to explain the process by which environmental cues come to elicit urges or cravings involved in the initiation and maintenance of AOD abuse. According to this theory, addicts and alcoholics develop a conditioned response to the setting (including people) associated with their drug and alcohol abuse. Wikler (cited in Childress, Ehrman, Rohsenow, Robbins, & O'Brien, 1992, p. 57) observed that former drug users, when talking about their prior drug use, often began to experience actual physiological symptoms of opiate withdrawal. Wikler hypothesized that the environmental cue of simply talking about the drug use was enough to elicit a "conditioned withdrawal" response through the process of classical conditioning. Subsequent experiments proved the hypothesis to be correct.

Wikler also discovered that when heroin addicts injected an inert solution that looked like heroin, they experienced a high from this process (cited in Rotgers, 1996, p. 170):

> Based on these findings classical conditioning theorists postulate that substance users actually condition many stimuli in the environment to the rituals, paraphernalia, and use of their drug of choice by repeatedly using the drug in specific settings with specific people, and according to a specific ritual. (Rotgers, 1996, p. 179)

Cue reactivity studies focus on the conditioned response of the AOD-dependent individual to external, environmental cues as well as internal cues such as negative mood states. Childress et al. (1992) have extensively studied cue reactivity issues in cocaine and opiate addicts. The experiments focused on differential physiological and subjective responses of opiate or cocaine addicts to neutral versus opiate- or cocaine-related cues. For example, one group of participants was shown a video featuring simulated drug buying, selling, and use, whereas another video of equal length featured a non-drug task such as playing a computer video game. Both physiological measures (e.g., galvanic skin resistance and heart rate) and subjective ratings reflected striking differential responses to drug-related rather than neutral stimuli (Childress et al., 1992, p. 59).

Childress et al. (1992) also focused on internal cues such as mood states and the way that they interact with external cues to become powerful drug signals themselves. They demonstrated that hypnotically induced mood states such as depression and anger could directly trigger opiate craving and, to a lesser extent, withdrawal-like symptoms in abstinent opiate abusers. Similar cue reactivity has been demonstrated with cocaine addicts (Childress, McLellan, & O'Brien, 1988).

On the basis of these findings, a variety of behavioral strategies have been incorporated into the treatment of substance abuse disorders. These strategies focus on relapse prevention and involve procedures that attempt to "break the conditioned connection between particular aspects of a client's environment and the conditioned withdrawal or cravings presumed to form the motivational basis for substance seeking and subsequent use" (Rotgers, 1996, p. 180). These procedures include "cue exposure treatments (e.g., Childress, [Hole, Ehrman, & Robbins,] 1993; McLellan, Childress, Ehrman, & O'Brien, 1986), stimulus control techniques (e.g., Bickel & Kelly, 1988), relaxation training (e.g., Monti, Abrams, Kadden, & Cooney, 1989), covert sensitization and other aversion therapy techniques (Rimmele, Miller, & Dougher, 1989)" (Rotgers, 1996, pp. 179–180). Aversion therapy attempts to apply classical conditioning techniques to "condition a new aversive response to substance use and the cues associated with it" (Rotgers, 1996, p. 180).

Operant Conditioning

Operant conditioning theorists believe that behavior patterns are determined by the positive and negative reinforcements that occur as a result of the behaviors. AOD abuse is influenced by two kinds of reinforcers: the positive reinforcement of euphoria and relaxation and the removal of subjectively negative effects such as anxiety and tension (Rotgers, 1996, p. 180).

Operant conditioning theorists assume that "voluntary behaviors are increased or decreased in frequency depending on the environment's responses to them" (Rotgers, 1996, p. 180). AOD abuse both brings positive affect such as euphoria and serves to medicate or decrease negative affect such as anxiety or tension. For these reasons, operant conditioning theorists focus on the reinforcing properties of alcohol and drugs to explain the initiation and maintenance of AOD abuse.

Reinforcing properties that are closer in time to the actual behavior exert a greater influence than reinforcing factors that occur later. Thus, an alcoholic person who drinks in the morning to avoid withdrawal symptoms achieves an immediate reinforcing effect. This effect is greater than the negative consequences that may occur later. Virtually all operant-conditioning–related treatment techniques involve rearranging the contingencies or responses to drinking such that rewards and punishments for not drinking are more apparent and immediate. One such method is the community reinforcement approach (Azrin, Sisson, Meyers, & Godley, 1982). This approach involves rearranging variables within the community such that reinforcement for not drinking as well as punishment for drinking is maximized. In general, operant theories assume that reinforcing factors for not drinking are more important than negative reinforcement or punishing factors.

Modeling Behavior

Modeling behavior involves observation of another person's behavior as a means of developing more appropriate coping skills. Modeling is seen as an efficient and rapid means of behavior change. Bandura (1977) believed that the individual develops a process of cognitive mapping in which aspects of behavior are stored and can be reproduced at a later time. Modeling behavior has been used to explain the initiation of AOD abuse, especially in adolescents (Rotgers, 1996, p. 182). A variety of data suggests that peer-group influences are extremely important for adolescents in the initiation of AOD abuse. Peer-group factors also play a strong role in the maintenance of AOD abuse for both adults and adolescents. Modeling theory plays a role in intervention strategies such as social skills approaches, relaxation, and anger management (Rotgers, 1996, pp. 182–183).

Cognitive–Behavioral Model

The fourth approach in learning theory models is a cognitive–behavioral model derived from social learning theory. Social learning theory postulates that conditioning not only affects behaviors but that it also leads to the development of thoughts and emotions that shape behavior: "A central concept in SLT [social learning theory] is reciprocal determinism, which states that people both influence and are influenced by their environments" (Rotgers, 1996, p. 184). Thus, changes can be initiated both by changing the environment and by changing the self-control processes that shape the individual's response to the environment.

A key variable in determining how the individual responds to the environment is a concept called *self-efficacy*. Self-efficacy refers to a person's confidence and self-assurance that he or she will be able to respond appropriately and deal effectively with a given situation. The greater the expectation that one can effectively manage a particular situation, the less the likelihood of an inappropriate or dysfunctional response. For this reason, cognitive–behavioral theory also focuses on techniques to enhance self-efficacy (e.g., assertiveness training, anger management, relaxation techniques), as does modeling theory. Social learning theory views addictive disorders as being a failure of coping, so that individuals must learn skills for coping with the stresses of problems. They also must learn to anticipate future stresses by avoiding situations in which the individuals know that they have a low self-efficacy about performing particular skills. These processes have been brought to bear in a relapse prevention model (Marlatt & Gordon, 1985), which attempts to identify triggers and high-risk situations for the addicted individual. Relapse prevention plans develop alternative coping strategies to deal with these situations. Cognitive–behavioral, marital, and family interventions also have been developed (Rotgers, 1996, p. 185).

Two models for AOD abuse treatment, rational–emotive therapy developed by Albert Ellis and colleagues (Ellis, McInerney, DiGiuseppe, & Yeager, 1988) and cognitive therapy developed by Aaron Beck and colleagues (Beck, Wright, Newman, & Liese, 1993), are derived from a cognitive–behavioral framework. Both of these theories suggest that irrational thoughts and feelings contribute to the development of AOD abuse. They attempt to reprogram or change these thoughts and feelings in a more functional direction (Rotgers, 1996, p. 185).

Conclusion of Learning Theory Models

Learning theory models have added a tremendous amount to the understanding of the initiation and maintenance of addictive disorders. An impressive body of data indicates the importance of environmental and contextual variables in the development of addictive disorders. Research by Childress and others demonstrates that cues in the environment such as drug paraphernalia, exposure to old "using" environments, and simulated drug use trigger physiological and subjective craving responses. This research has led to treatment interventions designed to assist the individual in developing a sense of self-efficacy as well as specific techniques to avoid situations for which coping skills are lacking. Relapse prevention work has assumed an ever-increasing and important role in all treatment environments, including traditional 12-step programs. Despite the fact that Marlatt's work on relapse prevention is not widely used in these programs, other theorists (Gorski, 1989) have adapted Marlatt's basic concepts to be compatible with a 12-step model. The notion of expectancies also has been valuable in explaining how individuals' responses to alcohol and drugs can be enhanced or diminished according to their expectation of the beneficial effects of this substance. Thus, alcohol expectancies can be a powerful force in the initiation and maintenance of AOD abuse problems. Many adolescents are especially vulnerable to peer influences, which in turn are shaped by larger societal factors such as the media and adult role models. Alcohol expectancy research has contributed to the understanding of this relationship and has shown that factors other than physiological or biochemical cravings play a role in the development of addictive disorders. Finally, learning theorists have advanced the field by developing a solid database supporting the efficacy of their interventions.

The controversy over controlled drinking (see chap. 1) has alienated learning theorists from the mainstream treatment community to the detriment of both the psychological community and the mainstream treatment community. It has kept otherwise valuable strategies and interventions from being incorporated into the majority of treatment programs today. In our opinion, this problem stems from a failure by some learning theorists to acknowledge genetic and biochemical factors in addictive disorders. If addiction is simply a bad habit that has been learned, then why can it not be unlearned? This criticism is not meant to undermine the major contributions of learning theorists but simply to point out that reductionistic thinking can lead to serious problems in the field of addiction theory and treatment.

In total, the evidence for the role of environmental and contextual variables in the initiation and maintenance of AOD abuse is compelling. It seems reasonable, however, with the large body of data available on both ends of the spectrum, to postulate that both biochemical as well as psychosocial variables play a potent role in the development and maintenance of addictive disorders. It is likely that different factors play a greater or lesser role in the development of addictive disorders for a given individual. As theorists such as Cloninger and others have surmised, there may be certain individuals who are uniquely biochemically predisposed to addictive disorders. On the other hand, there are individuals who find their way into an addictive lifestyle as a result of environmental and psychological deficits that are overwhelming and in response to which the attraction of an addictive lifestyle is sustainable even in the face of increasingly negative consequences. Some theorists from both the disease and learning theory models currently speak of addictive disorders in a biopsychosocial context rather than in the more reductionistic sense of one or the other.

Psychoanalytic Theory

Early psychoanalytic theories focused on addiction as a regressive attempt to return to an infantile, pleasurable state. By contrast, contemporary psychoanalytic theories, based on ego and object relations theory, view addiction as a progressive response to deficits of self-regulation. Contemporary theorists view the addictive use of alcohol and drugs as an adaptive mechanism by which the individual attempts to cope with self-regulatory deficits arising from early infantile deprivation and maladaptive parent–child interactions. This theory has been labeled the *self-medication hypothesis* (SMH) and has primarily been associated with Khantzian (Khantzian, 1981, 1982, 1985b, 1997).

The SMH states that

> rather than simply seeking escape, euphoria, or self-destruction, addicts are attempting to medicate themselves for a range of psychiatric problems and painful emotional states. Although most such efforts at self-treatment are eventually doomed, given the hazards and complications of long-term, unstable drug use patterns, addicts discover that the short-term effects of their drugs of choice help them to cope with distressful subjective states and an external reality otherwise experienced as unmanageable or overwhelming. (Khantzian, 1985b, p. 1263)

The theory evolved in the course of Khantzian's extensive clinical experience working in public-sector outpatient substance abuse programs, a Massachusetts inpatient facility for severely mentally ill patients, and in private practice (Khantzian, 1997). After creating an empathic bond with the patient in recovery and helping the patient establish abstinence, Khantzian explored the issue of how the patient experienced the drug in the initial period of use, before tolerance developed (Khantzian, 1997).

The theory is supported by the work of other researchers. Gerard and Kornetsky (1954, 1955) viewed adolescent addiction as an attempt to escape the overwhelming anxiety of preparation for adult role models. Weider and Kaplan (1969) viewed addiction as a pharmacological attempt to reduce stress by the addict. They emphasized that "individuals self-select different drugs on the basis of personality organization and ego impairments" (Khantzian, 1985b, p. 1260). Thus, drugs are not selected indiscriminately; they are chosen to act as "prostheses" (Khantzian, 1985b, p. 1260). The work of Milkman and Frosch (1973) suggested that heroin addicts prefer the calming effects of opiates, whereas amphetamine addicts use the stimulating action to enhance their sense of self-worth and grandiosity (Khantzian, 1985b, p. 1260). Alcohol and other central nervous system depressants minimize feelings of isolation, emptiness, and related anxiety and tension: "Patients experiment with various classes of drugs and discover that a specific one is compelling because it ameliorates, heightens, or relieves affect states that they find particularly problematic or painful" (Khantzian, 1997, p. 232).

Self-Regulatory Impairments

According to the SMH, several types of self-regulatory impairments can lead to substance abuse problems: deficits in affect tolerance, self-care, self-esteem, and relationships (Khantzian, 1997).

Affect tolerance. Several researchers have noted and described the deficits in affect tolerance exhibited by alcohol- and drug-dependent individuals (Brehm & Khantzian, 1992; Krystal, 1988; McDougall, 1984; Wurmser, 1974): "These patients alternate between intense emotions of rage and suffering and vague feelings of dysphoria and discomfort. . . . They experience their affects in the extreme" (Khantzian, 1997, p. 234). Not only do these individuals "feel too much or not at all" (Khantzian, 1997, p. 234), but they also sometimes find their affect confusing and inexplicable. They sometimes cannot find the words to express their emotions. Krystal believed that the drug abuser lives in terror of being overwhelmed by primitive preverbal affective experiences and that the use of drugs functions to shore up the addict against this danger.

Furthermore, Krystal believed that this preverbal over-whelming experience of affect can result in a condition called *alexithymia*, in which patients are unable to verbalize the feelings that they are experiencing. These patients are unable to connect the feelings that they are experiencing with the stories behind them. Although they experience intense affect for brief periods of time, they are unable to identify these feelings as angry, tired, sad, and so on. These individuals also have difficulty fantasizing and, as a result, can "experience only the physiological aspects of their affect, which are painful. Thus, they turn to drugs to alleviate or block the affective responses" (Brehm & Khantzian, 1992, p. 112). The theory states that it is much easier for these individuals to minimize their affect with alcohol or drugs than it is to verbalize these overwhelming traumatic affective experiences that occurred at a preverbal level. As a result, they are led to reduce their suffering by using alcohol and drugs.

Impairments in self-care. Many individuals who are drug dependent show a flagrant disregard for their sense of personal well-being and engage in risk-taking behaviors. These behaviors are viewed as an inability to provide for self-care: "Disturbances in self-care are the result of an impairment in the ego wherein the individual fails to be aware, cautious, worried, or frightened enough to avoid or desist in behavior that has damaging and/or dangerous consequences" (Khantzian, 1982, p. 589). The ability to provide for self-care is associated with ego functions related to "signal anxiety, reality testing, judgment, and synthesis" (Khantzian, 1981, p. 165). Studies have supported this theory that affect and self-care deficits are related to AOD problems. Khantzian cited the work of Kellam, Brook, Moss, and Cloninger (Khantzian, 1997).

Another impairment in self-care involves the inability of addicts to soothe or calm themselves appropriately or to mobilize for action when action or activity is called for. According to the theory, this vulnerability is caused by problems internalizing the caring functions of the mother at an early age.

Vulnerabilities in self-development and self-esteem. Still another self-regulatory deficiency concerns vulnerabilities in self-development and self-esteem. Kernberg (1975) described states that a child must go through to achieve healthy ego development. These states represent increasingly sophisticated differentiation of self from others until, in the final stage, "the child integrates the positive and negative self in object. When this stage is achieved, the child has a stable, cohesive sense of self and a constant representation of mother" (Brehm & Khantzian, 1992, p. 111).

Kernberg (1975) believed that the addict has not progressed to this final stage of development. Rather, a pathological "grandiose self" develops that is constantly refueled by alcohol:

> This entitled grandiose self perceives that the self is perfect and the object is loving, and any other perceptions are denied. The alcoholic then uses rigid and primitive defenses of splitting, denial, and projection to keep from his or her awareness the bad self or inadequate self at all costs. (Brehm & Khantzian, 1992, p. 111)

Just underneath this grandiose self, however, is the perception of failure and lack of self-worth. The SMH postulates that it is only by the constant abuse of alcohol and drugs that the addict can defend against this lack of self-worth and self-esteem surfacing.

Troubled relationships. A fourth area of self-regulatory deficiency concerns troubled relationships. The SMH states that difficulties with self-esteem and self-worth invariably cause conflicts in developing relationships and intimacy. Addicts and alcoholics desperately need the support that relationships can provide; however, they are constantly disguising this need by being oppositional, distancing themselves from others, and manipulating others. They tend to go to extremes. They either immerse themselves in a relationship and become completely dependent or they become hostile and rejecting and sever relationships at the slightest affront to their fragile self-esteem. From a psychodynamic standpoint, troubled relationships can emerge from the mother not displaying an ability to provide a nurturing, caring, and safe environment for the infant (Brehm & Khantzian, 1992). Brehm and Khantzian noted that McDougall (1984) hypothesized that certain mothers are "addictive." Because of their own needs, they foster the idea that their infant should depend on them for all of their self-regulatory needs. Later in life, it is natural for that individual to turn to alcohol and drugs in an effort to re-create the environment of total dependence that existed in the infant–mother relationship (Brehm & Khantzian, 1992, pp. 111–112).

Conclusion of Psychodynamic Theory

Theorists such as Khantzian have gone a long way toward reintegrating psychoanalytic thought into the mainstream of addiction treatment. The SMH is intuitively intriguing and appeals to both common sense and experience. It is supported by many clinical observations, although it is difficult to study in a methodologically rigorous manner. The lack of empirical support is generally considered to be a weakness of this model, but the tenets are difficult to confirm through empirical studies because they are based on clinical judgments about the internal experiences of the alcoholic or addict. The concept that addicts are attempting to address early disorders of self arising out of impaired object relations has clinical utility. Many therapists will verify that addicts speak about wanting to "feel normal" or avoid painful affective experiences as a reason for abusing substances. Many theorists talk about the extreme difficulty addicts and alcoholics have with tolerating affective material (S. Brown, 1985). Through these concepts, Khantzian enhanced the understanding of the addict's experience from an internal, intrapsychic position. By implication, the therapist is to assist the patient in becoming more comfortable with affective states and in developing healthy alternatives to cope with them.

In addition, Khantzian related his theories to mainstream addiction treatment, stressing the role that traditional self-help groups such as Alcoholics Anonymous can play in the overall recovery process:

During the initial stage of therapy, where control is of paramount importance, the use of self-help groups such as Alcoholics Anonymous (AA) and Narcotics Anonymous (NA) can provide the patient with a social family in which life is bearable and manageable without alcohol and drugs. AA helps the individual to recognize the "powerlessness" that he or she feels and/or denies in relation to alcohol. It provides alcoholics with the steps whereby their "powerlessness" can be changed into power to manage their impulsivity. The function of AA is to provide the individual with a framework of "self-governance" in a social context. (Brehm & Khantzian, 1992, p. 114)

Khantzian viewed his theory as being a complement to sociocultural and biogenetic theories of the etiology of AOD disorders. In this manner, he added a richness and a depth to the understanding of addictive disorders by enhancing the understanding of the intrapsychic, psychodynamic world of the alcoholic and drug addict.

Family Theory Models

There are three family theory models that are commonly used within the AOD abuse field. These include family systems models, behavioral models, and family disease models. Although these three models are each distinct and have their own unique characteristics, most treatment centers use an amalgation of the three models, borrowing elements from each model (McCrady & Epstein, 1996, p. 123).

Family Systems Model

The family systems model views the family as the major unit of analysis. Families are viewed as units governed by rules. In many cases, these rules are implicit or unspoken but serve to maintain a balance or homeostasis within the family unit. The principle of homeostasis is central to family systems theory and refers to the families' attempts to maintain stability and balance within the system. Any action or behavior on the part of one family member affects the entire system. To the extent that this behavior becomes a destabilizing force within the family, the system adjusts to try to restore a sense of homeostasis.

In alcoholic families, even introducing sobriety can become a disruptive force after years of living with and adapting to a drinking lifestyle. In fact, many theorists believe that alcohol may serve an adaptive function within the family (McCrady & Epstein, 1996). An example of this type of adaptive function might be a teenager who begins to drink in response to marital conflict between his or her parents. The drinking then serves the function of distracting the parents away from their own marital discord and focusing their attention on the teenager's drinking. In fact, the teenager's acting-out behavior may unify the parents in an effort to deal with the child's emerging crisis. Other possible adaptive functions of drinking would include dealing with anxiety about intimacy or avoidance of conflict.

As alcoholism or addiction progresses within the family system, family rules often become increasingly rigid and inflexible. Once again, these rules serve the function of maintaining homeostasis. These rules might include things such as "Don't talk about Dad's drinking" or "Don't confront Mother about her drinking because she is fragile and this may push her over the edge." Gradually, family members learn that certain topics are taboo and must not be discussed. Children growing up in these environments often have difficulty identifying their feelings or trusting their perceptions. Living within this type of rigid family structure encourages them to deny the validity of their own perceptions and feelings. Steinglass (1979, 1981) did research that supports the notion of rigid functioning within families of drinking alcoholics. Steinglass found that families with a drinking alcoholic were the most rigid in their functioning, followed by families who were in a transitional phase from drinking to sobriety, followed by families with a recovering alcoholic. The latter group was the most flexible and open in their functioning.

Family systems theorists also focus on family boundaries (Thombs, 1994, p. 140). In alcoholic families, traditional boundaries or patterns of relationships (husband–wife or parent–child) often become disrupted. An example would be a mother whose son begins to abuse drugs. In an attempt to rescue her son, the mother becomes overinvolved and exhibits both smothering and enabling behavior. She attempts to rescue her child, becomes overprotective, and makes excuses for him. The father, on the other hand, may go to the other extreme, becoming overly punitive or completely disengaging. As time progresses, the mother becomes more aligned with her son and the father feels more like an outsider. In this way, traditional family boundaries and alliances become disrupted.

Family systems theorists talk about roles that individuals play within the family. These roles describe functions that individuals play to maintain the homeostasis. Within alcoholic families, a classification of different roles might include the chemically dependent person, the chief enabler, the family hero, the scapegoat, the lost child, and the mascot (Thombs, 1994, p. 174). The chemically dependent person is, of course, the addict who is prone to acting irresponsibly. As stated previously, this behavior may serve a variety of different functions, including avoidance of marital conflict or intimacy. The chief enabler is usually the nondependent spouse. This is the one who makes excuses for the addict and tries to cover up or conceal the addict's drug- and alcohol-using behavior. Enablers are often completely unaware of the fact that their behavior is shielding the users from the consequences of their actions and thus contributing to the problem. The family hero may sometimes be the oldest child who takes on responsibilities at a level that is developmentally higher than would be expected. They often overperform in athletics and scholastic activities. This person helps to ease the tension in the family by overperforming and overfunctioning. These individuals often tend to "burn out" later in life (Thombs, 1994).

The scapegoat is frequently another child who is blamed for all the family's problems. This child may act out the emotional turmoil that is just under the surface in alcoholic families. This child often identifies with an alcoholic parent. Scapegoats serve to direct blame and focus away from the alcoholic parent and onto themselves (Thombs, 1994). The lost child is often difficult to recognize because he or she is so quiet. He or she seeks to avoid conflict and to smooth over tension at all costs. Later in life these individuals may become depressed or exhibit a variety of other emotional symptoms (Thombs, 1994). Their goal is to reduce tension by disappearing and not causing any conflict. The mascot is known as the family clown and is useful in helping the family dissipate tense or conflicting situations. Mascots often do silly, immature acts and make jokes even at their own expense (Thombs, 1994).

Family systems theorists view this model as useful in explaining both the initiation and maintenance of addictive behavior. As mentioned previously, the use of alcohol can serve an adaptive function and systems theorists believe that explains why certain individuals engage initially in AOD abuse and continue with this abusive behavior in spite of a variety of negative consequences. They emphasize the power of family systems to influence individual behavior such as drug abuse. Furthermore, they suggest that the family roles, the rigid set of rules, and the boundary problems contribute to the maintenance of AOD abuse problems as the disorder progresses.

Therapeutic efforts generally focus on making explicit the implicit family rules, changing the family structure to reinforce traditional boundaries, and educating the family about the ways in which family roles have helped to perpetuate the problem. A review of the literature reveals a robust database of studies indicating that family therapy is an important component of treatment for AOD abuse patients (McCrady & Epstein, 1996, p. 130).

Family Behavioral Model

The second family therapy approach that has been incorporated into AOD abuse treatment is the family behavioral

model. The family behavioral model relies heavily on observations of family members with specific focus on behavioral
interactions and patterns. This approach also involves using
behavioral change techniques, such as contracting, to encourage new interactional and problem-solving modalities
within the family. In 1973, Hersen, Miller, and Eisler observed
interactions between alcoholic husbands and wives (cited in
McCrady & Epstein, 1996, p. 121). They discovered that the
wives looked at their spouses more closely when they were
discussing alcohol than when they were discussing a neutral
topic. In addition, Becker and Miller (1976), in a similar study
of alcoholic husbands and their wives, found that the alcoholic spoke more when the topic being discussed was related
to alcohol and the wives spoke more when the topic was a
different issue. These researchers concluded that the marital
interactions were inadvertently reinforcing the alcoholic behavior by increased attention from the spouse, by the dom-
inance of the conversation by the alcoholic husband, or both.

McCrady and Epstein (1996) also reported on several other
interactional studies. They concluded that the "interactions
of alcoholic couples change when alcohol is present or discussed, and that these changes have a variety of positive features that may reinforce and maintain the drinking" (Mc-
Crady & Epstein, 1996, p. 122). As stated previously, the
behavioral models rely on specific structured interventions to
help couples change their interactional patterns. O'Farrell
and Cowles (1989) have developed a behavioral management
therapy that has specific change goals incorporated into the
process. This is a highly structured program involving a set
number of sessions. Both the alcoholic and the spouse must
commit to specific goals, including abstinence, self-help, and
meeting attendance. The program also has the spouse specify
what he or she will do in the event of a relapse. In this way,
O'Farrell and Cowles attempted to alter behaviors that may
have been enabling or dysfunctional and provide a structure
from which the family can move toward a healthy state of
recovery.

Family Disease Model

The third major model of addiction-related family therapy is the family disease model. This model arises from the traditional disease model concept and incorporates many of the traditions and techniques of the AA program. It also is the model that is most commonly used within traditional treatment centers. However, most programs incorporate elements of all three models.

The disease model describes alcoholism as a "family disease." The disease being referred to, however, is not alcoholism but *codependence*. The "disease" is characterized by a preoccupation that the family member has with the addict, especially an investment in trying to change the behavior of this person. Codependents most often become enmeshed and obsessed with the behavior of the alcoholic or addicted spouse. They gradually lose their sense of self-esteem, self-worth, and even a sense of personal identity as they continue to lead a crisis-filled life centered on the behavior of the drinking or drug-using partner. The codependent spouse is driven by a need to change the behavior of the addicted spouse. Family disease model theory believes that a return to normalcy is possible only when that individual gives up this attempt to try to control the situation and is able to "detach with love." Thus, the focus of therapy within the family disease model centers on helping the codependent spouse achieve this sense of detachment. This typically involves a personal program of recovery for the family member involving Al-Anon, Nar-Anon, or other self-help groups. Although family disease model theory strongly encourages continued family therapy attendance, it is believed that only through a personal program of recovery using the 12-step process (see chap. 8) can the codependent become truly healthy and fully functioning.

Conclusion of Family Therapy Models

Family therapy models and techniques have contributed a great deal to the understanding of addictive disorders. In particular, the concepts of homeostasis, the rules and goals that govern the interactions between family members and addicted families, the ways in which these rules become increasingly rigid and fixed, and the manner in which they contribute to the maintenance of the addictive cycle are all valuable concepts with true clinical utility. In addition, there is now a substantial database (McCrady & Epstein, 1996, p. 130) suggesting that the inclusion of family therapy into the mix of treatments for AOD abusers is significant in enhancing outcomes with this population. Family systems theory has added to the understanding of factors that might initiate alcohol and AOD abuse within an individual. Specifically, these factors are related to secondary gains that derive from the abuse of chemicals. Situations such as an adolescent who begins abusing marijuana to defocus his parents' attention away from marital conflict might explain the initiation of AOD abusing behavior. It also is true, however, that some family systems theorists overstate the importance of these factors and slide into reductionism when they begin to explain the full complexity of addictive disorders in these terms. It is likely that these factors play a role in the initiation of AOD abuse. It is also likely that these factors serve as motivating forces for individuals to continue abusing drugs or alcohol in the early stages of their disorder. It is unlikely, however, that individuals would continue to suffer the major life-threatening negative consequences associated with addictive disorders simply as a result of secondary gains. This is not to deny that these factors are important and powerful factors that enhance the understanding of addictive disorders. Rather, it is to emphasize the point that addictive disorders are extremely complex and involve familial, intrapsychic, biogenetic, and learned behavior patterns that all contribute to the initiation and maintenance of this disorder. The family therapy theorists have made a major contribution in the understanding of this disorder by emphasizing the need to include family members and to address family dynamics so that the alcoholic or addict can return to a more healthy, stable, flexible, and open family environment after treatment.

The Biopsychosocial Model: An Integrated Approach

The four major theoretical models discussed in this chapter offer a wealth of theoretical insights, research data, and clinical observations about the nature of addictive disorders. The difficulty of integrating these approaches into a unified model is complicated because each seems to offer a self-contained view of addictive disorders. In fact, in many cases these views seemingly conflict with each other. Most addiction professionals and treatment centers, however, use an integrated biopsychosocial model to explain the complexity of this disorder. A biopsychosocial model accounts for multiple pathways to addiction with specific factors playing a greater or lesser role for any given individual. This section represents our attempt to integrate the four major theoretical models and their supporting data into a biopsychosocial model. Table 1 shows the multiple pathways, the contributions of the models, and the progression from use to abuse to dependence.

Biochemical Factors

In this model, biochemical factors play a significant role in the initiation and maintenance of AOD problems for many addicted individuals. The strongest evidence for a genetic transmission of addictive disorders exists for alcohol (NIAAA, 1993, pp. 61–120), but a growing body of research data also suggests a biochemical if not genetic basis for addiction to other drugs (NIAAA, 1993, p. 120).

Neurotransmitter systems play an important role in modulating affective states, attention, and concentration. Some individuals may have genetic impairments in the neurotransmitter system that may create a hypersensitivity or predisposition to the effects of alcohol, drugs, or both. Within the complex neurotransmitter system, different individuals may have different impairments that may predispose them to the abuse of specific chemicals. For example, because the neurotransmitter system has both excitatory (stimulating) and inhibitory (calming) effects, we hypothesize that individuals with deficits in the excitatory neurotransmitter system might be more susceptible to the effects of stimulant drugs. Individuals with deficits in the inhibitory neurotransmitter chemicals, on the other hand, might be more predisposed to the effects of depressants. Other individuals might have a more global impairment predisposing them to the abuse of a wide range of drugs.

The introduction of mood-altering chemicals into the lives of these individuals may create powerful biochemical reinforcers that act like primary drive states (e.g., hunger, sex) precisely because mood-altering drugs mimic and even stimulate the action of these neurotransmitter chemicals in the brain. The more a person abuses psychoactive chemicals, the more this neurotransmitter system may become depleted and perhaps even permanently compromised, resulting in cravings for psychoactive chemicals in greater quantities and with increasing frequency. For individuals who were born with a compromised neurochemical balance, the introduction of psychoactive drugs might provide a powerful positive reinforcer by allowing these individuals some relief and control over affective states that previously seemed to dominate their lives.

It is also possible that other individuals may develop a biochemical susceptibility to alcohol and drugs as a result of years of abuse. This abuse may have started as a result of psychosocial factors such as painful affective experiences, family problems, or peer pressure, but over time the abuse of chemicals may have damaged the neurotransmitter system.

In either circumstance, the neurochemical imbalance may create a biochemical craving that acts like a primary drive state and powerfully reinforces the continued abuse of psychoactive chemicals despite a variety of negative consequences. The individual may experience the cravings as powerful enough to overwhelm cognitive factors such as judgment, insight, and impulse control, and they may propel the individual toward an alcohol- and drug-dependent life-

Table 1

Biopsychosocial Model: Multiple Pathways to AOD Disorders

Stage of disorder	Etiological factors						
	Biochemical	Expectancies	Cue reactivity	Self-efficacy	Family dysfunction	Psychoanalytic	Other risk factors
Prior to use	Individual is born with a neurochemical abnormality that may make affect regulation, concentration, etc. difficult. ADHD and aggression may predate AOD—stems from same abnormality.	As individual progresses from grade to middle to high school, expectancies about positive effects of AOD increase due to peer influence, adult role models, media messages.	Not applicable.	In certain situations efficacy expectations are low. Individual does not believe he or she can perform appropriately (e.g., lack of assertiveness).	Fragile family structure threatens to become overwhelmed (e.g., marital discord).	Early trauma leads to disorders of self, which leads to intense psychic pain. Impaired ability to trust others leads to increased likelihood that individual will trust external object (e.g., alcohol or drugs). Individual discovers feelings can be medicated via AOD.	ADHD, aggressive behaviors, substance-using peer group.
Point of contact (first use)	Desire to drink or use is abnormally stimulated due to drug–neurotransmitter interaction. Person's genetic tolerance results in lack of feedback about when to stop.	Because individual is primed to expect positive results, he or she experiences positive results. Social reinforcement glamorizes heavy drinking.	Rewarding stimulus (AOD use), coupled with environmental cues and internal cues, begins to develop conditioned response to the cues. Presence of cues without AOD use can trigger psychological and physiological craving response.	AOD temporarily addresses problem by decreasing social uneasiness.	Family member uses drugs to defocus from marital discord and restore homeostasis.		

| Abuse | Individual discovers feelings can be modulated via AOD. Devotes larger amounts of time and energy to AOD. Begins to crave. Begins to have negative consequences, some loss of control. Feels more and more shame, desires to alter feelings, more AOD. | In teen years peer group is increasingly important. Increased contact with AOD peer group further reinforces use. | As person's life increasingly revolves around AOD use, cues assume greater power. Craving response increases as association between AOD use and cues is reinforced. AOD use increases. | AOD becomes self-reinforcing as individual learns to use AOD to address variety of social and emotional problems. Individual develops conditioned responses to set and setting of AOD behavior that reinforces use. Consequences increase. Loss of control increases. | Family structure is impaired. Mother aligns with drug-using child and becomes enabler. Father plays policeman role. AOD progresses as parents argue. | Individual begins to identify specific drugs to address specific ego deficits (e.g., cocaine fuels grandiose self-image). |

(Table continues)

Table 1 (*Continued*)

Stage of disorder	Etiological factors						
	Biochemical	Expectancies	Cue reactivity	Self-efficacy	Family dysfunction	Psychoanalytic	Other risk factors
Dependence	AOD becomes like primary drive state. Depletion of or permanent damage to neurotransmitter system may trigger stronger craving. Intense craving driven by physiological and psychological realities. Achievement of euphoric effects increasingly difficult. Goal is now avoidance of pain. Consequences have no meaning. Increased loss of control.	As individual continues to use, nonusing peers are discarded. Increased negative consequences. Increased loss of control.	Exposure to cues becomes powerful factor in increasing abuse and triggering relapses if there are attempts to stop. Increased loss of control.	Learned patterns of behavior are entrenched. Alternative coping strategies are unavailable. Increased loss of control.	Family is increasingly crisis focused, reacting to drug user's behavior. Other family needs ignored. Family communication breaks down as rules become rigidified (e.g., don't talk about his or her drug use). Family has increased consequences and loss of control.	Rigid narcissistic personality structure emerges that must be protected at all costs. Guards against enfeebled self that lurks beneath the surface. Increased craving. Increased loss of control.	

Note. More than one set of factors can and often does play a role in the development of this disorder for a given individual. There are not only multiple pathways to AOD disorders for different individuals, but for a particular individual the etiology is determined by a variety of factors. AOD = alcohol and other drug; ADHD = attention deficit with hyperactivity disorder.

style. Many addicts speak of needing drugs to feel normal rather than to feel high. Opiate addicts often talk of needing to get their fix to feel normal or to "get right."

Once the individual develops a dependency on alcohol and drugs, the disorder becomes a primary entity in and of itself. This entity has its own set of symptoms and natural progression toward increasingly destructive consequences. The individual will progress toward a lifestyle characterized by greater degrees of unmanageability and loss of control. The biochemical imbalances may help to explain why AOD-dependent individuals are no longer able to return to moderate levels of use.

Expectancies

Although the biochemical factors may be important, a number of other factors also contribute to the initiation, maintenance, and progression of AOD disorders. Not only the pharmacological properties of the drug itself, but also the individual's expectation of the drug's effects contribute to the desire to use drugs (Marlatt & Gordon, 1985; Marlatt & Rohsenow, 1980; Monti et al., 1988). Expectancy studies show that individuals who expect greater effects from alcohol and drugs in terms of tension reduction, euphoria, and avoidance of negative affect states are more likely to use and abuse these drugs. Expectancies may play a significant role in the initiation of AOD disorders, especially for adolescents. Peer-group influences are extremely important in explaining the initiation of adolescent substance abuse (Bukstein, 1995; Rotgers, 1996, p. 182). In today's society, adolescents are exposed to many messages that may reinforce positive expectancies of AOD use. These messages come from their peer group, adult role models, and the media. In many adolescent peer groups, there is widespread AOD use that serves to normalize this behavior for others. The peer-group influence may glamorize it and provide respect for the ability to consume large amounts. The peer-group attitude may lead to the expectation that AOD use will provide special status of increased popularity. Media and mass marketing through TV,

radio, movies, and magazines also may create positive expectancies.

As adolescents progress into a substance-abusing lifesyle,
they associate less and less with non–drug-using peers. They
are less likely to be exposed to negative information and messages that might alter their expectancies. They also may dis-
count negative messages about AOD use because the messages would challenge their increasingly rigid defense and
denial structure. Thus, positive AOD expectancies remain intact even as the AOD use progresses and negative consequences accumulate. In this way, expectancies play a powerful role in the initiation, maintenance, and progression of
AOD disorders.

Cue Reactivity

Like expectancy studies, cue reactivity studies also show that
factors other than genetic or biochemical factors contribute
to the maintenance and progression of the disorder. These
studies show that alcoholics and addicts develop a conditioned response to the set and setting of their drug use (Childress et al., 1988, 1992). Addicts who are exposed to drug
paraphernalia or video presentations of drug-using situations
develop powerful physiological reactions as well as powerful
craving responses. These studies help to explain how addictive disorders are maintained in spite of the negative consequences. As alcoholics and addicts become enmeshed in a
drinking and drug-using lifestyle, they may become aware
of the need for change and they may achieve periods of abstinence on their own. However, the exposure to an environmental cue can threaten to pull them back into their old lifestyle. The alcoholic who passes by the bar or liquor store on
the way home from work or the cocaine addict who sees a
movie with cocaine use experiences powerful cues and stimuli to resume use of his or her drug. Without effective training in how to handle these cues, a substance-dependent person may relapse.

Self-Efficacy

Self-efficacy is the ability and confidence to cope with the environment and emotions in successful ways. Individuals who lack self-efficacy also may be more likely to abuse alcohol or drugs. Many substance-dependent individuals indicate that when they began to use, the substances seemed to help or medicate various psychological or functional deficits. They speak of alcohol making them more relaxed in social situations or relieving stress during traumatic events such as divorce, loss of job, or death of loved one. Adolescents talk about marijuana helping them to forget poor academic performance. For example, "After I began smoking pot I was still getting bad grades and my parents were still yelling at me, but it just didn't bother me anymore." As the AOD problem progresses, the physiological and functional impairments worsen rather than improve other problems, but the individuals do not view the AOD use as a complicating factor. Instead, they frequently increase their use to further medicate and the disorder progresses into more negative consequences and increased loss of control.

Attempts to enhance their functioning through social skills training, assertiveness training, anger management skills, and so on are all valuable interventions for addressing these impairments in self-efficacy (McCrady & Epstein, 1996; Steinglass, 1979, 1981). Both therapists and self-help groups recognize the need to develop nonchemical coping skills for these problem areas. If AOD-dependent individuals have effective nonchemical coping skills and believe in their own ability to manage stress, they will be more likely to give up the AOD behavior (Hester, 1994; W. R. Miller, Westerberg, & Waldron, 1995; Rotgers, 1996).

Family Dysfunction

Family dysfunction also plays a causative role in the development of AOD problems (Kaufman, 1994; McCrady & Epstein, 1996; Steinglass, 1994). If the family structure is threatened by marital discord or other stress, some individuals may adapt by using AOD. As the AOD use increases, family rules become increasingly rigid and fixed. Family members adopt roles such as enabler that unwittingly perpetuate the cycle of addictive disorders. The family may develop its own dysfunctional system, referred to as codependency. A major focus of family systems therapy, behavioral family therapy, and disease model family therapy is to elucidate these roles and intervene to improve family functioning. Interventions also involve dealing with underlying adaptive functions of AOD use and addressing these issues more functionally.

Psychoanalytic Contributions

Psychoanalytic theory posits that impaired nurturing during infancy or other early trauma may be a factor in the development of AOD dependence. As a result of these early traumas, people may develop disorders of self, ego deficits, and intense psychic pain. These people discover that alcohol or other drugs can medicate their pain and distress. Indeed, specific drugs address their specific deficits and such a drug becomes their favorite to abuse. As abuse continues, a narcissistic or grandiose ego develops that hides a much more fragile sense of self-esteem just below the surface (Khantzian, 1981, 1982, 1985b, 1997). The narcissistic ego must be defended at all costs, resulting in more AOD use, increased craving, and increased loss of control. S. Brown (1985) believed that as individuals continue to abuse alcohol and drugs, there is a narrowing of perceptions or a need for them to filter out information from the environment to maintain their alcohol- and drug-abusing lifestyle. The more they abuse, the greater the narrowing of perceptions and filtering out of contradictory data. Eventually, they become more and more self-absorbed and more attuned to their own internal justifications and rationalizations for continuing to abuse alcohol and drugs. They are less able to process data from the environment that might provide a more objective assessment of a situation. S. Brown (1985) believed it is this filtering process that accounts for the increasingly narcissistic and grandiose character presentations observed with many alcoholics and drug addicts, especially in the early phases of recovery. This narcissistic character structure also accounts for the presence of denial, which is often described as a defining characteristic of this disorder.

Conclusion of the Biopsychosocial Model

The integrated biopsychosocial model is based on the premise that biochemical factors, disorders of self, learned or conditioned factors, and family and social factors contribute to the initiation and maintenance of these disorders. The theory stresses that there are multiple pathways to addiction and that the differential effect of these factors varies from individual to individual. Once the individual progresses to the point of substance dependence, however, the disorder becomes primary and has its own set of symptoms and a somewhat definable progression.

A defining symptom of the disorder is craving. Both biochemical and conditioned or learned reinforcers contribute to the intensity level of this craving. This craving or emptiness assumes the nature of a primary drive state that is sufficient to overcome judgment, insight, and reasoning for addicted individuals. It is this craving response that explains why addicts and alcoholics are unlikely to return to a state of moderate or controlled use. Cue reactivity studies indicate that once the dependency cycle has been established, any contact with mood-altering substances is likely to retrigger this powerful craving response. This notion that addicted individuals are not good candidates for moderate or controlled use is supported by research data that suggest a 2%–3% success rate in attempts to teach alcohol-dependent individuals to consume alcohol moderately (Wallace, 1989). As the disorder progresses, their life is characterized by an increasing degree of loss of control. The concept of loss of control is difficult for some to comprehend; however, the analogy of comparing drugs to other primary drive state deficits such as hunger may help to explain it. For addicted individuals, the notion of living without alcohol and drugs seems overwhelming if not impossible. Increasingly desperate (e.g., out of control) measures are used to ensure that this possibility does not become a reality. As the disorder progresses, these individuals become more self-centered and grandiose and less able to process information appropriately from the environment. As a result, they develop a strong denial system that serves to perpetuate the disorder. Finally, families, in an attempt to respond to the increasingly disrupted and out-of-control lives of the addicted individual, become increasingly dysfunctional. Their efforts to control the situation invariably result in rigid and fixed interactional patterns such as enabling, scapegoating, and distracting, which unwittingly perpetuate the substance abuse. Most professionals today agree that successful treatment of an addicted individual involves participation on the part of significant others to alter these dysfunctional relationship patterns.

This biopsychosocial model attempts to integrate theoretical and empirical data from the different schools of thought into an integrated conceptual framework. Much more research is needed before the differential impact of biopsychosocial factors can be determined definitively. In addition, the impact of larger societal factors has not been explored in great depth. The fact that epidemiologists have noted secular waves of ascending and declining drug-use patterns suggests, however, that societal factors may play a significant role in the overall process.

Conclusion

In this chapter we have reviewed five theories of addiction. Each theory has much to offer to both model and the treatment of AOD disorders. A theory or model is only of value to a clinician if it informs clinical practice in some meaningful way. For example, an understanding of the complex biopsychosocial factors that account for the addicted person's attachment to and craving for psychoactive chemicals might help the therapist to devise behavioral strategies for coping with cravings. It might also help the therapist to react in a more empathic and less punitive manner when relapses occur. We hope that clinicians will keep an open mind regarding the theories and use whatever treatment methods are effective for their patients. Research continues to bring new light to the etiology and new evidence of effective treatment methods. Fortunately, it is not necessary to fully understand all of the etiological factors to compassionately and effectively intervene in the lives of addicted individuals to help them cope with this most overwhelming and destructive disorder.

Chapter

3

Assessment

The assessment of substance abuse problems is a challenging task but one that is vital for the well-being of patients in any clinical setting. Studies indicate that substance abuse disorders are frequently undetected or misdiagnosed and that professionals are "even less likely to detect these problems when the patient is employed, married, White, insured, or a woman (Clark, 1981; Cleary, Miller, & Bush, 1988; Moore, Bone, & Geller, 1989; Wolfe, Chafetz, & Blane, 1965)" (Schottenfeld, 1994, p. 25). J. W. Smith (1983) reported that only 1 in 10 alcoholic patients is appropriately diagnosed and treated.

R. C. W. Hall, Popkin, Devaul, and Stickney (1977) studied therapist reaction to patients who entered psychotherapy while covertly abusing drugs. They obtained urine samples from 195 psychiatric outpatients and divided the patients into those who tested positive for drugs and those who did not. A retrospective review of patients' charts revealed that patients who abused drugs were significantly more likely to be misdiagnosed. Substance-abusing patients were seen as fragile and unstable. Therapists viewed these patients as dependent and sick out of proportion to their social behavior. Interestingly, therapists were 7 times more likely to cancel appointments and 13 times more likely to transfer substance-abusing patients than patients in the control group. In follow-up interviews, many of these patients indicated that they felt abandoned by their therapists. The substance-abusing patients were significantly less likely to benefit from therapy than were nonabusers. The results of this study suggested not only a failure to correctly assess substance abuse problems but also countertransference reactions toward these patients leading to inappropriate treatment and poor outcomes.

The second reason for the importance of the assessment process is that the clinician in private practice is most likely to encounter substance abuse problems at the assessment and diagnosis stage. Substance abuse treatment, like other areas of psychological treatment, is becoming highly specialized. The generalist clinician who does not specialize in substance abuse treatment may well refer difficult substance-abusing patients to either a treatment center or a specialist private practitioner. The ability to make an appropriate referral, however, depends on the ability to screen patients for substance abuse problems, conduct an intensive substance abuse evaluation, and match the patient with the appropriate treatment provider. In this chapter we focus on the assessment process as we discuss the criteria from the fourth edition of the *Diagnostic and Statistical Manual of Mental Disorders* (*DSM–IV*; American Psychiatric Association, 1994) for abuse and dependence, the diagnostic interview, screening and assessment measures, as well as patient feedback and treatment goals.

There are several elements in the assessment process. Assessment includes determining the degree of substance abuse or dependence, the need for medical detoxification, the existence of comorbid psychiatric disorders, the degree of physical or sexual abuse, and the current and past role of the family. The final stage of the process involves establishing treatment goals with the patient, determining the appropriate level of care needed, and linking the patient with the appropriate provider. Throughout the process the clinician will be examining the patient's readiness for change and enhancing the patient's motivation for further change. Keeping these elements of the assessment process in mind facilitates the overall success of the process.

These elements suggest the complexity and length of time required for this process. The assessment should involve more than one session and a variety of different measures, including clinical interviews, screening or assessment instruments, and possibly more focused psychological testing (e.g., neuropsychological or personality assessment). There may be times when this complexity is not possible. For example, in a crisis situation the clinican may do an initial triage and refer the person to an inpatient treatment setting. Nevertheless, in most cases substance abuse evaluation should be done as an ongoing process with care and thoroughness. An extended assessment may require 3–4 weeks and may be done in an inpatient or outpatient treatment setting or even partial hospitalization.

Diagnostic Interview

The centerpiece of any addiction assessment is the diagnostic interview. This interview requires the same set of interviewing skills that clinicians use with other disorders. A nonjudgmental attitude and empathy for the patient bring more effective results than a confrontational approach. In the beginning the therapist needs to develop a sense of rapport with the patient by listening to the patient's concern and joining in a mutual exploration of the problems. Many therapists who are uncomfortable working with these clients may believe that they should adopt a confrontational therapeutic style and convince the patient to do something that the patient does not want to do (e.g., stop drinking). In fact, research suggests the opposite. Therapists who are more empathic, open, and nonjudgmental generally experience more positive outcomes with their clients (W. R. Miller & Baca, 1983; W. R. Miller, Taylor, & West, 1980; Valle, 1981).

Substance-abusing patients often suffer within a shame-based system and receive many messages from society and family members that they are failures and bad people. Premature confrontation or labeling only serves to reinforce these messages, often resulting in premature termination of treatment. Washton (1995a) pointed out that "the intense shame, guilt, and self-loathing commonly associated with substance abuse place additional demands on the clinician to convey an empathetic, non-judgmental and accepting attitude towards these patients" (pp. 24–25).

The diagnostic interview should help the clinician to determine the nature of the individual's relationship to psychoactive chemicals. The clinician needs to investigate the degree of loss of control and functional impairment, the chemical use profile, developmental and family history, comorbid psychiatric disorders, physical and sexual abuse, and the current role of the family.

Loss of Control

The individual with abuse or addiction problems has an increasing loss of control and continued use of the substance despite negative consequences. The term *loss of control* has frequently been misunderstood as implying a complete or total loss of control every time the person uses psychoactive chemicals. In fact, individuals in the early stages of abusive drinking may lose control infrequently. For example, the individual may drink three times with no significant consequences. On the fourth episode, however, the individual may drink uncontrollably, experience a blackout, and drive the car into a tree.

The defining characteristic of loss of control is the inability to predict or guarantee that the individual will maintain control when he or she drinks. As abusive drinking and substance abuse increases, the individual experiences a progressive loss of control and more frequent hardships and crises. Although the loss of control increases, the individual denies that the drinking is out of control in an attempt to sustain the relationship with alcohol and drugs. The individual sustains the relationship by minimizing and rationalizing consequences and by failing to connect the drinking and increasingly negative consequences.

This denial system is the only way in which the individual can manage the cognitive dissonance that inevitably occurs as increasingly negative consequences and destructive incidents mar the lives of addicted individuals. As S. Brown (1995) pointed out,

the individual's life gradually becomes dominated and organized by alcohol. The person's behavioral, cognitive, and emotional world—outer and inner—begins to shrink so that all incoming information and the individual's perceptions and interpretation of it will be shaped and colored by the need for alcohol and denial of that need. (p. 31)

Washton (1995a) indicated that in many cases addicts and alcoholics "are most likely to appear for treatment when faced with an acute crisis or emergency that demands immediate attention" (p. 26). Whether the crisis is marital, job related, or legal, the individual usually fails to see the connection between the drinking or drug use and this particular crisis as well as a whole history of past negative consequences. The clinician's job in the diagnostic interview is to listen for examples of loss of control. The degree of loss of control ultimately determines the patient's relationship with alcohol. It is the degree to which "the turn towards alcohol" (S. Brown, 1985) is complete and the individual now views his or her alcohol and drug use as a part of life that must be sustained at all costs.

The clinician may find the job of identifying and labeling loss of control and negative consequences more difficult than it might appear. Patients who have been denying the role of alcohol and drugs in their life for many years become highly adept at devising alternative explanations for the difficulties they experience. Therapists who are understandably invested in forming a bond with their patients may be susceptible to believing these explanations, thereby endorsing the patients' distorted rationalizations and minimizations. To the extent that therapists can maintain a clear and consistent focus on loss of control during the diagnostic interview, they can arrive at an accurate determination of the role that alcohol plays in that individual's life and the degree of impairment that exists secondary to alcohol and drug abuse. This clear-sighted and unswerving focus on loss of control is the clinician's ally in arriving at an appropriate diagnosis: "We listen for the organizing role of alcohol and label its central function and presence in the individual's life and the life of the family. We help bring this secret partner out of hiding" (S. Brown, 1995, p. 32).

Determining the "organizing role" (S. Brown, 1995, p. 32) of alcohol and other drug (AOD) abuse for the patient is exactly what the *DSM–IV* criteria are designed to accomplish. Placing the patient on the continuum from abuse to dependence is a vital part of the clinical interview and requires familiarity with these criteria.

The *DSM–IV*

To arrive at a proper diagnosis, the clinician needs to be familiar with the American Psychiatric Association's (1994) *DSM–IV*. Certain core concepts such as loss of control or continued use despite negative consequences form the basis for much of the modern diagnostic and classification system (*DSM–IV*) for substance abuse and dependence. Older classification systems relied on tolerance and withdrawal as the hallmarks of the substance dependence syndrome. This emphasis sometimes fostered confusing situations in which a patient who abused a substance that did not create physical dependence (e.g., cocaine) could not receive a substance dependence diagnosis despite a highly malignant pattern of abuse.

The *DSM–IV* includes five behavioral indicators in addition to tolerance and withdrawal in arriving at a definition of dependence. The five behavioral criteria are as follows: (a) The substance is taken in larger amounts over a longer period than was intended; (b) there is a persistent desire or unsuccessful effort to cut down or control substance use; (c) a great deal of time is spent in activities necessary to obtain the substance; (d) important social occupational or recreational activities are given up or reduced because of the substance; and (e) the substance use is continued despite knowledge of persistent or recurrent physical or psychological problems. In addition to physical tolerance and withdrawal symptoms, there are now seven criteria for substance dependence. Patients can meet criteria for dependence without manifesting tolerance and withdrawal. To qualify for a diagnosis of substance dependence, the patient must exhibit three or more of these symptoms at any time in the same 12-month period.

In the *DSM–IV* substance abuse is less severe than substance dependence. The *DSM–IV* lists four criteria for substance abuse with the patient needing to exhibit only one of the symptoms within a 12-month period. These criteria are as follows: (a) recurrent substance abuse resulting in a failure to fulfill major role obligations such as those at home or work; (b) recurrent substance use in situations in which it is physically hazardous; (c) recurrent substance-related legal problems; or (d) continued substance use despite having persistent or recurrent social or interpersonal problems created or exacerbated by the effects of the substance. The definitions of both abuse and dependence focus on impairments of behavioral functioning reflecting an increasingly significant loss of control and continued use despite negative consequences. Both conditions reveal themselves in failure to fulfill major role obligations and continued use despite knowledge of physical or psychological problems that have been caused by the substance use itself. In substance dependence the classic criteria of tolerance and withdrawal also may be part of the overall dependence syndrome.

To the extent that therapists can make this abuse and dependence determination in a nonjudgmental and nonthreatening tone they can successfully conduct a diagnostic interview without alienating the patient from the treatment process. Washton (1995a) suggested phrasing the *DSM–IV* criteria as questions during the clinical interview. These questions are repeated here:

1. Have you often ended up consuming much more than you expected or intended to?
2. Have you found it difficult to limit or stop your use?
3. Have you ever spent so much time using and/or re-

covering from the effects that you had little time for anything else?

4. Has your use caused you to neglect responsibilities at work or home?

5. Has your use ever led you to give up or greatly reduce important activities such as sports, and/or time with family/friends?

6. Have you continued to use despite being aware of these negative consequences on your life?

7. Do you ever get tolerant to the effects so that you need to take larger doses or have reached a point where you no longer get the desired effects from the amount you had been accustomed to taking?

8. Do you experience any withdrawal or other physical discomfort when you try to cut down on your dose or stop all together?

9. Have you ever taken alcohol or other drugs to avoid having withdrawal or to relieve withdrawal symptoms you were already experiencing?

Asking these questions in a straightforward, nonjudgmental manner can help to place the patient along the continuum from abuse to dependence.

Many patients have difficulty giving objective answers to these questions. The degree to which patients have difficulty with these questions can often be an indication of their level of denial, which, for purposes of this discussion, can be defined as an inability to acknowledge or be aware of the connections between their substance use and loss of control. A clinical example may help to illustrate this point:

John is 25 years old and has smoked marijuana for 10 years. During the last 5 years he has smoked marijuana on a daily basis. Despite having a high school degree and vocational training in computers, John has never really developed a career. He lives at home with his mother and delivers pizza in the evenings. Both John and his mother are dissatisfied with this situation. John has a variety of explanations as to why his life is not progressing: "Good jobs are hard to come by," "I'm not in a good field," "My mother's nagging really brings me down."

> At no point does John acknowledge a connection be-
> tween the drug use and the life problems. When asked
> specifically about this he responds, "No, the drugs are
> not the problem. Besides, pot's not addicting. You should
> know that."

Clinicians sometimes mistake the individual's denial for an indication that the patient does not wish to get better. Rather, the denial results from the very real fear that to acknowledge the true relationship between alcohol and drugs and loss of control would be to threaten a relationship that has become increasingly important and central to the individual's existence. The perception that life without alcohol and drugs would be intolerable must be overcome in the early stages of the treatment process. Once the therapist addresses and lessens this perception, a strong desire for health and recovery often emerges. Frequently, this desire has existed all along, but it has been suppressed by an overwhelming fear of the perceived consequences, physical and psychological, that would accompany the stopping of alcohol and drug use.

Another common mistake for clinicians is to confuse denial with ignorance or lack of information. Patients often have mistaken notions about alcohol and other drugs, such as "Marijuana is a harmless substance because it grows naturally." This misconception has been offered by a number of patients. Also, many patients are unaware of negative effects of alcohol and other drugs, especially those removed in time from the actual use. Thus, an individual who is repeatedly late for work because of heavy drinking and then receives a negative performance appraisal several months later may not make the appropriate connection between the drinking and the poor job review. Spending some time initially providing information and focusing on consequences of use may help to overcome resistance later.

Functional Impairment

In addition to the loss of control, the clinician should listen for impaired functioning during the diagnostic interview. Be-

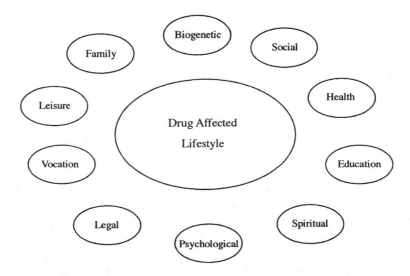

Figure 1.   Functional Impairment Model: The figure depicts the scope of diagnostic and treatment domains associated with substance abuse. The model facilitates a viable fit between the assessment, treatment, and aftercare services.

cause of a lack of understanding or denial, the patient may have little awareness of the role that alcohol or drugs play in the overall pattern of difficulties that he or she is experiencing. Although the clinician should not reach conclusions prematurely about the role of chemical abuse, the therapist must assess the degree to which the individual's functioning is impaired. In doing this, a simple *functional impairment model* (see Figure 1) may be helpful. This model specifies domains of functioning on which the clinician can focus in the initial interview. These domains of functioning (e.g., work, family, peers) typically become increasingly impaired as substance abuse progresses over time. The clinician may frequently see these areas of functional impairment emerging before he or she fully recognizes the extent of substance abuse. When the clinician does note severe functional impairment, the clinician should not rule out possible chemical abuse and dependence even when the patient denies significant levels of abuse.

Another advantage of focusing on functional impairment is that it avoids arguments and labeling, such as whether the patient actually is an alcoholic or addict. The clinician can simply note these areas of functional impairment and relate them to substance abuse as appropriate. The patient can form his or her own conclusions. This model can help the clinician not only to assess the degree of severity and the progression of the disorder but also to focus on domains of functioning that are most impaired in the treatment plan. For example, patients with dysfunctional family systems may need intensive family therapy or even primary addiction treatment for an impaired family member. This model also can be used later in the course of treatment to evaluate treatment effectiveness and to develop continuing care plans.

Chemical Use Profile

The clinician needs to obtain the complete alcohol and drug use profile during the diagnostic interview. At this point, the clinician needs information to determine the present danger to the patient and the need for medical detoxification. The therapist should be prepared to ask specific questions regarding the types, amounts, and frequency of drugs used. The specific questions on drug use should detail the use for the past week. The answers will help to determine precisely the nature and severity of the patient's current drug use. The need for medical detoxification is based not only on the type of drug use but also on the amount and frequency of use.

The clinician needs some knowledge of psychopharmacology. Withdrawal from some drugs such as alcohol, barbiturates, and benzodiazepines can be life threatening. For the benzodiazepine-dependent patient, medical detoxification is almost always indicated. In the case of benzodiazepines, which are slow-acting drugs, the withdrawal can be protracted. Seizures can occur as late as 2 weeks after cessation of use. Thus, if the patient reports he or she is dependent on benzodiazepines but has not used in the past 5 days, it is not safe to assume that the person no longer needs medical detoxification. The patient must be referred to a physician to assess the need for medical detoxification. Drugs that can be stopped abruptly without potentially dangerous medical consequences include opiates and cocaine. Unfortunately, cessation of these drugs creates such intense craving and physical discomfort that many opiate and cocaine users require structured, medically supervised residential care to successfully withdraw from these drugs. Finally, even in the case of opiates and cocaine, older, frail, or psychologically impaired patients may be at high risk when they stop use abruptly without medical supervision. For example, an individual with a heart condition may experience medical complications from the stress of withdrawal. A depressed individual may become suicidal during the "cocaine crash" phase of withdrawal. In fact, for patients who have not had a routine physical examination recently, a referral to an internist is appropriate as part of the assessment process.

In the diagnostic interview the chemical use profile should cover past history and focus on the progression from earliest use of psychoactive chemicals to the present day. This history gives the clinician a well-rounded picture of how the individual's disorder has evolved over time and it helps the individual to see how the loss of control has increased. During this part of the interview, the clinician frequently will hear the patient make statements such as "As a teenager I smoked pot, but told myself I would never go on to harder drugs. It was only 6 months later that I was doing LSD and cocaine." Another relevant statement might be "I told myself that I couldn't be an alcoholic because I would never drink in the mornings. Just a few months later I realized I could become someone who needed a drink to get going." The patient can hear these statements as examples of crossing personal boundaries or violating internal limits, and this reflection can help the patient to comprehend the concept of loss of control.

Developmental History, Family History, and Family Dynamics

Another significant portion of the diagnostic interview is obtaining a thorough developmental history. When focusing on the usual developmental milestones, the therapist should pay special attention to those areas that are correlated with substance abuse and alcohol problems such as learning disabilities, attention deficit disorder, and antisocial or aggressive behavior. The clinician also can focus on the individual's peer group, especially how it has changed and evolved as the individual became increasingly enmeshed in a drinking and drug-using lifestyle.

The therapist can cover family history and family dynamics during the diagnostic interview. Chemical dependence tends to run in families, and the presence of alcohol and drug dependency in one or more family members places an individual in a high-risk category. It suggests that an added degree of concern is appropriate. Thus, for individuals with a history of chemical dependence in their family, even occasional or sporadic abuse should be viewed with more concern than if family chemical dependence were not present. It is often difficult to obtain an accurate family history of chemical dependence. The therapist sometimes must ask questions in such a way that the person or family thinks of the issues in a new light. Addiction and psychiatric problems frequently are "in the closet" and emerge only after repeated questioning. If the family history indicates chemical dependence, the clinician should inquire about the outcome of the disorder for those family members. Did the individuals die at a young age? Did they eventually get sober and lead successful lives, or was the outcome somewhere in between? Did these individuals ever receive treatment and were they helped? This information will most likely color the individual's view of the treatment process.

Finally, it is most important to know what degree of support the individual is going to receive from the immediate family. The therapist should try to ascertain not only whether family members will participate in the treatment process but also the role they may have played in perpetuating or enabling the overall using behavior of the individual. Without this information, the clinician runs the risk of having therapeutic efforts overtly or covertly sabotaged by family members for whom change in the person's behavior can be threatening or disruptive. Family members sometimes accompany the patient to the initial interview or attempt to contact the therapist to round out the clinical picture. When the patient is an adolescent, the family members should be included in the assessment as a matter of course. In other cases, how the clinician deals with these collateral contacts is extremely important. In order not to violate the patient's confidentiality and trust, any contact between the therapist and family members must take place with the full knowledge and consent of the patient. Information from other family members may provide valuable clinical information. These contacts also may help the family to realize that its involvement in the change process is essential and that changes in its own behavior patterns will help the patient deal with the addiction problem.

Coexisting Psychiatric Disorders

Part of the diagnostic interview is assessing coexisting psychiatric disorders. In making this assessment, the clinician may be tempted to overdiagnose psychopathology. There is a simple reason for this phenomenon; alcoholism and addiction can and do mimic virtually every other form of psychopathology. The clinician should be aware of how individual drugs may affect the patient's mental status, especially in the early days of withdrawal. For the patient who abuses stimulants such as cocaine, the withdrawal may produce an agitated depression (Kosten & Kleber, 1988). For these patients, the risk of suicidality is high and must be assessed carefully. In addition, prolonged cocaine or other stimulant abuse can lead to paranoid reactions that may be difficult to differentiate from paranoid schizophrenia or other paranoid delusional states. Patients under the influence of hallucinogenic drugs may appear to be psychotic. Even after cessation of use, flashbacks may occur some weeks or months later. Differentiating schizophrenia from hallucinogenic flashback experiences challenges many clinicians. Chronic abusers of marijuana may appear listless and lack motivation for weeks or months after cessation of use. In most cases, motivational levels return to normal after discontinuing use, but in the early weeks of abstinence this amotivational syndrome may mimic depression. Opiate addicts have a higher rate of depression than the general population (Kosten, Rounsaville, & Kleber, 1982). Individuals withdrawing from opiates may not only appear depressed but may also exhibit signs of anxiety. Finally, adolescents who have been chronic inhalers of solvents may appear to have organic brain syndrome or exhibit schizophrenic symptoms. Schuckit (1986) and Washton (1995a) suggested waiting 4–6 weeks before making a psychiatric diagnosis. In today's climate of managed care, such a delay may be impractical. Shortening the time period from 4 to approximately 2 weeks is suggested by some experts (Rounsaville & Kranzler, 1989), but this is less likely to permit an accurate distinction between AOD use and an independent disorder. The important point is that it is often impossible to differentiate substance-induced behavior from true psychiatric disorders. Premature labeling before a period of sustained abstinence can lead the therapist in the wrong direction.

When a coexisting psychiatric disorder is present, Rounsaville, Kosten, and Weissman (cited in Schottenfeld, 1994) found that treatment of this disorder improves outcome in both opioid- and alcohol-dependent patients. McClellan et al. (cited in Schottenfeld, 1994) demonstrated that appropriate matching of different degrees of psychiatric disturbance with different treatment modalities was the best predictor of overall outcome. Bukstein (1995) listed common comorbid psychiatric disorders that are statistically associated with addiction problems. These include the following: (a) conduct disorder, especially aggressive type in adolescents and antisocial personality disorder in adults; (b) attention deficit hyperactivity disorder; (c) mood disorders, especially major depression; (d) dysthymia, bipolar disorder, and cyclothymia; (e) anxiety disorders such as social phobia, posttraumatic stress disorder, and generalized anxiety disorder; (f) bulimia nervosa; (g) schizophrenia; and (h) borderline personality disorder. The clinician should be able to recognize psychiatric symptoms and, when they persist, to integrate the comorbid psychopathology into the treatment plan. For example, Kadden, Getter, Cooney, and Litt (1989) and Litt, Babor, DelBoca, Kadden, and Cooney (1992) demonstrated that antisocial alcoholic patients do better in structured group settings that provide coping skills training than they do in more traditional psychodynamic groups. These patients also benefit from longer term therapeutic community interventions. A knowledge of these disorders and how they interact with substance abuse problems is central to designing an effective treatment plan.

Physical and Sexual Abuse

Many patients suffer physical and sexual abuse secondary to their substance abuse. Still other patients were the victims of physical or sexual abuse before getting involved in alcohol and drug abuse. Because a high number of patients who appear in treatment centers grew up in alcoholic homes, many of these individuals have suffered neglect, abuse, and trauma at an early age. Substance abusers also are sometimes perpetrators of physical and sexual abuse. They may have medicated these traumas with alcohol and drugs and may experience painful affect bubbling to the surface while they achieve sobriety. For this reason, the clinician should be aware of the level of trauma and should anticipate the needs of these patients because painful affect gets uncovered during the therapeutic process. The clinician should ask specific questions about physical and sexual abuse during the diagnostic interview. In addition to the clinical interview, the clinician also has available a number of screening and assessment measures that can provide valuable information.

Screening and Assessment Measures

Urine drug screens should be done as part of the diagnostic screening and assessment. Some clinical judgment is appropriate in determining when to use the screens. We have found the following guidelines helpful in our practices. We recommend drug screens as part of the initial workup for all patients for whom AOD use is an identified problem and as part of an ongoing monitoring program agreed to by the therapist and patient. We also use them when working with patients with legal charges, impaired professionals, or in any situation in which the therapist may want to document treatment compliance for the benefit of the patient. It is also helpful to use drug screens whenever there is reason to doubt the accuracy of the patient's self-report. In addition, we use drug screens more frequently with adolescents than with adults.

Urine Drug Screens

Urine drug screens should be done as part of the diagnostic screening and assessment. Although some clinicians hesitate to use drug screening for fear of the patients' reactions, our experience shows that therapists' attitudes heavily influence patients' responses. When clinicians present drug screening as a normal part of the assessment process rather than as a confrontation about the patients' veracity or commitment to change, the patients usually accept the test. Becoming overly apologetic or appearing distrustful of patients may sabotage therapists' efforts. Therapists who approach the situation in a matter-of-fact manner and stress that urine drug screening is a matter of course for all substance abuse patients often can enlist compliance in even the most difficult patients. To be effective urine drug screens must occur on a truly random and regular basis during the assessment and treatment period. Additionally, these tests should be either observed or monitored (e.g., temperature tested) to ensure their validity.

The quality of urine drug screens varies with the type of the test. The Emit Process test is commonly used for an initial screen. Positive results should then be confirmed through gas chromatography and mass spectroscopy, a more sensitive but more costly process.

Clinicians should be aware that drugs such as cocaine leave the body rapidly. Except in cases of heavy use, they can be detected only within 48–72 hr after use. On the other hand, marijuana remains in the system for an extended period of time and may be detected from several weeks to a month after cessation of use. Other drugs such as LSD and inhalants are extremely difficult to detect and require specialized and costly procedures. For this reason they are not often included in the regular panel of drugs in a typical urine drug screen. Alcohol leaves the body quickly, within 12–24 hr, and thus urine drug screening is not effective. Breathalyzers or Alco strips can be used to detect alcohol use. Alco strips react with any alcohol present in the body when they are placed on the patient's tongue.

The CAGE

A number of screening and assessment tools may help the clinician in assessing alcohol and other drug dependence in patients. One of the most common such tools is the CAGE. The CAGE is widely used in emergency rooms and medical settings because it is quick and simple to administer. The test consists of four questions whose key words form the acronym (Ewing, 1984). The questions are as follows: (a) Have you ever felt you should cut down on your drinking? (b) Have people annoyed you by criticizing your drinking? (c) Have you ever felt guilty about your drinking? and (d) Have you ever had a drink first thing in the morning (an eyeopener) to steady your nerves or get rid of a hangover? It is, of course, easy to give the "correct" answers on a straightforward test such as the CAGE, so corroborating information is essential. Despite this fact, Mayfield, McCloud, and Hall demonstrated that "90% of the 142 known alcoholics could be correctly identified by their CAGE responses" (cited in Jacobson, 1989, p. 22). The CAGE is not effective when used with driving while intoxicated (DWI) defendants (Mischke & Venneri, 1987). A score of 2 or 3 on the CAGE is recommended as a cutoff for identifying patients with alcohol-related problems.

The Michigan Alcoholism Screening Test

The Michigan Alcoholism Screening Test (MAST; Selzer, 1971) is perhaps the most widely used of all screening tests. This test lists 25 items of common behaviors and symptoms of alcoholism. Although the traditional cutoff point for positive identification is 5, several studies (Jacobson, 1989) have shown that using a cutoff score of 5 results in "unacceptably high false positive rates when checked against other criteria" (Jacobson, 1989, p. 23). Jacobson suggested an alternative scoring as follows: 0–4 points = no problem; 5–9 points = possible problems; 10–11 points = probable problems; 12+ = likely problems. The MAST is not copyrighted and is available from its designer (Selzer, 1971). It also is available from its designers in several shorter forms: the Brief MAST (Pokorny, Miller, & Kaplan, 1972) and the Short MAST (Selzer, Vinokur, & van Rooijen, 1975).

The Alcohol Use Inventory

The Alcohol Use Inventory (AUI), a more thorough assessment tool, attempts to measure a variety of dimensions associated with alcohol problems. These dimensions can be grouped into four domains: (a) benefits from drinking (i.e., reasons for drinking such as improving sociability and avoiding negative affect states); (b) styles of drinking (e.g., gregariously, compulsively); (c) consequences of drinking (i.e., self-harming behaviors, belligerence); and (d) concerns and acknowledgments regarding drinking that may help to assess readiness for treatment. This multidimensional conceptualization of alcohol and alcohol-related problems is more sophisticated than traditional screening tools, which are laundry lists of alcohol-related concerns and symptoms. An impressive body of research suggests that the AUI helps in predicting outcomes and matching patients to appropriate levels of care (Jacobson, 1989):

> The instrument authors (Horn, Wanberg, & Foster, 1987) indicate that the AUI scales have demonstrated good to

excellent levels of internal consistency, test–retest reliability, and both concurrent and construct validity. These
findings have been replicated and extended by other investigators (e.g., Isenhart, 1990; Rohsenow, 1982; Skinner
& Allen, 1983; Tarter et al., 1987). (Donovan, 1995, p. 105)

The AUI can be purchased from National Computer Systems,
P.O. Box 1416, Minneapolis, Minnesota 55440.

The Addiction Severity Index

Another tool, the Addiction Severity Index (ASI), developed
by McLellan, Luborsky, O'Brien, and Woody (1980), is widely
used in research, especially government-funded projects. The
ASI measures the degree of impairment secondary to alcohol
and drug abuse in seven different domains, including medical, employment and support, drug and alcohol use, legal
status, family and social relations, and psychological or psychiatric status. The test requires a structured interview of
about 30–40 min and consists of approximately 180 items.
"In a number of studies, the ASI has consistently been shown
to be psychometrically sound (McLellan, Luborsky, O'Brien,
& Woody, 1980; Kosten, Rounsaville, & Kleber, 1983), with
good test-retest and interrater reliability and concurrent validity" ([W. R.] Miller, Westerberg, & Waldron, 1995, p. 77).
The ASI assesses addiction not just in terms of the amount
of alcohol and drugs that the individual consumes but also
in terms of the impairment in different domains of functioning related to alcohol and drug abuse. The Joint Commission
on the Accreditation of Healthcare Organizations has referred
to the ASI as "a model instrument for satisfying its requirements for a comprehensive patient admission assessment
leading to an individualized treatment plan" (McLellan et al.,
1985). This test is in the public domain, supported by grants
from the Veterans Administration and the National Institute
on Drug Abuse. It can be obtained at no cost other than minimal charges for photocopying and mailing from Delta-
Metrics/TRI ASI Information Line, (800)238-2433.

The Chemical Dependency Adolescent Assessment Project and the Personal Experience Screening Questionnaire

With regard to adolescent substance abuse, the federal government has developed the Chemical Dependency Adolescent Assessment Project (CDAAP; Winters & Henly, 1987). The CDAAP represents an attempt to address the specific diagnostic needs of adolescents and includes several different measures of adolescent alcohol and substance abuse. Although the entire CDAAP is probably too lengthy for most clinicians, a brief screening instrument based on the CDAAP, the Personal Experience Screening Questionnaire (PESQ), should suffice. This instrument focuses not only on the type, frequency, and onset of use but also on psychosocial functioning as well as defensiveness (Winters, 1992):

> Winters (1992) reported that the problem severity portion of the PESQ has a high internal reliability estimate (.92), that the PESQ as a whole demonstrated satisfactory discriminant validity, and that overall scores were related to assessment referral recommendations. Also PESQ scores were found to be highly predictive of scores on a more comprehensive assessment instrument, the Personal Experience Inventory (PEI; Winters & Henly, 1989). (W. R. Miller et al., 1995, p. 70)

This test can be purchased from Western Psychological Services, 12031 Wilshire Blvd., Los Angeles, California 90025.

Feedback and Treatment Goals

A final objective of the assessment process is to provide feedback to the patient and begin to formulate treatment goals. This is a delicate process that requires the ability to communicate the nature of the problem in a way that is clear but not overwhelming to the patient. It also involves enlisting the cooperation of the patient in formulating an initial treatment plan.

Washton (1995a) pointed out the need for the therapist to be nonjudgmental and to avoid conclusions or specific recommendations before the patient is ready: "Simply stated, the goal is to present information in an objective, dispassionate, straightforward manner so the patient will be able to hear it and, it is hoped, reflect on it" (Washton, 1995a, p. 41). Although direct confrontations are to be avoided during the feedback stage of the assessment, making connections between the alcohol and drug use and behavioral and interpersonal consequences for the individual is a legitimate and desirable goal of the feedback session. The desired connections between drinking or drug using and negative consequences often become obvious by simply restating the data gathered during the assessment. We offer a clinical example that concerns Michael, a 29-year-old man who was referred by the court for evaluation after his second DWI arrest:

> Michael, you told me that you were referred by the court after your second DWI. This DWI occurred 6 weeks ago and your blood alcohol level was just over the legal limit. You also told me that your first DWI occurred when you were 19 years old, and you stated that you used to drink a lot more at that time. During your teenage years and up until about the age of 22 you would frequently abuse alcohol and occasionally have blackouts. After you graduated from college and began your first job, you made a decision to cut down on your use of alcohol and were able to successfully do so for a number of years. Your alcohol use increased at about age 27 when your marriage broke up. At that time, your wife indicated her concern about your drinking; however, you believe that this was simply her excuse for wanting to get out of a marriage that she really did not want to be involved in. For the past 2 years you have occasionally overdone it but have tried very hard to keep your drinking in moderation. Despite these efforts there have been times, especially when you were under stress at work, when you were prone to drink more than you should and this causes some concern for you.

We also talked some about your family background. As I understand it, your father was an alcoholic and he was verbally abusive to you as a child. He died at age 55 of alcohol-related causes. You grew up in a small town, and your father was not well regarded. He was looked down on by others in your community, and this caused you great embarrassment. One of the statements that you made when we discussed whether you might be an alcoholic was that you were determined never to be like your father.

As I see things now, you are in a state of some confusion. On the one hand, you are beginning to get concerned. Your second DWI is a serious situation. You have only been partially successful at moderating your drinking, and others around you, in addition to your ex-wife, have registered some concern about your drinking. On the other hand, it is your sincere determination not to grow up like your father. I think that this is an issue that we need to explore further. I would be interested in your thoughts. What do you think or how do you feel about what I have just said?

The goal of this feedback is not to hammer Michael over the head but to reveal the connections between his drinking and the negative consequences in his life. Over time, as the relationship with the therapist progresses, the consequences will be easier for Michael to acknowledge. Once he is secure that therapy is not a shame-based environment, he will see the connections and begin to honestly explore the possibility of his alcoholism. As Liftik (1995) pointed out, the progressive nature of the client's disorder can be counted on to make the consequences more apparent: "The client's alcoholism is our ally; we can count on it to create pain and suffering, losses and failures that our clients will reveal to us in different ways. Making the connection between these difficulties and drinking is our task" (Liftik, 1995, p. 88).

Abstinence Contract

Once the connections become apparent, the therapist can begin to discuss treatment recommendations. Often a time-limited abstinence contract is desirable at this point. The purpose of abstinence contracts is not only to see if individuals are able to maintain sobriety but also to determine their thoughts, feelings, and moods during this time. For example, do they have night dreams or daydreams about using? Do they become increasingly irritable and moody? Do they become more dysfunctional at work, or do they isolate themselves more at home? For those patients who cannot maintain a period of abstinence of at least 30 days, some form of structured treatment program, either outpatient or inpatient, is generally indicated.

Another technique that might be suggested during the feedback session is for the individual to attend a self-help meeting such as Alcoholics Anonymous or Narcotics Anonymous. The patient can approach such a meeting as a learning experience about the dynamics of addiction. The therapist can emphasize that patient and therapist together are working mutually to try to solve the perplexing and sometimes confusing problem. To the degree that the patient learns more about addiction, he or she will be better able to participate in this ongoing assessment process.

Readiness for Change

As stated earlier, patients come for assessment for a variety of reasons and under differing circumstances. Some come under coercion from the courts. Many come because of a marital or family crisis. Patients also come in different stages of readiness for change. Prochaska and DiClemente (1986) have developed a model consisting of five different levels in the stages of change. Their model can be used to assess the patient's willingness to change. Briefly, the stages are precontemplation, contemplation, preparation, action, and maintenance.

Patients in the precontemplation stage have no awareness that a problem exists. They rarely enter treatment centers unless they are coerced. Patients in the the contemplation stage are ambivalent about seeking change. They consider the possibility that a problem exists, but they are not yet prepared to take specific action. Although they may express an awareness of the consequences of their substance use, they are still attached to the feelings that they experience while using alcohol and drugs. They are reluctant to consider positive steps toward change.

Patients in the preparation stage are beginning to recognize that the negative effects outweigh the positive benefits of their alcohol and drug use. They may indicate a sincere desire to learn more about how they can stop using or correct the problem and they may have already experimented with attempts to control the situation on their own.

Patients in the action stage are actively engaged in efforts to reduce or stop their substance abuse. They are good candidates for entering treatment.

In the maintenance stage, the patient has already initiated and put into place effective change strategies. The therapist can focus on sustaining the gains that have already been made and developing specific skills such as relapse prevention.

Patients in the precontemplation stage will have much different treatment goals than patients in the action stage. The therapist needs to assess both the readiness for change and the patient's personal goals for treatment. A man in the precontemplation stage who arrives under coercion from the courts may want a letter stating that he does not have a problem and does not need treatment. The therapist will treat this patient differently from another patient who has serious concerns about drinking and strongly wants sobriety. Assessing the patient's readiness and goals can help establish realistic treatment interventions without imposing the therapist's agenda.

Enhancement of Motivation

Because the therapist pays attention to the readiness for change, the therapist also will want to enhance the patient's motivation to change and the desire to move to the next level of readiness. W. R. Miller and Rollnick (1991) have developed specific techniques to enhance motivation for treatment (these techniques are discussed in greater detail in chap. 6). Although enhancing motivation is most frequently used in the treatment phase, it also is important in assessment. Anything that the clinician can do in the early stages to help the patient "see the light at the end of the tunnel" will enhance motivation for change and energize the patient toward investing in recovery.

Treatment Matching

After determining the degree of abuse or dependence, the coexisting psychiatric conditions, the level of readiness for change, and the patient's own treatment goals, the clinician can match the patient to an appropriate level of care and treatment setting (this is discussed later in further detail; see chap. 5). The clinician should state in specific terms the recommended treatment, the appropriate setting, the frequency, and who is responsible. The level of care should match the patient's needs. For example, a crack-cocaine addict wanting to achieve abstinence may experience such intense cravings that an inpatient setting is necessary to allow the initial cravings to subside before the individual enters a partial hospitalization or intensive outpatient program.

Link With the Treatment Provider

The clinician should then link the patient with the appropriate provider or setting. Many psychologists experience some difficulty at this point because treatment centers have not welcomed psychologists in the past. Fortunately, many treatment centers have changed and now allow psychologists to function as a primary therapist while their patients are in inpatient and partial hospitalization programs. Clinicians should establish their own connections with treatment centers before working with substance-abusing patients. For psychologists who do not wish to do this, assessing and referring some patients to providers who are connected with treatment centers are essential.

Professional Enabling

One professional caution is in order. Therapists risk becoming professional enablers when they continue to work with patients who drink and use drugs abusively and fail to maintain a focus on this behavior as a top priority. It is not appropriate to discontinue therapy with the majority of patients, even those who are drinking and abusing drugs. The therapist must assess, however, when he or she is becoming a part of the enabling system surrounding the addict. This may occur in a variety of ways. For example, an employer refers a man for assessment; the individual reports back to his boss that he sees the professional in ongoing treatment and at the same time he continues to abuse drugs. Over time it becomes apparent that the patient has no intention of stopping drug use. The most difficult part of an addiction assessment may be knowing when to step back and set a limit. In some instances, the therapist may need to give the patient a choice: Either address the drug use problem directly (e.g., stop drinking and using or go into treatment) or psychotherapy will end. Continuing psychotherapy in the absence of a commitment to sobriety may not be helpful to the substance-abusing patient.

A Sense of Hope

Assessment is something much more than putting together pieces of a puzzle such that diagnosis emerges and the patient is told what the nature and the severity of his or her disorder is. An effective assessment assesses severity and risk factors through diagnostic interviews and structured instruments, makes connections between drug or drinking behavior and negative consequences, determines the readiness of the patient for change, enhances motivation for further change, and engages the patient in a process of mutual exploration.

At the end of the assessment process, the clinician wishes to leave the patient with a sense of hope. The resistance that individuals experience on diagnosis of alcoholism or addiction comes from an overwhelming hopelessness of the out-come. When this despair arises, the therapist must counter with an attitude and words of hope. Contact with other re-covering individuals often helps the patient to see the con-tinuum from withdrawal to ongoing recovery, from the most difficult and frightening of times to a most rewarding and self-enhancing process.

Conclusion

In this chapter we have covered the diagnostic interview, screening and assessment measures, feedback to the patient, and treatment goals. Becoming proficient in the assessment of AOD disorders is especially important for a number of reasons. AOD problems are very widespread and thus certain to appear in any therapist's office. As discussed earlier, they are difficult to detect and frequently mimic other disorders. Failure to detect these disorders can have grave conse-quences for the patient. For these reasons an awareness of the risk factors and warning signs of AOD problems is es-sential for all clinicians.

4

Treatment Modalities and the Continuum of Care

There is a remarkably wide range of activities and interventions in the substance abuse treatment field, and it is likely that psychologists will interact with only a few depending on their own base of activity. However, it is important to appreciate the range of possibilities to give a perspective for referral. In this chapter we briefly describe these diverse subcultures, starting with an overview of the separate evolution of the alcohol and drug treatment systems. We then examine how major models and modalities arose, their assumptions about how people change, key interventions or activities, sources of information and data evaluating the effectiveness of each model, showing its strengths and limits. Some of the treatment settings are more accessible to working people with insurance; others are funded by federal or state governments for the indigent population. Ironically, the latter may offer highly innovative programs (e.g., long-term residential programs for mothers and their children) not usually available to the middle-class or even the very wealthy. In general, long-term programs are more common when the target population is indigent because the clients have fewer interpersonal, social, and vocational skills to reclaim. Thus, they are more likely to need "habilitation" rather than rehabilitation. However, these distinctions may blur in practice. Many clients in public-sector programs are originally working- or middle-class but downwardly mobile because of their alcohol and drug use and return to a working- or middle-class lifestyle once in recovery.

In the next chapter, we approach the question of matching patient needs and type of care, reviewing current frameworks for making decisions about levels of care. The rapid transition of the health care delivery system makes it difficult to outline realistic possibilities. Extensive treatment outcome studies suggesting the importance of retention in treatment for a positive outcome are less influential when short-term funding commitments are the norm. Under conditions in which health care delivery organizations are responsible for the patient over the long term, different decisions will be made. Further complicating the process of sound decision making is the fact that many of the cost savings from treatment are realized not only in health care itself but also in reductions in other systems. Recent studies suggest that every $1 invested in substance abuse treatment saves $5–$7 in health care costs, and $11 when reductions in criminal justice and social services are factored in (Gerstein, Johnson, Harwood, Suter, & Malloy, 1994; Lewis, 1994). When local, state, and national government entities insist on a planning framework that crosses the systems, the extensive outcome data in the addiction field will be put to better use and greater revenue savings should result.

Evolution of the Alcohol and Drug Research and Treatment Systems

Although awareness that alcoholism is a clinical and not a moral problem dates back to the signing of the Declaration of Independence (Jaffe, 1979), key events that shaped our current system took place in the 1960s and early 1970s. It was during that period that government entities were developed to address policy issues and allocate resources, in a manner which continues to shape our national capacity to respond to alcohol and drug problems. This brief overview highlights some of the key issues and developments.

The National Institute on Alcoholism and Alcohol Abuse (NIAAA) was founded in 1970 as a center within the National Institute of Mental Health, and has sponsored important research on the biology of alcoholism as well as psychosocial issues affecting alcohol use and more recently treatment. Although it has produced educational material to use in prevention efforts, the NIAAA did not take a leadership role in the treatment field. Pressure to expand into the treatment field came from community groups responding to perceived need. Programs derived from the 12-step model proliferated and became the standard when they were adopted by hospital programs funded by insurance. Their development was not guided by controlled evaluations demonstrating efficacy but by ideology fueled by the enthusiasm of recovering people. Betty Ford made an enormous contribution to opening discussion and reducing stigma when she revealed her dependence on alcohol and prescription drugs in 1978. This further legitimated programs and encouraged expansion. However, the anti-empiricism of this segment was a barrier to improving its efficacy and made it vulnerable once managed care took hold (Rawson, 1990–1991).

The drug treatment system had a completely separate evolution from the alcohol treatment system, and throughout the 1970s there was little mixing. Approaches developed in the 1950s and 1960s received increasing attention as concerns grew about the expanding population of heroin users and the associated increase in crime. In 1971, President Nixon created the Special Action Office for Drug Abuse Prevention within the Executive Office of the President. Through the leadership of Jerome Jaffe (1979), there was an explicit commitment at the highest levels of government to make treatment more available.

In 1972, the National Institute on Drug Abuse was founded to promote the creation of a treatment system accompanied by research to investigate clinical issues. A major goal was to determine whether programs were contributing to reducing the social costs of addiction. In the ensuing decades, the treatment system for indigent people developed. It was funded by a variety of federal, state, and local agencies, adapting to the changing demographics and drug-use patterns that emerged. This treatment system attempted to meet the needs of those who had always been disadvantaged as well as those who were downwardly mobile (and hence uninsured) because of their drug use. As was the case in the alcoholism treatment programs, former users played a central role in designing and implementing programs in several major treatment modalities. Research on treatment modalities and strategies was a major emphasis (De Leon, 1993; Rawson, 1990–1991). De Leon (1993) observed that

> this federal initiative has yielded the most comprehensive assessment of short- and long-term stability of treatment effects for any behavioral disorder in the social sciences. The depth of this literature can be appreciated in terms of the number of clients in treatment who have been followed longitudinally (over 15,000), the length of time followed (1–12 years), the array of variables surveyed, the number of different treatment agencies evaluated in both multimodality comparisons and single-program based studies, and the similarity in design and measures across studies. (p. 104)

In 1990, the federal government formed the Office for Treatment Improvement, later renamed the Center for Substance Abuse Treatment, to focus on expansion of effective services with evaluation components. The National Institute on Drug Abuse continued to concentrate on more rigorous research.

From our viewpoint and experience, several key elements warrant highlighting. Before and into the 1970s, professionals either provided inappropriate intervention or ignored the alcohol and other drug (AOD) problem. Many psychotherapists favored psychodynamic orientations that not only had no empirical basis supporting efficacy but that often yielded inadequate results in the eyes of family members and others affected by the addictive behavior. During this period, professionals, including psychologists, social workers, and others involved in therapy or counseling activities, became distrusted by recovering people as a source of assistance. During the 1980s professionals became integrated into the recovery effort in more constructive ways through their research contributions and by bringing in a wider intervention repertoire, which was welcomed as recognition grew of the clinical complexity of problems.

We have noted, however, that despite its strong research base, the addiction field remained out of the mainstream of the university as well as mainstream medicine and mental health. Research was often conducted outside of the university to protect funding. The typical university had huge overhead, and those organizations providing the funds wanted as much service as possible without bearing the overhead burden. This served to maintain the insularity of the addiction field and the professionals in it (J. Jaffe, personal communication, December 26, 1996). Lack of attention to alcohol and drug use in graduate training and medical schools perpetuated the insularity despite evidence of the high prevalence of AOD users in the social services, health care, and criminal justice systems.

By the 1980s, the cocaine epidemic began to bring the separate alcohol and drug treatment systems together in serving both the insured and indigent. Cocaine users needed "downers" to counteract their edginess and alcohol was the prevalent choice. For the first time, alcohol and drug treatment providers began to attend the same training and were forced to grapple with their differences. Alcohol programs changed their names to "chemical dependency units" and continued to command the support of insurers without having to provide evidence of efficacy. Public-sector programs evolved at first more slowly, then with more solid encouragement as the role of drug use in spreading AIDS became clearer. By that time, however, financial support was limited and there was a movement toward reduced treatment with fewer services (Rawson, 1990–1991). Negative public attitudes remain high despite increasing emphasis on encouraging interventions that can demonstrate effectiveness. With this brief overview, we look at the major treatment modalities in more detail.

Treatment Settings and Modalities

The individual therapist plays a key role in preparing the patient to address alcohol and drug issues, and in working on early and ongoing recovery issues. However, the therapist must be flexible enough to shift the degree of involvement and the nature of his or her activity during the period when the patient is engaged in specialized treatment programs and activities. If the patient is in residential or hospital-based treatment, the individual therapist will, it is hoped, be in a collaborative role (e.g., attending case conferences and participating in treatment planning), but will usually not be in charge of the treatment for the duration of the residential stay. In the various forms of outpatient treatment, the therapist retains a more central role. However, outpatient addiction treatment is more highly structured than psychotherapy, and the therapist is advised to be familiar with program expectations and to establish a working relationship quickly with the outpatient provider to discuss ongoing issues as they arise. Collaborating appropriately requires some knowledge of specialized addiction treatment modalities.

Residential and Inpatient Treatment

Live-in programs include a range of treatment environments in which there is 24-hr supervision, thereby offering a protected setting in which the client or patient is insulated to some extent from the triggers and stressors of drug use. These may be hospital based, such as inpatient programs offering medical interventions (e.g., medically managed withdrawal), or programming aimed at psychosocial issues. The term residential is applied to a wide range of programs that exist outside medical settings as free-standing programs of variable duration using a variety of approaches. These include therapeutic communities (TCs), inpatient programs, and social model recovery homes.

TCs. TCs are long-term residential programs that emerged in the 1960s as an alternative treatment for heroin addiction. They are based on a self-help model developed by Charles Dederich and a group of recovering alcohol and drug addicted members, with major influences from Alcoholics Anonymous (AA) and religious healing communities dating back many years (Deitch, 1973; De Leon, 1994b, 1995). Over time, the resident population diversified and professionals were integrated. Currently, there are a wide range of settings, a variety of lengths of stay, and numerous adaptations that may or may not conform to the therapeutic community model. Two of the best known programs are Day Top and Phoenix House.

The traditional, long-term residential programs have been studied continuously since their inception. Although it does not appear possible to conduct randomized, blind clinical trials, the empirical data support the conclusion that TCs result in positive outcomes of reduction of illicit drug use, other criminal activity, and an increase in economically productive behavior and other measures of positive outcome (Gerstein, 1994; Gerstein & Harwood, 1990). Newer adaptations such as programs serving severely mentally ill individuals or in adaptation of the model for outpatient settings are currently under study.

In the TC model, drug abuse is viewed as a disorder of the whole person that can affect some or all of the person's functioning (De Leon, 1994b). Thus, the intervention must be comprehensive, addressing in particular those psychological difficulties or social deficits that will undermine the ability to maintain a drug-free lifestyle. Indeed, TCs are often said to promote habilitation rather than rehabilitation because residents frequently never acquired prosocial attitudes and skills. Thus, the program must develop qualities that were never there instead of reclaiming those temporarily lost. Recovery entails a shift in personal identity as well as lifestyle. The essential ingredient in change is affiliation, with the community being the primary agent. Table 2 describes the key features assumed to produce change (De Leon, 1994a).

TCs typically define stages of treatment: orientation induction, primary treatment, and reentry. In contrast to the assumption that treatment readiness can be assessed quickly, TCs assume that the initial period will clarify such issues as the resident becomes a participant in the activities of the community. Ambivalence is a given, and the orientation period (0–60 days) is designed to assimilate the individual and promote understanding and acceptance of its norms. The isolation of the individual from the wider community, which is often a source of misunderstanding by professionals and significant others, is designed to bond the resident to the community by eliminating outside influences as much as possible. Dropout is greatest during this early period. Primary treatment (2–12 months) consists of educational and therapeutic meetings, groups, job functions, and peer and staff feedback. As residents display an understanding and acceptance of both the TC perspective and the daily regimen, they ascend in status and privileges in the leadership structure of the community, including job hierarchies. In this way, they set an example for others at the end of their stay in primary treatment. Additional privileges include things such as greater privacy and desirable job responsibilities. The therapeutic process takes place in all facets of community life, ranging from groups specially designed to focus on psychological issues (e.g., traumatic experiences, sex role identity and conflicts) to job performance in which the feedback process is ongoing.

The reentry process prepares the individual for more autonomous functioning outside direct contact with the community. There typically is a reduction in structure, and the resident progresses to a looser form of affiliation. Many TCs offer gradations such as satellite apartments in which residents who shared the common program experience live together without program supervision. In this way, the culture of the TC is transplanted into the wider community setting, so that gradual transitions can promote stable progress.

Common stereotypes of the TC assume harsh confronta-

Table 2

Community as Method: Eight Essential Concepts

Use of Participant Roles	Individuals contribute directly to all activities of daily life in the TC, which provides learning opportunities through engaging in a variety of social roles (e.g., peer, friend, coordinator, tutor). Thus, rather than spectator, individuals are active participants in the process of changing themselves and others.
Use of Membership Feedback	The primary source of instruction and support for individual change is the peer membership. Providing observations and authentic reactions to the individual is the shared responsibility of all participants.
Use of the Membership as Role Models	Each participant strives to be a role model of the change process. Along with their responsibility to provide feedback to others as to what they must change, members must also provide examples of how they can change.
Use of Collective Formats for Guiding Individual Change	The individual engages in the process of change primarily with peers. Education, training, and therapeutic activities occur in groups, meetings, seminars, job functions, and recreation. Thus the learning and healing experiences essential to recovery and personal growth unfold in a social context and through social intercourse.
Use of Shared Norms and Values	Rules, regulations, and social norms protect the physical and psychological safety of the community. However, there are beliefs and values that serve as explicit guidelines for self-help recovery and teaching right living. These are expressed in the vernacular and the culture of each TC and are mutually reinforced by the membership.
Use of Structure and Systems	The organization of work (e.g., the varied job functions, chores, and management roles) needed to maintain the daily operations of the facility is a primary vehicle for teaching self-development. Learning occurs not only through specific skills training, but in adhering to the orderliness of procedures and systems, in accepting and respecting supervision, and in behaving as a responsible member of the community on whom others are dependent.

(Table continues)

Table 2 *(Continued)*

Use of Open Communication	The public nature of shared experiences in the community is used for therapeutic purposes. The private inner life of the individual, feelings and thoughts, are matters of importance to the recovery and change process, not only for the individual but for other members. Thus, all personal disclosure is eventually publicly shared.
Use of Relationships	Friendships with particular individuals, peers, and staff are essential to encourage the individual to engage and remain in the change process. And relationships developed in treatment are the basis for the social network needed to sustain recovery beyond treatment.

Note. From "The therapeutic community: Toward a general theory and model," by G. De Leon, 1994a, *Therapeutic Community: Advances in Research and Application* (National Institute on Drug Abuse Research Monograph No. 144). In the public domain: No permission to reprint required. TC = therapeutic community.

tion, a feature of the original Synanon model that has evolved in productive directions in the more mature TC systems. In the 1970s, more participation by professionals led to the introduction of gestalt techniques, cognitive–behavioral strategies, and other approaches intended to broaden the repertoire of tools. Most TCs also endorse a family model in which the community is seen as a substitute family, often an improved version of what residents may have experienced in childhood. The TC family participates in holiday rituals and graduation for those who complete the program and offers support and caring as the context for exploration of difficult issues. Certainly, TCs vary in the extent to which they establish a healthy and positive climate, but there are many examples in which the family spirit is vigorous and the TC provides a culture for all people involved that is more cohesive and inspiring than many available in the fragmented world of the typical addicted individual.

The Minnesota model. The dominant paradigm for short-term inpatient treatment was developed in Minnesota during the 1950s at the fledgling facilities of Hazelden and Wilmar (McElrath, 1997). Before that time, the prevailing belief that alcoholism was a psychological vulnerability to be treated in mental health units had failed to produce effective treatment. Guided by their successful experiences in AA, the founders of Hazelden and Wilmar adapted these principles to create a new treatment model and brought it into hospital-based treatment. Over time, proponents of the model refined their treatment practices and restructured institutional relationships to emphasize the collaboration between professionals and noncredentialed recovering individuals. By 1954, non-degreed counselors on alcoholism, usually recovering alcoholics, shared the responsibility and decision making for the treatment. This has developed into the certified addiction counselor program carried on through national and state certification programs.

The essential features of the model are its goals of complete abstinence and behavior change, its intimate link with the 12-step process of AA (discussed in more detail in chap. 8) and program participation, and its multidisciplinary approach (McElrath, 1997). Key leadership at Wilmar eventually joined Hazelden, blending their models to produce the Minnesota model, which became the prototype for hospital-based inpatient programs. McElrath (1997) described the key elements as follows:

> 1) the grace of a beautiful environment which promoted respect, understanding, and acceptance of the dignity of each patient; 2) a treatment based essentially on the program and process of AA; 3) the belief that a respite from the familiar environment and association with other alcoholics was central to recovery; 4) simple behavioral expectations, including: make your bed, comport yourself as a gentleman [sic], attend the daily lectures on the 12 steps, and talk with one another; 5) a multidisciplinary

team approach; 6) a systematic approach to the treatment
of an illness defined as a primary disorder distinct from
mental illness; 7) the need and value of an aftercare program. (p. 142)

Thus, a model developed and was disseminated that viewed
recovery as a physical, psychosocial, and spiritual process
with recovering personnel as the primary element in deliv-
ering the service.

The term *chemical dependency* emerged during the cocaine
epidemic and the existing terminology was extended to all
mood-altering drugs. Although this term is widely used, it is
not necessarily accepted by providers in other treatment modalities. Differences in historical origin and in populations
served (e.g., heroin users on methadone maintenance) make
the term alien to some providers; hence, one should not assume the term will be used by all addiction treatment providers.

As has occurred a number of times in the history of addiction treatment, a practical decision based on seasoned clinical opinion but no data shaped the modality for decades to
come. McElrath (1997) reported that in the mid-1970s, when
the State of Minnesota asked how much time was necessary
to treat alcoholics, the response was "at least a month." With
the subsequent mandate of 28 days of insurance coverage in
the 1970s, the Minnesota model became more defined and
proliferated. In McElrath's (1997) opinion, the huge expansion of inpatient programs in the 1980s also fostered a cal-
cification because incidental elements (e.g., the 28-day duration of treatment) rigidified and creativity diminished.

Much controversy existed about the necessity for 28-day
rehabilitation programs even before the period of their rapid
demise as a result of changing insurance reimbursement
policies. Several decades of studies yielded equivocal results, partly because of inadequate methodological strategies.
Within the private sector, the Chemical Abuse/Addiction
Treatment Outcome Registry was developed to document
positive outcomes. This private Minnesota corporation contracts with treatment programs to track individual patients.

Data are collected during treatment and transmitted to the Outcome Registry, which conducts and reports on the follow-ups (Institute of Medicine, 1990). Although these data are useful in exploring treatment issues, the information is often used in marketing efforts without adequate cautions that it is unwarranted to assume that a positive outcome reflects treatment efficacy. For example, researchers following a matched sample have concluded that given certain patient characteristics, improvement will follow minimal or no intervention as well as intensive intervention. W. R. Miller and Hester (1986) reviewed outcome data comparing inpatients and outpatients and concluded that, in general, the data did not justify costly inpatient treatment. However, intensive treatment may be differentially beneficial for those who are more severely deteriorated and less socially stable; these are not the individuals who have ready access to such programs. Randomized controlled trials provide the most rigorous means of evaluating outcome, but they are expensive, time-consuming to conduct, and may be precluded by human participant safety concerns.

Meanwhile, managed care companies established in the 1980s to contain rapidly escalating costs dramatically reduced access to inpatient treatment and shifted the emphasis to outpatient modalities (Rawson, 1990–1991). Currently, these programs demonstrably reduce costs, but the impact on effective outcome is unclear. Researchers are in the process of clarifying questions of how to match people to programs or treatments (e.g., criteria for intensive services), and guidelines are rapidly evolving and being refined.

Social model and other environmental approaches. Social and community model approaches represent an important influence on a variety of treatment and prevention activities. They can form the basis of complete programs or can be components or elements in other types of programs. The goals of social model programs are to provide recovering people with alternative social environments that support recovery and to alter larger communities to prevent alcohol problems and support abstinence on the basis of recovery (Dodd, 1997). Emphasis is on the micro- and macro-community, rather than on the individual, who is generally the focus of clinical model programs. Although others may have an influence on an individual's recovery, it cannot be induced:

> Perhaps the hallmark of social model recovery programs, which is also an indication of its AA roots, is that recovery is considered a "gift of God." From this perception, recovery is not an act of an individual's will, nor the result of a therapist's skill. Recovery is an act of God's *grace*; a gift of *unconditional* love that *cannot be earned*, but only accepted. (emphasis added, Dodd, 1997, p. 134)

In this framework, the creation of an environment that is conducive to recovery is the primary goal. The characteristics of social model programs can be summarized as follows (Wright, 1990):

1. Experiential knowledge about recovery is the basis of authority, especially when decisions are made about program design and operation. Other recovering individuals serve as examples and guides.
2. The primary therapeutic relationship is between the person and the program rather than between the person and a staff member, therapist, or other professional. The group is the agent of change.
3. Everyone both gives and receives help. The program is peer oriented and distinctions between staff, volunteers, and program participants are less distinct than in clinical programs. Any hierarchy is minimized.
4. The fundamental framework of social model programs is derived from the basic principles of AA and emphasizes the values of honesty, tolerance, willingness to try, and emphasis on helping others. Unlike AA, however, social model programs endeavor to make good use of community resources such as public health clinics, social services, therapists, and any other activities that benefit participants.
5. A positive, sober environment is crucial, with clean, homelike, comfortable surroundings setting the tone.
6. Alcohol problems are not only individual problems but

are defined in terms of families, communities, and the larger society. They are centered in the reciprocal relationship between the individual and his or her surrounding social unit. Because this relationship is central, effective intervention must include the overall environment.

The range of social model programs includes social setting detoxification, alcohol recovery homes (short and long term; also referred to as halfway houses), and community recovery centers. Social model detoxification programs were developed initially at the Addiction Research Foundation in Canada in 1970, and shortly thereafter a model was opened as a demonstration in Stockton, California. The goal was to create a system to provide services to intoxicated people in crisis or emergency situations when there was no medical indication for costly hospitalization or outpatient medical management. This system also was designed to foster appropriate use of alcoholism programs and other community agencies, organizing the referral process and creating a continuum of care in a network of community services. Consistent with the larger social model perspective, the physical setting and environment were designed to protect the alcoholic from the stigma frequently encountered in other settings and to promote constructive behavior changes. Medication is not used in most of these settings, but staff are trained to observe warning signs of potential problems. Linkages with hospitals permit immediate transfer in the case of medical complications (O'Bryant & Peterson, 1990).

Alcoholic recovery homes surround the alcoholic with a community that supports the lifestyle changes needed to promote recovery. Like therapeutic communities, residents participate fully in the operation of the home, but the atmosphere of recovery homes tends to be less structured and confrontational. The presence of role models and community reinforcement are key change factors. Peer influence, rather than control by the social service, health care, or criminal justice systems, is the dominant force.

Community recovery centers are another form of social

model program that may include the "sobering services" and residential services described earlier as well as a very wide range of other activities identified as useful to support recovery. Typically, center staff are knowledgeable about community resources and are willing to devise strategies to create resources that are needed but do not currently exist. They view themselves as "guides" rather than case managers, coaching participants in the appropriate use of resources outside the program itself. Other activities include discussion groups on specific topics such as parenting skills, stress reduction, women's issues, and recreational activities designed to promote clean-and-sober fun, especially during weekends, holidays, and other times when recreation was previously organized around drinking. Centers also create a comfortable environment to provide unstructured opportunities to relax and meet people in a friendly, undemanding, alcohol-free setting (Wright, Clay, & Weir, 1990). These centers provide important safe havens in drug-infested inner cities.

Although it is common to find social model elements in a variety of settings, it also is possible to have strong ideological antagonism between social and clinical treatment model proponents in some communities. Many of those who became involved with the social model in its early years, the 1970s, were responding to the failure of professional treatment to meet the needs of the alcoholic. In elaborating their rationale, they took strong public policy stands that sometimes included attempts to extinguish competing models in certain communities:

> The fundamental differences between clinical and social model programs have major implications for the development of social policy for responding to alcohol problems. . . . The principal contribution that social model programs make to such a strategy is a conceptual approach to alcohol problems that *mandates an internal logic and consistency* [italics added] in service structure, funding mechanisms, and systems responsibility. (Reynolds & Ryan, 1990, p. 38)

In statements such as these, the successful effort to create a funding mechanism for a group of programs that could not fit neatly into medically oriented third-party reimbursement systems evolved in the 1980s into a determination to impose that single framework on all activities. For example, one California county prohibited the use of the words *treatment*, *patient*, *client*, and *counseling* in county contracts under the banner of promoting consistency in contract language. Although such divisive efforts are fortunately rare, they leave a legacy that impedes efforts to collaborate to integrate systems in the community.

The great contribution of social model programs is to emphasize, by example, the importance of the support system outside the boundaries of professional treatment. In many cases, this may be entirely adequate to promote the transition to an alcohol- and drug-free lifestyle. Clinicians may forget that they see a subgroup of people in distress; there are many who find the path to healing outside professional treatment. For those who use professional assistance, social model programs provide a context for that effort with the potential to greatly amplify the impact of the treatment effort. It also is a model with applicability to mental health and other social problems.

Continuing care and aftercare. Although it is not considered a separate modality, there is widespread understanding of the importance of a continuum of care designed to assist the recovering individual to maintain his or her gains (particularly after residential or inpatient treatment) and continue to integrate or reintegrate into society (Brown & Ashery, 1979). The term *aftercare*, although still used in some settings and circumstances, is viewed with some caution because of its implication that when one is "done" with treatment, the main event is over and subsequent activities are less important. Continuing care conveys more appropriate expectations because recovery is seen as a process requiring life-long attention to factors such as stress management, good self-care, and avoidance of known hazards. The recovering person acquires tools while participating in treatment, capitalizing on the knowledge of the treatment staff, and begins to apply skills as stress management before formal treatment is ended.

The self-help system provides a subculture that supports recovery and offers continuing growth opportunities without financial and other barriers to access.

Outpatient Treatment

Outpatient care, intensive outpatient care, and partial hospitalization. Throughout the 1980s, 28-day programs dominated the landscape for insured populations, and outpatient treatment was viewed as being "second best." Under pressure to offer a service that was less disruptive to employed patients, short-term outpatient models were developed, often by scaling down the inpatient version and offering programming for 3–4 hr on weekday evenings. These programs typically lasted 5–8 weeks, following which the patient participated in aftercare of considerably reduced intensity. In the sector serving the indigent population, outpatient programs were of longer duration and increased their range of services as the Center for Substance Abuse Treatment appeared in 1990 and began to encourage the provision of comprehensive services. Currently, many outpatient programs exist that vary considerably in content, intensity, and duration. The lack of standardization in program design (e.g., the same program may be called *intensive outpatient* or *partial hospitalization* by different providers) and evaluation methodology makes it difficult to identify effective ingredients. However, with the development of patient placement criteria by the American Society of Addiction Medicine (ASAM; 1996), greater consistency in definitions will presumably promote research efforts. Given the length of time needed to plan, fund, conduct, and publish research studies, it will likely be near the end of the decade before basic issues of effectiveness are clarified.

Despite the variety of programs available, ASAM offers general guidelines. Level 1, outpatient treatment, is described as a professionally directed alcohol and other drug treatment occurring in regularly scheduled sessions usually totaling fewer than 9 hr a week. It consists of a combination of individual and group sessions in conjunction with self-help group participation. Level 2, intensive outpatient (also referred to as partial hospitalization or day treatment), is a more structured program with a minimum of 9 treatment hr a week. Patients can live at home or in special residences supervised to ensure they remain clean and sober (ASAM, 1996). Program sites include hospital-based facilities, homeless shelters, and community-based organizations. The Center for Substance Abuse Treatment offers a treatment improvement protocol (Nagy, 1994) describing in detail the essential and desirable components of an intensive outpatient treatment program.

Methadone maintenance treatment. Methadone maintenance treatment (MMT) is a major treatment modality for opioid (primarily heroin) users who have tried to become abstinent without medication but did not succeed. It is considered the treatment of last resort for "intractable" heroin addicts. In the middle 1960s, the upsurge of heroin addiction and its higher visibility in young (15–35 years) and middle-class populations led to increased federal efforts to develop effective treatment modalities. This era produced the resources to establish, proliferate, and study both MMT and TCs, which have been the subject of continuous study since that time. Currently, approximately 150,000 of an estimated 1 million U.S. heroin addicts are in MMT (Center for Substance Abuse Treatment, 1997).

MMT was developed in the mid-1960s by two physicians, Vincent Dole and Marie Nyswander, who postulated that a metabolic defect accounted for the inability of heroin addicts to remain abstinent for more than brief periods of time. They intended for methadone to be used as a corrective medication indefinitely. As it was being formally approved for clinical use, professional and public opinion shifted to a new goal: to use methadone to wean off heroin to achieve a drug-free lifestyle. Once this was accomplished, methadone was to be discontinued. Research in the following decades indicated that less than 20% of addicts would be able to discontinue methadone and remain drug free (Zweben & Payte, 1990). In more recent work for which he won the Lasker Award, Dole (1988) postulated that a receptor system dysfunction resulting from chronic heroin use leads to permanent alterations that physicians do not know how to reverse. Thus, indefinite maintenance is corrective, but not curative, in much the same way that thyroid or insulin replacement normalizes body functioning. Studies indicate that methadone is a benign drug that shows stability of receptor occupation and thus permits interacting systems to function normally (Zweben & Payte, 1990). It is this stability that results in evenness in functioning. This distinguishes it from heroin, a short-acting narcotic producing rapid changes that make a stable state of adaptation impossible. An addict maintained on heroin would go through 4-hr cycles of intoxication and withdrawal; even if supplied with a clean and legal source, the short duration of action makes heroin undesirable as a maintenance drug. Even with long-term use (20 years or more), methadone continues to have a withdrawal prevention effect in which patients do not experience craving or other withdrawal phenomena and are able to function normally without somnolence (Zweben & Payte, 1990).

MMT, in combination with educational, medical, and counseling services, has been thoroughly documented to assist patients in reducing or discontinuing illicit drug use and associated criminal activity; improving physical and emotional well-being; becoming responsible family members; furthering a patient's education; and obtaining and maintaining stable employment and resuming or establishing a productive lifestyle (Gerstein & Harwood, 1990; Hubbard et al., 1989). Despite three decades of research confirming its value and safety, MMT remains perhaps the most stigmatized of all drug treatment modalities and the one that is the least understood (Murphy & Irwin, 1992). It remains a source of contention among treatment providers, the general public, and health care policymakers. After a long period of isolation from other forms of treatment and recovery interventions, the AIDS epidemic stimulated a reexamination and renewed interest in this modality. MMT has been demonstrated, through education, reduced needle use, and increased safer sex practices, to slow the spread of HIV disease and to slow the progression of the disease in those who have contracted it (Selwyn & Batki, 1995; Zweben & Payte, 1990). On closer examination, the "controversies" about MMT usually reflect several common misunderstandings rather than a difference of opinion between informed parties.

In our experience, one primary source of opposition is the notion that use of methadone is "just substituting one addicting drug for another." This notion is often shared by the patients themselves, who may lack information and have usually internalized the stigma. Technically, this is correct: MMT is drug-replacement therapy in which a long-acting, orally administered medication is substituted for a short-acting illicit opioid that is used intravenously. These differences have significant consequences. The long duration of action of methadone (24–36 hr) allows most patients to receive a daily dose and function in a stable manner because their blood level remains relatively constant. This stands in contrast to the 4-hr cycles of euphoria and withdrawal that are characteristic of heroin use. It is this feature that promotes lifestyle changes by permitting normal functioning.

In addition, there is widespread misconception among both the public and professionals about what constitutes addiction. Addiction treatment professionals increasingly distinguish between physical dependence and addiction. Physical dependence itself is a factor to be considered but one that in and of itself does not constitute addiction, which is characterized by behavior that is compulsive and out of control and persists despite adverse consequences. The key question is whether functioning is improved or impaired by use. Benzodiazepines are an example of a medication that is dependence producing at therapeutic doses but that can be used beneficially for long periods for people with anxiety disorders. Patients with chronic pain are another group for whom assessment focuses on whether their functioning is improved or impaired rather than on physical dependence itself as the deciding factor.

Another common misconception is that "methadone keeps you high," which reflects misunderstanding of a properly adjusted dose. While a patient's dose is being stabilized, he or she may experience some subjective effects, but these usually diminish or disappear once stabilized. This is precisely why methadone is a good tool; once stabilization is achieved, the patient should be able to function normally.

Extensive research on safety indicates that long-term use of methadone results in no physical or psychological impairment of any kind that can be perceived by the patient, observed by a physician, or detected by a scientist (Zweben & Payte, 1990). There is no impairment of balance, coordination, mental abilities, eye–hand coordination, depth perception, or psychomotor functioning. Recently, we became familiar with methadone patients identified through workplace drug testing who were threatened with negative consequences and who succeeded, through advocacy efforts, in keeping their jobs. The Americans with Disabilities Act may also help protect them.

Because of historical disputes and political controversies, the current treatment system is overburdened by regulations and inappropriate expectations (Rettig & Yarmolinsky, 1995), producing a delivery system so dehumanizing that programs usually make efforts to assist the patient wishing to taper off methadone. However, it is important to remember that studies indicate that although it is common for patients to remain opiate free for a short time, relapse is the norm for 80% or more (Ball & Ross, 1991; McLellan, 1983). Because a history of treatment failures is required, only a subset of heroin addicts qualify for methadone maintenance, and it is likely that neurobiological factors are decisive (Dole, 1988). High motivation is necessary but not sufficient for successfully tapering off methadone. Unfortunately, it is common for uninformed professionals, family members, and others to encourage or coerce methadone patients to discontinue their medication (Zweben & Payte, 1990). The decision to taper should be made by the patient in collaboration with professionals experienced in MMT and should not be based on bias against this medication. The relapse rates of methadone users are so extraordinarily high that the risks are considerable. Therapists should be cautious about encouraging a patient to discontinue MMT because pressure is often applied by the family or by other treatment providers based on stigma instead of careful review of the case. The results of misguided interventions such as this can be lethal.

Because of the features of the MMT delivery system, the majority of patients are indigent or working class; of these, many are downwardly mobile from the middle class as a result of their drug and alcohol use. However, depending on clinic location, there may be surprising numbers of successful and high-functioning individuals who conceal their participation in MMT from colleagues and even family members. It is possible that under better circumstances, MMT would be the treatment of choice for opioid users with more middle-class characteristics.

Clinicians have observed patients who flounder for long periods, unable to maintain abstinence, or who substitute alcohol and deteriorate. The chemical dependency programs in which they were likely to seek treatment often claimed an expertise they did not have in treating heroin users, and lacked long-term follow-up studies to assess the efficacy of their efforts. In our experience, such patients report being highly stigmatized by the more populous cocaine users because their drug preference was heroin, and they were labeled "more disturbed" by treatment staff. Results of an Empire Blue Cross and Blue Shield study (Eisenhandler & Drucker, 1993) showed that there is a large population of opiate users who may be excluded from the estimates of overall number of opiate users because they are less likely to be counted via contact with government agencies. They estimated that between 1982 and 1992, Empire Blue Cross and Blue Shield (New York Metropolitan Area) insured approximately 141,000 opiate users, of which 85,000 were currently insured with them at the time of the study. They recommended that the social characteristics of opiate users should be reconsidered because many middle-class heroin users may be overlooked and undertreated.

Smoking cessation. Until relatively recently, treatment for smoking cessation was offered mainly in primary health care settings or by smoking cessation specialists and remained relatively unintegrated with the rest of the addiction field. Attention began to focus on it in the mid-1980s, as reflected in

Wallace's (1986) editorial, *Smoke Gets in Our Eyes: Professional Denial of Smoking*. He challenged the minimization of health consequences and the complacency about addressing it, especially given the high percentage of smokers among patients in treatment for addiction. He also noted that the prevalence of smokers among recovering staff members presented a troublesome role model and constituted a source of resistance to no-smoking policies. Since that time, researchers have documented the significantly higher frequency of smoking among alcoholics and polydrug users, established that smoking cessation does not in itself increase relapse as previously feared, and refined intervention techniques to promote success (Jarvik & Schneider, 1992). Smoking cessation is gradually becoming integrated into addiction treatment, although it continues to be provided by health care organizations and private practitioners. As insurers and the government focus on the many costs associated with smoking-related illnesses, one can also expect increasing support for identification and treatment outside addiction treatment settings.

Short-term behavioral therapies have long been prominent in smoking cessation. Many are able to achieve high initial cessation rates, but success rates at 1 year averaged 15%–30%, unrelated to the initial quit rates (Jarvik & Schneider, 1992). This may be related to a lack of emphasis on relapse prevention. In our opinion, the behavioral strategies that are effective in initiating abstinence are different from those needed to maintain it, and reliance on short-term treatment makes it less likely that long-term maintenance strategies will be provided at the time they actually become relevant.

The recent development of effective pharmacological withdrawal agents has been shown to greatly augment the success of behavioral strategies (Smoking Cessation Clinical Practice Guideline Panel, 1996). Nicotine dependence and craving varies among smokers, and these agents significantly decrease discomfort. Nicotine replacement in the forms of transdermal patches, gum, nasal spray, and inhalers are available. The Agency for Health Care Policy and Research (AHCPR) smoking cessation guidelines (Smoking Cessation

Clinical Practice Guideline Panel, 1996) summarize the issues pertaining to the selection and application of both pharmacological and psychosocial treatments. Studies support the view that combination therapies show greater effectiveness than pharmacotherapy or behavioral interventions alone, but effective treatment matching protocols have not been established (Smoking Cessation Clinical Practice Guideline Panel, 1996). Social support is a key element in smoking cessation, as with other drugs; hence, the proliferation of antismoking regulations at the work site and in other public settings will likely improve treatment success rates.

Psychiatric comorbidity has emerged as a key element in successful smoking cessation; hence, treatment planning should take this into account. Strong relationships have been reported between depression and smoking. Glassman (1993) reported that both major depression and depressive symptoms are associated with a high rate of cigarette smoking, and a lifetime history of major depression has an adverse impact on smoking cessation. In this vulnerable group, there is also a significantly higher likelihood of the patient developing a depressed mood during the first week of withdrawal, and the entire withdrawal syndrome is more severe. The emergence of depressive symptoms predicts a failure of the attempt to quit (Glassman, 1993). Thus, it is important that the clinician assess depression and include appropriate interventions in the treatment plan. For example, it may be advisable to wait until the patient has been stabilized on antidepressant medication before encouraging action on quitting. Cognitive–behavioral strategies designed to enhance affect regulation also have been demonstrated to be effective for this group (S. M. Hall, Munoz, & Reus, 1992, 1994).

Clinicians working with schizophrenic patients have a more complex dilemma. Although the serious health risks are undisputable, it appears that nicotine confers some benefits that must be considered in smoking cessation efforts (Goff, Henderson, & Amico, 1992). Reviews note the high rates of smoking among schizophrenics: 74%–92%, compared with 35%–54% for all psychiatric patients and 30%–35% for the general population (Goff et al., 1992). Current smokers received significantly higher neuroleptic doses and displayed less parkinsonism and more akasthisia (i.e., restless movements induced by neuroleptics). Patients report that it produces relaxation, reduces anxiety, reduces medication side effects, and ameliorates psychiatric symptoms (Goff et al., 1992). It has been postulated that nicotine provides transient symptomatic relief by stimulating cholinergic nicotinic receptors, enhancing the gating mechanism that permits schizophrenics to filter out irrelevant stimuli (Freedman et al., 1994). Thus, efforts to promote smoking cessation in schizophrenics, especially abruptly when they enter smoke-free hospital environments, must take into account these complex considerations. Success will likely depend on a better understanding of the mechanisms of the positive benefits of smoking and development of alternatives (e.g., transdermal patches). In summary, wide recognition of health consequences for smokers and those around them and stricter laws about smoking will likely result in increasing demand for assistance, in which both clinicians and researchers will play an active role.

Psychotherapy in the treatment of addiction. Although psychotherapy alone is not usually considered an appropriate treatment for addiction, in reality many therapists in the community diagnose and attempt to address addictive behaviors ranging from mild to severe. Increasingly, they combine their efforts with a referral or insistence on AA or Narcotics Anonymous attendance. For many, the issue is given priority and the combination of psychotherapy with self-help group participation is considered adequate, although there is no referral to formal addiction treatment. To our knowledge, there are no empirical data on how often this process occurs and how effective it is. Many addiction specialists view the community therapist as being in a prime position to do effective early intervention, arresting problems before serious deterioration occurs. However, it also is apparent that some therapists in the community are not sufficiently concerned about lack of progress in changing behavior. It would be valuable to study this therapeutic process in more detail, defining parameters for effective intervention in this context, looking at outcome, and formulating guidelines for when referral to the specialty system is advisable.

Conclusion

We hope that this brief review will assist the treatment provider in seeking resources on the basis of the patient's resources. Unfortunately, barriers to access have multiplied even as documentation of the effectiveness of treatment has grown. Capacity is inadequate in most communities. Insurers and managed care organizations have focused on cost containment and are only beginning to be held accountable by the public to provide an effective level of intervention. Patients, long accustomed to having such services covered by insurance, may be resistant to paying private providers out of pocket even when they are able to afford to do so. However, there are growing numbers of trained providers who can fill in important gaps in what benefits cover. Services for the indigent are usually funded through county health departments or are coordinated by them. These departments usually maintain some kind of directory or clearinghouse (e.g., central intake) for those seeking help. Individual providers need to be prepared to advocate (sometimes vigorously) to get their patients' needs met from the multiple systems with which they interact. The ability to collaborate with providers across disciplines is a great asset. We hope that more public–private partnerships will emerge to help maximize limited resources and fill gaps in the treatment delivery system. Advocacy by informed professionals is a key element in securing effective services within a community.

5

Determining Appropriate Treatment: The Collaborative Challenge

Before reviewing treatment options for individual patients, we think it is useful to consider what constitutes effective collaboration because this is as important as therapeutic skills in addressing addiction. It is rare to find an addicted patient for whom there is no need to collaborate with other professionals and systems. Precisely because addiction is a bio-psychosocial disorder, the clinician must be prepared to interact with physicians, social workers, psychologists, lawyers, probation officers, and other addiction treatment professionals with specialty credentials. It is useful to think of the other disciplines as "subcultures" with their own language and assumptions about what people need in order to change. Mental health providers often underestimate the need for integrated addiction treatment, assuming that if the mental health disorder were addressed, the addictive behavior would correct itself. Physicians may underestimate the importance of sustained participation in psychosocial interventions. In working with the criminal justice system, divergent interests (e.g., promoting public safety vs. individual welfare) may overshadow the common interest of achieving stable recovery. The more the practitioner understands the perspectives of those with whom he or she is collaborating, the greater the likelihood of the kind of teamwork that leads to success. The individual therapist may need to be the patient's advocate, educate other professionals, and assist in problem solving to formulate and implement a treatment plan.

The existing system is fraught with obstacles that multiply with the number of problem areas in the individual patient. The separate systems in which various disorders (e.g., psychiatric disorders, medical problems) normally are treated have different assumptions about what goals are desirable and how people can achieve them, a different language, and to some extent different values. For example, goals are formulated differently when one focuses on a terminal illness such as AIDS than when one has a relatively normal life expectancy. Abstinence goals, the usual organizing principle of addiction treatment, may result in harsh treatment when inflexibly applied to a deteriorating patient with AIDS. The right of the individual to make certain value judgments about drug use must be weighed against the social cost of permissiveness about alcohol and drug use.

Those working with severely mentally ill individuals have other collaborative challenges. Jerrell, Hu, and Ridgley (1994) documented how interventions to address substance disorders in people with severe mental illness reduce acute and subacute service use. There is an abundance of other evidence that alcohol and drug use increases medical costs in an otherwise healthy population. Except for those recently trained, most mental health practitioners are not skilled in motivating their patients to address their alcohol and other drug (AOD) use; this issue was seldom addressed in their basic training. They attempt to address the AOD use by referring the patients to the addiction treatment system, which is not well equipped to deal with those who are highly ambivalent in their motivation and not prepared to make a wholehearted commitment. Thus, a large group in need of attention, and amenable to appropriate intervention, does not usually get its needs met in either system. Private practitioners or therapists in other settings are in an excellent position to develop "treatment readiness" in the patients by applying the motivational enhancement strategies described in chapter 10.

Sequential, Parallel, and Integrated Treatment Models

Although it is widely acknowledged that the social service, mental health, addiction, and criminal justice systems are seeing many of the same people, in many communities it is still necessary to deal with multiple systems in order to get an appropriate treatment plan implemented. Many obstacles are inherent in this process. At best, it is time-consuming and frequently overwhelms the patient with the task of meeting contradictory expectations. HIV adds the dimension of fatigue, susceptibility to other people's diseases, as well as the inability to drive or use public transportation. By contrast, integrated treatment models permit addressing multiple client needs within one system. Ries (1993, 1994) discussed the strengths and limits of sequential, parallel, and integrated models for different patient profiles and described treatment approach similarities and differences (see Table 3). Private practitioners doing psychotherapy may need to match the patient with mental health or addiction treatment services in the community to provide missing elements. It is important to consider which model best meets the goals that need to be achieved.

In *sequential treatment*, the patient is treated by one system (addiction or mental health) and then by the other. Many clinicians believe that the addiction treatment must always be initiated first and that the patient must be abstinent before treatment for psychiatric disorders can be effective. Some psychotherapists, impressed by the futility of ignoring AOD use, insist that the patient address the addictive behavior first before working on other issues. Indeed, there are times when this is the preferred approach, although the rigidity of some clinicians is cause for concern. It is more likely that the therapist will need to make the case for an abstinence commitment over a period of time and focus on exploring the pa-

Table 3

Treatment Approach Similarities and Differences

	Mental health system	Dual disorders approach	Addiction system
Medications	Central to the management of severe disorders in acute, subacute, and long-term phases of treatment: antidepressants, antipsychotics, anxiolytics, and mood stabilizers.	Central to the treatment of many patients with dual disorders. Caution is used when prescribing psychoactive, mood-altering medications.	Central for acute detoxification; less common for subacute phase. Few used during long-term treatment: disulfiram, naltrexone, methadone, and LAAM.
Therapeutic confrontations	Minimal to moderate use, depending on setting, patient, and problem. Not central to therapy.	Generally used, but use is modulated according to fragility of mental status.	Use by staff and peers is one of the central techniques in AOD treatment.
Group therapy 12-Step groups	Central to treatment. Although historically underused, use is growing. Examples include Emotions Anonymous, Obsessive–Compulsive Anonymous, and Phobics Anonymous.	Central to treatment. Dual Disorders Anonymous groups not yet widespread. Use of 12-step groups for AOD problems is central, but actively psychotic or paranoid patients may not mix well in meetings. "Double Trouble" AA groups are becoming more numerous.	Central to treatment. Use of 12-step groups is central to AOD treatment. Great availability. Examples include Alcoholics Anonymous, Narcotics Anonymous, and Cocaine Anonymous.

| Other self-help groups | Numerous national organizations. Growing numbers of local groups. Use depends on availability and awareness. Examples include Anxiety Disorders Association of America, National Depressive & Manic–Depressive Association, Recovery, Inc., and National Association of Psychiatric Survivors. | Use of self-help groups regarding AOD and mental health problems is increasing. | Numerous organizations and groups, often specialized. Examples include Women for Sobriety, Rational Recovery, Secular Organizations for Sobriety, International Doctors in AA, Recovering Counselors Network, and Social Workers Helping Social Workers. |

Note. From *Assessment and treatment of patients with coexisting mental illness and alcohol and other drug abuse* (p. 13), by R. Ries, 1994, Rockville, MD: Substance Abuse and Mental Health Services Administration. In the public domain: No permission to reprint is required. LAAM = levo-alpha-acetul-methadol, used in opioid maintenance pharmacotherapy; AOD = alcohol and other drug; AA = Alcoholics Anonymous.

tient's resistance to doing so. Patients with severe psychiatric disorders may need to have those addressed first. Addiction treatment may be ineffective until symptoms of the mental health disorder are stabilized, such as until antipsychotics take effect or antidepressant blood levels are up to the therapeutic level.

In *parallel treatment*, the patient is simultaneously involved in addiction and mental health treatment. For example, a depressed woman may be placed on antidepressants, participate in psychotherapy, and attend classes on coping with depression at a mental health center while participating in 12-step meetings, a recovery group, or alcohol- or drug-refusal classes in an addiction treatment program. These forms of treatment are provided by clinicians within different systems, or peripheral to them, who may rarely if ever communicate with each other. If the patient becomes caught between conflicting expectations and philosophies, there may be no obvious mechanism to resolve issues. This situation is likely to interfere with a good treatment outcome.

In *integrated treatment*, both mental health and addiction treatment are combined into a unified and comprehensive treatment program involving clinicians who have been cross-trained in both approaches. This includes a unified case management approach that makes it possible to monitor and treat patients through both psychiatric and AOD crises. The burden of treatment consistency and continuity is placed on staff in a setting designed for the simultaneous treatment of both disorders.

Models for the treatment of coexisting disorders are rapidly evolving and under extensive study, but it is not currently possible to make data-based comparisons between models. Many clinicians working in this area are convinced that the integration of psychosocial and medical treatment within the treatment and recovery setting has the greatest chance of success with most patients. Even with aggressive case management, follow-through on referrals may be difficult, especially because multiple diagnoses magnify stigma and patients are keenly sensitive to the negative attitudes they encounter. Bouncing between two or three systems usually results in the patient being given conflicting messages with inadequate opportunity for resolution and diminishes the chance of compliance with any treatment plan. However, sequential or parallel treatment may work well when patients have a severe problem in one area but a mild problem in the other. The therapist in private practice should be prepared to play a coordinating and advocacy role to assist the patient who becomes caught in conflicting expectations or practices.

The current transition in the health care delivery system poses other problems for which solutions may not be immediately apparent. The impetus to shorten the length of stay and reduce the intensity of treatment runs counter to the needs of patients with not one but several chronic relapsing disorders. In the addiction field, treatment outcome research done on public-sector populations over the past three decades is consistent in its findings about the relationship between retention and outcome (Gerstein & Harwood, 1990; Hubbard et al., 1989). The longer people stay in treatment, the better they do. Gains begin to be enduring after about 6 months' participation in treatment. Such findings suggest that in a managed care environment, many with multiple disorders will not receive care that is effective by objective measures. The "positive outcomes" described by some managed care organizations appear to be based on an absence of immediate casualties or protest by members. They do not use the same treatment outcome criteria as the addiction or mental health provider.

Individual psychotherapy can fit into the following models and situations in a variety of ways. The patient often arrives at the door of the addiction treatment system referred by his or her therapist, who may continue to see the patient during and after specialty treatment is completed. Others seek psychotherapy after a period of sobriety to address many painful issues once obscured by AOD use. Limited psychotherapy is even becoming available to adjudicated populations as recognition grows that inadequate resources have brought many with psychiatric disorders into the criminal justice system as their untreated symptoms escalated and appropriate help was unavailable. It is imperative that the individual therapist familiarize himself or herself with the expectations and constraints of the relevant systems and be flexible enough to tailor treatment to accommodate the extensive and sometimes conflicting demands on the patient.

Formulating a Treatment Plan

We now look in more detail at attempts to standardize principles for deciding the level of care and a range of services that should be included and how they can be matched with patient needs. Although these principles are under continuous revision, they provide sensible guidelines for current practice. Note that most of the vast literature on matching in both alcohol and drug treatment modalities has failed to yield dependable, practical methods for assigning patients to programs or particular treatments. For example, a recent national study showed that three commonly used approaches were effective but did not get support for most of the hypotheses about which matching variables indicated which treatment. Only psychiatric severity demonstrated relevance as a matching variable (National Institute on Alcohol Abuse and Alcoholism Project MATCH Research Group, 1997). Most of these studies used a patient–program matching strategy in which efforts were made to match particular types of patients to particular types of programs. Attempts to apply these matching principles encountered access barriers in the programs selected, long waiting lists made admission difficult, and geographical obstacles limited participation. Programs rapidly emerged and disappeared in the unstable funding climate. Patient–program matching has increasingly come to be viewed as impractical.

McLellan and Alterman (1991), who are part of a well-known group of researchers in Philadelphia, reviewed conceptual and methodological issues to chart a more productive course for this complex endeavor. Recent research by this group has focused on problem–service matching, a promising strategy that can be used by individual private providers and agencies. We examine this approach and then describe two other frameworks in common use: the Center for Substance Abuse Treatment's (CSAT) comprehensive care model and the American Society of Addiction Medicine's (ASAM) patient placement criteria (PPC). Taken together, these frameworks may be helpful in guiding the clinician in treatment planning and implementation.

Problem–Service Matching

In the course of several decades of treatment outcome research, the Philadelphia group has been refining ways to use the Addiction Severity Index (ASI), described in chapter 2, as a tool for measuring outcome. The ASI provides a severity score in the areas of alcohol and drug use, employment, illegal activities, family and other social supports, and medical and psychiatric conditions. In their recent work (McLellan, Alterman, Woody, & Metzger, 1992), this group devised the treatment services review (TSR) as a means of tracking whether the patient received services relevant to his or her individual profile. For example, if the patient was high in psychiatric severity, did he or she receive appropriate services? This measure is simple and can be administered in a brief (5- to 10-min) weekly inquiry that asks in how many services, or in how many activities, did the patient discuss or address a particular problem. Thus, a visit to a psychiatrist would count, as would discussion in a group therapy session. McLellan and his colleagues then examined the relationship between close problem–service matching and outcome.

This approach shed light on the mystery of why much of the literature on 28-day inpatient programs failed to demonstrate differential effectiveness for the population treated. In a study of private treatment programs, McLellan, Grissom, Brill, et al. (1993) concluded that the setting (inpatient vs. outpatient) was a poor indicator of what the patient might actually receive. Inpatient programs provided significantly more AOD counseling sessions and medical services. In the areas of family, employment, and psychiatric severity, there were great differences between the programs, unrelated to setting. All programs in this study were accredited by the Joint Commission on Accreditation of Healthcare Organizations (JCAHO) and enjoyed good reputations in the community; nonetheless, the variability was striking. The goals of treatment, operating rehabilitation philosophies, and core components of the program were similar or identical (e.g., 12-step meetings, education, group therapy), but there were substantial differences in the types and quantities of services actually delivered. Despite the presence of psychiatrists, psychologists, and social workers on the regular or consulting staff, the majority of patients had little contact with those providing these specialized services. However, the programs that provided the most services focused on a specific treatment problem (as measured by the ASI) generally showed the best outcome. Thus, the specificity and relevance of the treatment services actually delivered to each individual appears to have a major influence on differential effectiveness.

In a subsequent study, McLellan et al. (1997) provided participating treatment programs (again, JCAHO licensed and well regarded) with ASI profiles under standard and matched conditions. In the standard condition, treatment providers were given the scores and handled the patient according to the program's usual protocols. In the matched condition, the research team "prescribed" a minimum of three professional sessions in any of three areas (i.e., psychiatric, family, and employment) indicated as problematic on the basis of the ASI profile. Standard patients were less likely than matched ones to receive professional services, and, although all patients improved in treatment, the matched patients showed significantly greater improvement. Although unsettling, it is perhaps not surprising given the predilection of clinicians to focus on the areas of their own interests and skills. However, it does indicate the need for a more disciplined approach by both private practitioners and institutions. These methods are simple enough to be integrated into information management systems and evaluation reports.

CSAT Comprehensive Care Model

The CSAT model offers a detailed framework for matching patient needs with services in public-sector programs. These patients typically have far more complex practical problems (e.g., housing, medical, educational, vocational) and often require more comprehensive services to stabilize their psychosocial functioning. In 1990, the CSAT began (as the Office for Treatment Improvement [OTI]) with the task of expanding the availability of effective services for addiction treatment. Resources are targeted to the indigent population because

> those who suffer from extreme socioeconomic dislocation are at highest risk for addiction by virtue of their exposure to crime, poverty, abuse and homelessness, as well as their lack of access to good primary health and mental health care, social services, vocational training, and education. (Primm, 1990, p. 1)

A key element in the CSAT's mission is to facilitate the application of the vast body of knowledge generated by the National Institute on Drug Abuse and the National Institute on Alcohol Abuse and Alcoholism (NIAAA). This necessitated engaging the system of state and local government agencies and public and private treatment providers responsible for the delivery of addiction treatment services (Primm, 1990). To upgrade the standard of care, the CSAT articulated in detail the ingredients in effective treatment for the population it serves.

The extensive research literature generated several basic principles that guided the activities of OTI, which became CSAT in the course of a government reorganization in 1992. The first recognizes that there are multiple physiological, psychological, and environmental factors that contribute to the onset and maintenance of addiction. It cannot be effectively treated without addressing the individual's primary health, mental health, and socioeconomic deficits and disorders. Second, it is well established that addiction is a chronic, relapsing disorder appropriately likened to diabetes or hypertension (O'Brien & McLellan, 1996), thus requiring a series of interventions along a continuum to sustain recovery. The comprehensive treatment model, which forms the basis for CSAT's initiatives, reflects this understanding (Primm, 1990).

Research data accumulated over 30 years indicate that treatment does work in effectively reducing the use of alcohol and illicit drugs, criminal activity, rates of HIV seroconversion, and overall patient morbidity and increasing employment rates and family functioning (Gerstein & Harwood, 1990; Hubbard et al., 1989). Hence, the thrust of the CSAT's activity is to foster the application of treatment and recovery interventions known to be effective. Within the treatment system for the indigent population evolved comprehensive and sophisticated clinical programs, as providers sought to apply the mandate to the needs of their community.

The largest portion of the funds were the Alcohol, Drug Abuse, and Mental Health Services block grants, allocated to each state by a formula legislated by the U.S. Congress and distributed to counties and cities on the basis of need and other criteria. This program expanded the availability of funds while allowing the states considerable latitude to design solutions to specific problems. The CSAT's other initiatives, particularly the demonstration grant programs, had more rigorous guidelines intended to encourage application of research-based, state-of-the-art treatment practices to specific populations. These included racial and ethnic minorities, adolescents, pregnant and parenting women and their children, homeless people, residents of public housing, criminal justice populations, and those with a high instance of physical and mental illness as well as their substance use disorders. These comprehensive services can be provided within the program itself or through linkages with community agencies providing the needed service, such as primary medical care.

Guidelines for model treatment programs were disseminated widely by the CSAT through vehicles such as its request for applications for funds, treatment improvement protocols (e.g., Nagy, 1994), and various other publications

carrying a range of economic and other incentives. Guidelines adapted from Kleber (1994) include the following:

1. *Assessment,* to include a medical examination, drug
   use history, psychosocial evaluation, and, when war-
   ranted, a psychiatric evaluation and a review of socioeconomic factors and eligibility for public health, welfare, employment, and educational assistance
   programs.
2. *Same-day intake,* to retain the patient's involvement
   and interest in treatment.
3. *Documenting findings and treatment,* to enhance clinical
   case supervision.
4. *Preventive and primary medical care,* provided on site if
   possible.
5. *Testing for infectious diseases,* at intake and at intervals
   throughout treatment, for infectious diseases such as
   hepatitis, retrovirus, tuberculosis, HIV and AIDS,
   syphilis, gonorrhea, and other STDs.
6. *Weekly random drug testing,* to ensure abstinence and
   compliance with treatment.
7. *Pharmacotherapeutic interventions,* by qualified medical
   practitioners as appropriate for those patients having
   mental health disorders, those addicted to opiates,
   and HIV-positive individuals and AIDS patients.
8. *Group counseling interventions,* to address the unique
   emotional, physical, and social problems of HIV and
   AIDS patients.
9. *Basic substance abuse counseling,* including individual,
   family, or collateral counseling, trained and certified
   when possible. Staff training and education are integral to successful treatment.
10. *Practical life skills counseling,* including vocational and
    educational counseling and training. These can be
    provided through linkages with community pro-
    grams.
11. *General health education,* including nutrition, sex and
    family planning, and HIV and AIDS counseling, with
    an emphasis on contraception counseling for adoles-
    cents and women.
12. *Peer support groups,* particularly for those who are

HIV-positive or who have been victims of rape or sexual abuse.

13. *Liaison services*, with immigration, legal aid, and criminal justice system authorities.

14. *Social and athletic activities*, to restore patients' perceptions of social interaction.

15. *Alternative housing*, for homeless patients or for those whose living situations are conducive to maintaining the addict lifestyle.

16. *Relapse prevention*, which combines aftercare and support programs such as 12-step programs within an individualized plan to identify, stabilize, and control the stressors that trigger and promote relapse to substance abuse.

17. *Outcome evaluation*, to enable refinement and improvement of service delivery.

On the basis of our experience, implementation of these guidelines was imperfect, but the impact was to enlarge the vision of treatment providers and map out a process for upgrading quality. Demonstration programs were intended to provide a model for others in the community to emulate. The insistence of knowledge of state-of-the-art practices allowed for the introduction of new approaches into a community, dislodging complacency with familiar approaches. The CSAT provided support in the form of technical assistance to grantees directly in regular meetings or through the state offices and in materials available to providers or the public at large. Recipients of such funding for a sustained period of time had unparalleled exposure to learning opportunities and access to resources to refine treatment approaches for specific populations. Some of these, such as long-term residential treatment for women and their children, do not exist in private-sector programs. When there was interaction with private-sector programs, the opportunity for cross-fertilization was productive. Thus, although treatment capacity for the indigent population remains seriously inadequate, in a given community one could find programs that are unusual in creativity and comprehensiveness. By 1996, the demonstration grant program had been modified to place more emphasis on the development and application of new knowledge in a more rigorously evaluated format. We hope that, despite the increasing restriction in scope, these grant programs will continue to yield important knowledge on how to improve treatment.

The ASAM's PPC

As the addiction treatment field evolved and changed, clinicians in the private sector relied on a variety of guidelines in selecting appropriate settings. Decision making necessarily took into account various barriers to access, particularly financial limitations. Those with health insurance coverage had access to different types of programs than those without, although the relationships among quality, cost, and outcome were often elusive. Programs with fine reputations and impressive staffing did not necessarily produce outcomes that were superior to what occurred without such treatment in populations with good prognostic factors at the outset. Although assessments were conducted, placement often had more to do with ideology and availability of reimbursement rather than empirically derived matching criteria. Outcome data often emanated from the marketing department and did not stand up to rigorous scrutiny. Communities varied in the options available for the indigent population; federal funding provided more opportunities in some locations than others. Recent efforts are intended to systematize this process and strengthen its empirical database.

The ASAM has developed and is refining a biopsychosocial model to specify the treatment that matches the patient's clinical severity. This necessitates accurate assessment of the nature and severity of the patient's medical, psychological, and social problems and the availability of services to respond to the needs identified. The ASAM's eventual goal is to arrive at uniform patient placement criteria to determine appropriate levels of care. To lay the groundwork for developing them, the ASAM's current PPC, originally published in 1991 (Hoffman, Halikas, & Mee-Lee, 1991), were revised in 1996

(ASAM, 1996). The following dimensional criteria are used to select levels of care (Gartner & Mee-Lee, 1995; Gastfriend, 1995; Hoffman et al., 1991; see Appendix A).

The ASAM criteria specify levels of care according to the following dimensional criteria:

1. Acute intoxication, withdrawal potential, or both.
2. Coexistence of biomedical conditions or complications.
3. Emotional and behavioral conditions and complications (e.g., psychiatric conditions, psychological or emotional and behavioral complications of known or unknown origins, poor impulse control, changes in mental status, or transient neuropsychiatric complications).
4. Treatment acceptance or resistance.
5. Relapse and continued use potential.
6. Recovery and living environment.

Level 0.5: Early Intervention

This is an organized service, delivered in a variety of settings, designed to explore and address risk factors and problems and facilitate recognition of adverse consequences of AOD use.

Level I: Outpatient Treatment

Nonresidential service or office visits totaling less than 9 hr a week.

Patients seen as suitable for outpatient treatment are those with no withdrawal risk and stable biomedical conditions or complications, if present at all. These patients should be stable in their emotional and behavioral conditions or complications, if these exist at all. The patient may need motivating or monitoring strategies but must be willing to cooperate. Relapse potential should be low; the patient should have the skills to maintain abstinence and recovery goals with minimal support. The recovery environment should be supportive.

Level II: Intensive Outpatient and Partial Hospitalization

Minimum of 9 hr a week, structured therapeutic milieu.

This level is for patients with minimal withdrawal risk and easily manageable biomedical conditions and complications, if these are present at all. There can be emotional and behavioral conditions and complications that detract from recovery, but these should be mild. Resistance can be high enough to require a structured program, but not so high as to render addiction treatment ineffective. This level of treatment is appropriate for patients who show an intensification of addiction symptoms and high likelihood of relapse without close monitoring or support. The recovery environment can be unsupportive but manageable if the patient is given structure and support.

Level III: Medically Monitored Intensive Inpatient Treatment

Twenty-four hour inpatient, multidisciplinary staff.

This level is for patients who have a severe withdrawal risk, require medical monitoring but not intensive treatment, or both. Moderately severe emotional and behavioral conditions and complications indicating the need for 24-hr structured setting can be handled here. Such patients have a sufficiently high relapse potential to warrant 24-hr structure (i.e., the patient appears to be unable to control substance use despite active participation in less intensive care). Their recovery environment is sufficiently dangerous to necessitate removal or there are logistical impediments to outpatient treatment.

Level IV: Medically Managed Intensive Inpatient Treatment

Inpatient, including primary and medical nursing services and the full resources of a general hospital; multidisciplinary staff.

This level is for patients who have severe withdrawal risk (e.g., barbiturates, sedative-hypnotics) or require 24-hr medical and nursing care because of their biomedical conditions and complications. It also is appropriate for those with severe problems requiring 24-hr psychiatric care, with concomitant addiction treatment. The factors of treatment acceptance and resistance, relapse potential, or recovery environment do not qualify the patient for this level of treatment.

Opioid Maintenance Therapy

Opioid maintenance therapy is a specialized set of services in which psychosocial interventions are combined with opioid medications (usually methadone) to eliminate drug craving and facilitate the patient's focus on rehabilitative tasks. It is usually offered as a Level I service but can be provided in other contexts.

In the process of treatment planning, the appropriate intensity of services can be selected on the basis of consistent criteria. It is hoped that this will result in placement in the least intensive (and expensive), safe level of care, permitting application of strategies from a range of modalities. Outcomes then can be monitored by assessing the improvement or deterioration in the various dimensions (Gartner & Mee-Lee, 1995). The success of this effort depends on the availability of a broad continuum of care to permit matching to services once the patient's physical, psychological, and social needs have been determined.

The ASAM's PPC were developed through a consensus process involving a range of clinicians, including counselors, social workers, psychologists, and physicians. However, the initial group had considerable homogeneity, and some elements of the treatment field (i.e., the public sector) were only partially represented. The revision currently under way aims to strengthen the criteria in areas such as dual diagnosis and adolescence. Nonetheless, the PPC represent a basic framework that encourages the use of multidimensional assessments to make placement decisions and provides criteria sufficiently objective to facilitate research. It is expected to be elaborated more fully and validated through empirical research over the next few years.

Coerced Treatment

The greatest expansion of addiction treatment services is occurring in the criminal justice sector, which is rapidly becoming a major employer of professionals. Treatment money is diminishing steadily in the health care system and increasing in the criminal justice system. As managed care creates discouraging work conditions, increasing numbers of professionals are migrating into the criminal justice sector, where they face new challenges to provide appropriate care.

It is estimated that the majority of those incarcerated have an AOD problem to which their offenses are directly or indirectly related (Vigdal, 1995). Programs to divert individuals from incarceration to treatment in the community have existed for a considerable period of time, but programs to provide treatment in prison are rapidly increasing. Concomitant with increasing demand for addiction treatment personnel with specialized training to work within the criminal justice system, it is likely that the need for systematic evaluation of outcome will increase.

A rigorous review by the Institute of Medicine (1990) suggested that despite disappointing findings in the overall research literature on prison-based treatment, addiction treatment programs that are sufficiently comprehensive and well integrated into the criminal justice system do achieve a significant reduction in recidivism (Anglin & Hser, 1991; Gerstein & Harwood, 1990; Vigdal, 1995). These findings are particularly important in light of a belief on the part of many professionals that coerced treatment does not work. In fact, in addiction treatment, retention is the variable most highly correlated with a positive outcome. Those who remain in treatment longer than 6 months look similar regardless of whether the treatment attempt was initiated voluntarily or through legal coercion. Clinicians have noted the positive effects of pressure from social services or Supplemental Security Income, which brought many individuals who had never sought treatment before and influenced them to remain long enough to begin to see benefits for themselves.

From the clinical perspective of the addiction specialist, this is not surprising. People who are actively using alcohol and drugs do not make good decisions. Once this cycle is interrupted and they get some distance from AOD use, they are more likely to take a different view of their circumstances, particularly if offered an opportunity for self-examination in a supportive treatment setting. Many current drug users come from families in which there may have been multiple generations of AOD users. They have no model for an alternative lifestyle or conviction that a better life is possible for them. Coercion may provide the opportunity and impetus to enter a recovery process, the motivation for which gradually becomes internal. The Alcoholics Anonymous nugget, "bring the body, the mind will follow" is wisdom that is repeatedly confirmed in the area of coerced treatment. We briefly review the major types and settings in which criminal justice system interventions take place.

Community-Based Interventions

Efforts to use the leverage of the criminal justice system to promote treatment efforts began in the 1960s. Civil commitment was one legal procedure that enabled addicted people to be committed to compulsory drug treatment programs that typically included residential treatment followed by outpatient services in the community as aftercare. The California Civil Addict Program, the most extensively studied program, demonstrated a reduction in daily narcotic use and associated crimes to one third the level of others not in the program (Anglin & Hser, 1991; Vigdal, 1995). The Treatment Alternatives to Street Crime, initiated in 1972, also demonstrated effectiveness (Anglin & Hser, 1991; Vigdal, 1995). More recently, there has been a rapid proliferation of drug courts, special courtrooms that focus on mandating or encouraging substance abuse treatment for individuals under close supervision of a judge. The leverage of the criminal justice system is applied to promote engagement in treatment by integrating substance abuse treatment with the pretrial processing of criminal cases. The postarrest period is seen as "a particularly good opportunity for interventions that will break the drug-crime cycle" (Sherin & Mahoney, 1996, p. 1). However, success depends on the availability of appropriate treatment in the community, a condition that is increasingly difficult to meet when federal funding is withdrawn. As funding for addiction treatment becomes more concentrated in health care systems, barriers to obtaining adequate treatment increase. It remains to be seen whether an increase in funding from the criminal justice system will fill the gaps.

Treatment for Incarcerated Offenders

Treatment is increasingly being provided to inmates of prisons and jails, with research components in some settings beginning to examine key issues (Leukefeld & Tims, 1992). Providing treatment not only engages the drug-dependent inmates in a rehabilitation process but reduces management problems in the institution. Prison overcrowding and growing recognition that the majority of inmates have alcohol and drug-related problems contributing to their incarceration has stimulated increased interest in this area.

Federal prison treatment for drug abuse began in 1938 in two U.S. Public Health Service hospitals in Lexington, Kentucky, and Fort Worth, Texas. Antirehabilitation research findings published in the late 1960s had a powerful effect on discouraging treatment efforts despite subsequent reversal in the interpretation of the findings. More recent research findings showing that treatment is effective (Gerstein & Harwood, 1990; Hubbard et al., 1989) stimulated a renewal of interest, particularly in areas in which crack-cocaine epidemics strain both correctional facilities and community treatment settings. The therapeutic community movement has been particularly influential in prison treatment, partly because of outcome data supporting effectiveness and partly because its tight structure makes it more acceptable to corrections personnel than more loosely structured models.

Some practitioners consider it preferable to separate those receiving treatment from the rest of the inmate population, so that a supportive social milieu can be established. Currently, there is variation in the extent to which the services provided constitute pretreatment (e.g., drug education, motivational enhancement, information on resources) or an extensive treatment effort, but it is agreed that linkages to the community to provide continuity of care is essential. The unique needs of special population groups, such as women and ethnic minorities, are receiving increasing attention. Modeling is acknowledged to be an important component of treatment; hence, the successful use of recovering individuals in correctional treatment programs. The transition from prison to community programs is emphasized, with increasing attention given to relapse prevention approaches. Self-help activities (12-step programs such as Narcotics Anonymous) are viewed as desirable but not sufficient components of community aftercare (Leukefeld & Tims, 1992).

Clinical Issues

The criminal justice system currently severely limits the clinician's ability to determine appropriate treatment because many options are simply not available. However, there are several reasons to believe that there is great potential for improvement in treatment outcome in criminal justice populations by wider application of existing approaches. Many clinicians share the perception that the people in treatment under coercion are not significantly different from those who voluntarily enter community-based treatment. It has been noted that addiction is viewed as a public health problem when it affects the middle class and a criminal justice problem in more impoverished communities. Outcome studies of therapeutic communities and methadone maintenance treatment consistently show a reduction in criminal behavior (Gerstein & Harwood, 1990; Hubbard et al., 1989). Making quality treatment more available to those in the criminal justice system can be expected to produce meaningful gains, reducing the cost of long-term incarceration for some in this system.

A second promising avenue of investigation is the value of consistently integrating treatment for psychiatric disorders within treatment efforts focused on criminal justice populations. In a recent large-scale epidemiological study, Regier et al. (1990) found that in institutional settings, the comorbidity of addictive and severe mental disorders was highest in the prison population. Schizophrenia, antisocial personality disorder, bipolar disorder, and dysthymia were the most common, with a 90% concurrence of an addictive disorder among this group. Abram and Teplin (1991) offered data that jails may contain disproportionate numbers of severely mentally ill individuals with alcohol and drug abuse disorders; they noted that police often arrested mentally ill individuals when treatment alternatives would have been preferable but were unavailable. McFarland, Faulkner, Bloom, Hallaux, and Bray (1989) interviewed family members about their chronic mentally ill male relatives and documented that substance abuse significantly predicted arrest. More than half were arrested after unsuccessful attempts by the family to commit the patients during a crisis. In Abram and Teplin's analysis, the narrow parameters of the caregiving systems serve as a formidable barrier to treatment. Mentally ill individuals, particularly those with comorbid disorders, engage in disruptive behaviors and become criminalized. Abram and Teplin (1991) noted that "jails, unlike many treatment facilities, have no requirements or restrictions for entry" (p. 1042).

Despite the fact that comorbidity is especially high in the criminal justice client, it is rare for treatment programs to provide adequate services to address both their needs. This is an area of investigation likely to be of increasingly great importance. Although skeptics may object that many of those in the criminal justice system are diagnosed with antisocial personality disorder, and thus have a poor prognosis, there are reasons to be cautious about such a conclusion. Overdiagnosis of antisocial personality disorder is likely to lead the clinician to assume a poor prognosis and discourage efforts to secure quality treatment. Gerstley, Alterman, McLellan, and Woody (1990) argued that it is crucial to assess antisocial personality disorder independent of substance abuse. When this is done rigorously, the percentage of those with a primary antisocial personality disorder declines dramatically. They speculated that those whose antisocial activity is directly related to their drug use might show a better treatment response, a view shared by other clinicians. Gerstley and his colleagues also discussed the possibility that antisocial behavior can be an expression of an affective disorder. Another important factor is the extent to which the context (i.e., court-related referral) biases the clinician to view the patient's pathology in antisocial terms (Travin & Protter, 1982). More recently, it has become clear that those who are high on the numbing cluster of posttraumatic stress disorder symptoms (e.g., avoidance, detachment, restricted range of affect) also can be misdiagnosed with antisocial personality disorder. Thus, childhood histories of abuse may be associated with violent behavior in adulthood. The clinical complexities of adjudicated populations is becoming better understood as professionals have increasing access to these populations.

Drinking Driver Programs

Often existing in isolation from other addiction treatment services, drinking driver programs are specialty referral, education, and treatment programs that vary state to state. They are known as driving while intoxicated or driving under the influence programs and are usually regulated by state authority, which sets the standards and monitors the programs. Participants have been arrested or convicted for alcohol-related traffic offenses and must complete the program to avoid further legal problems. In many states, there are programs for first offenders (more didactic, short term) and multiple offenders (more treatment oriented).

The Institute of Medicine's 1990 report on interventions for alcohol problems noted that there has been no recent review of the structural and operating characteristics of these programs nor any comprehensive evaluation of their effectiveness. The population is heterogeneous, ranging from social drinkers who drink occasionally but show few adverse consequences before their arrest, to severe alcoholics who are highly resistant to treatment. These differences make determining effective outcomes difficult. The Institute of Medicine study group concluded that although most existing studies support such programs' general effectiveness in decreasing abusive drinking and improving psychosocial functioning, more differentiated studies need to be conducted. The group noted that further progress depends on developing better classification systems for subgroups, better referral and matching procedures, better follow-up procedures, and more specific treatment methods. Such efforts would be a valuable addition to the growing literature on the effectiveness of coerced treatment.

Conclusion

There are a variety of conceptual frameworks used in the addiction field to determine appropriate treatment. The problem–service matching strategy permits assessment, quality assurance, and outcome evaluation to be accomplished in a relatively straightforward manner. The CSAT comprehensive care model offers a way of identifying basic elements of treatment that can be found in a wide variety of settings. The ASAM's PPC are becoming widely used as a means of determining what level of care is appropriate for the patient. All these frameworks are used, more or less explicitly, by practitioners in the addiction field. In the arena of coerced treatment, state-of-the-art practices combined with adequate evaluation will be important to justify allocating resources to treatment rather than to a purely punitive approach. Clinicians will increasingly find themselves interacting with these systems and will hopefully be able to meet the collaborative challenge.

6

Individual Psychotherapy

In this chapter we focus primarily on the role of the private practitioner in addressing addiction issues. Our goal is to assist therapists in addressing alcohol and other drug (AOD) use in situations in which the patient has sought help for other problems. Clinicians, especially those in private practice, have a long history of underestimating the role of AOD use in producing or exacerbating the presenting symptomatology and in negatively influencing the response to treatment (see chap. 2 in this book). AOD use has been documented in almost all clinical populations, and it is important that therapists and clinical supervisors be trained to address it. Mild-to-moderate abuse problems often can be handled by therapists in private practice or in agencies outside addiction treatment settings. Such early intervention can have a powerful impact on both the success of the treatment and the quality of the patient's life.

If treatment in a specialty setting is needed, therapists have an important role in helping the patient become "treatment ready." To accomplish these things, it is important for the therapist to build collaborative networks. This includes a variety of professional resources: a physician familiar with addiction medicine, options for inpatient or outpatient addiction treatment, and addiction specialists available for assessment and consultation. It also includes community resources, such as self-help groups and halfway houses. The therapist's collaborative task may be complex at particular points in the treatment. For example, many individual therapists do not manage the acute treatment alone but tap other resources in the early stages of treatment and at other times such as during a relapse episode or period of heightened relapse vulnerability. Issues such as eating disorders, gambling, compulsive sexual behavior, or spending (discussed in chap. 9 in this book) also frequently require collaboration. Therapists who develop strong networks can maximize the effectiveness of their own work.

Having established a context, we focus on the activities of the individual psychotherapist. We begin by considering several concepts that have served as barriers to good communication between psychotherapists and addiction treatment professionals. We then discuss strategies for enhancing motivation and present a model for intervention that is recovery oriented. The material included represents a blend of empirical studies and clinical experience. The literature in this area includes not only systematic investigations but also clinically based discussions from a variety of perspectives. The goal of the chapter is to provide a synthesis, a framework for prioritizing and integrating AOD interventions with those needed to address coexisting disorders.

Ideological Hot Buttons

Most therapeutic systems contain concepts and language that lend themselves to professional squabbles and disparagement or rejection of patients (e.g., "acting out, narcissistic"), and the addiction field is no exception. Enabling, codependency, and denial are examples of three concepts that capture important phenomena but also have been greatly misused. It is important to understand the essential meaning of these concepts, their utility, and their perils.

The term *enabling* refers to behavior that protects the AOD user from the consequences of his or her behavior and thereby colludes in perpetuating the behavior. Six styles of enabling derived from the literature include avoiding and shielding, attempting to control, taking over responsibilities, rationalizing and accepting, cooperating and collaborating, and rescuing and subserving (Nelson, 1985). These behaviors, although understandable attempts to cope with the situation and protect family members and others (e.g., employers), can postpone the alcoholic or addict's full recognition of consequences for long periods of time.

In the past, therapists acquired a reputation for being professional enablers by allowing patients to talk about their problems without recognizing the detrimental effects of AOD use and without emphasizing the need for a change in behavior. Indeed, one only has to attend 12-step meetings to hear painful stories of people who had been given poor guidance or had been actively discouraged from focusing on their AOD use by their therapists (e.g., "Deal with your underlying problems and it will take care of itself; You don't have an alcoholic personality"). Thus, some therapists might have allowed patients to preserve the illusion of working on problems without translating insights into meaningful action. Many recovering people felt they had lost years of their productive lives in this manner and formed a vocal subgroup in Alcoholics Anonymous (AA) that cautioned against involvement with therapists. Some of these people formed grassroots groups that succeeded in getting legislation mandating education in substance abuse for licensed therapists.

In recent years, the situation has improved. The latest AA membership survey (Alcoholics Anonymous, 1996) indicates that 60% of the members received some kind of treatment or counseling and that 77% of that group felt it played an important role in directing them to AA. After coming to AA, 62% received treatment or counseling and 85% of those said it played an important part in their recovery. Thus, the antipathy toward professionals appears to be lessening, but it is important for the therapist who encounters it to be mindful that its basis is understandable.

Codependency is another concept that refers to similar phenomena, in this case, the distorted adaptations made by others in an effort to cope with the behavior of the alcoholic or drug user. Several authors have critiqued the concept, particularly as a "symbol of stigmatization" that exacerbates guilt by labeling significant others as pathological and blameworthy, and have noted that the majority of those to whom this label is applied are women (Haaken, 1990; Harper & Capdevila, 1990). In clinical settings, these labels often substitute for distinguishing between individual and interpersonal problems and between what is healthy and what is emotionally destructive in the complex relationships between active users and their significant others.

Unfortunately, both concepts also have been repeatedly used to discourage appropriate forms of helping. An intact family or support structure is a key element in promoting positive treatment outcome, so the therapist needs to help significant others distinguish between constructive and undermining efforts. (These issues are discussed further in chap. 7.) Some therapists have been known to ban the use of the terms *enabler, codependent,* or *co,* imposing on patients the discipline of specifying the behaviors that they find objectionable or problematic. This discourages the use of jargon in the service of expressing anger, clarifies problem areas, and promotes constructive efforts at conflict resolution.

Denial is another concept so brutalized by misuse that it is wise to use it selectively and with caution. It refers to the "refusal to admit the reality of, disavowal of the truth of, refusal to acknowledge the presence or existence of" (Campbell, 1989, p. 190). Before invoking the label of denial, it is useful to hypothesize lack of information. For example, the elderly man who disputes that alcohol could be a problem because he drinks the same two glasses of wine with dinner as he has for 30 years needs first to be informed that aging changes the body's response to a wide range of drugs and medications and indeed that what was once not problematic may have become so. Before interpreting behavior as resistance, it is important to build a foundation of information. Even among highly educated individuals, the absence of information or the presence of misinformation can be striking. For example, many (men in particular) view a high tolerance for alcohol as evidence of a "better physical system," particularly because it is culturally valued in many subgroups. They are often surprised to hear that it is a marker for alcoholism. Education provides the foundation to interpret resistance and allows for charged issues to be introduced in a more neutral framework. The clinician can note areas of defensiveness while demonstrating empathy and support as he or she provides the information.

Stephanie Brown (1985) described denial as a cognitive phenomenon that she referred to as a thinking disorder. As negative consequences begin to accumulate, the drinking individual must construct a reality that externalizes the problem, often assigning another source of blame. Marital conflict or work stress become common explanations for drinking, and the role of drinking in exacerbating problems is minimized or ignored. Breaking down the denial involves connecting the drinking with its consequences and aiding the patient in accepting the reality of loss of control. The patient must begin to see drinking as the problem, not the solution. S. Brown noted that the question, Why do you drink? often elicits excuses. Better focus is achieved by asking about the function or purpose of the drinking. This facilitates recognition of the importance of drinking, and once acknowledging that it serves a purpose its merits can be called into question. Thus, the therapist helps the patient examine the possibility that the solution or coping mechanism has now become a problem.

S. Brown (1985) stressed the importance of the cognitive factors in this phase because these are what maintain and explain drinking behavior. The therapist repeatedly brings the patient back to a focus on alcohol, challenging the patient's illusion of free choice and the "accounting system" by which drinking is rationalized. Moving beyond denial requires a total revision of a belief system characteristic of the drinking phase, shifting two central beliefs. The conviction "I am not alcoholic; I can control my drinking" is gradually replaced by "I am alcoholic; I cannot control my drinking." It is this that provides the basis for the transition to abstinence.

It is evident from S. Brown's work that the time required for this process is highly variable from individual to individual. It is the therapist's consistent focus that dismantles the denial system, and there is no specified time frame or encouragement of harsh confrontation techniques. Thus, a sophisticated understanding of denial, as exemplified in S. Brown's work, is enormously helpful to clinicians seeking to move the patient into a serious recovery process.

In our experience, at its worst, the concept of denial is used to make practitioners feel better about their impotence and frustration. It allows clinicians to disclaim responsibility for difficult clinical problems and shift responsibility to the patient in ways that can leave the patient feeling misunderstood and criticized. When used in confrontation (e.g., "You are in denial"), it can be a form of invalidation that leaves many patients feeling frustrated and helpless:

> Sophie was in intensive outpatient treatment in a hospital affiliated with a prestigious university. She and her husband had had intense conflict over her marijuana smoking, which he deplored. He reported having several alcoholic relatives, but insisted his own drinking was not a problem. She had stopped smoking marijuana for 9 months until they had a major fight. She left to stay with a friend for a few days, during which time she smoked marijuana twice. When they made peace, he insisted she enter drug treatment, which she did. The otherwise extensive intake process did not include a careful assessment of his drinking pattern or the role of marijuana in their relationship. In groups in the treatment program, she was repeatedly assailed about "being in denial" when she stated she no longer smoked marijuana and did not think it was her main problem. No attempt was made to address the marital conflicts or to examine her husband's drinking despite his being at high risk for alcoholism. After 3 weeks of feeling her self-esteem was being battered and her concerns ignored, she dropped out of treatment.

This vignette illustrates a common dilemma: Denial is a

frequent characteristic and a legitimate hypothesis, but the clinician needs to avoid coming to this conclusion prematurely. In this example, the treatment program was strong in some areas but lacked the family perspective that would have generated further query into the marital dynamics. In other cases, the patient's report of a mild-to-moderate problem may reflect the changing cultural threshhold for recognition. In the past, alcoholics and addicts arrived at treatment after years of damaging consequences. With widespread media attention and a large popular literature, awareness is heightened in both users and significant others, causing people to seek help at earlier stages. In such cases, the therapist may not need to challenge the patient's perception of severity but can emphasize the desirability of taking the problem seriously in its early stages to avoid difficulties later on. If denial is in fact influential, this will become apparent, and the patient will likely be more cooperative than if challenged prematurely.

A Note on the Timing of Insight-Oriented Psychotherapy

In a recovery-oriented model, the tasks of the recovering individual determine the nature of the therapist's intervention. These tasks can be summarized as follows: recognizing AOD use is a problem and becoming willing to address it; establishing abstinence; and consolidating abstinence and changing lifestyles to support a comfortable and satisfying sobriety (Zweben, 1993). Therapists with an eclectic intervention repertoire will find this work more congenial. Those who rely on a single approach, especially psychodynamic psychotherapy, will find some of the necessary shifts more difficult. A psychodynamic model is frequently useful in clarifying the issues presented by the patient. However, as an intervention strategy, it can be a trap, particularly in early recovery. Many people can and do stop drinking and using drugs with little understanding of why they initiated or continued their substance use. Conversely, many others avoid making behavior changes for years while engaged in an inner exploration they believed would "naturally" bring an end to the AOD use once they resolved the "underlying" issues. In a recovery-oriented model, insight-oriented explorations are useful to help the patient understand and address ambivalence about giving up alcohol and drugs. Once the commitment to become abstinent occurs, the most useful interventions are cognitive–behavioral strategies focused on how to become clean and sober. An AA slogan, "Bring the body, the mind will follow," reflects an effective approach at this stage. Psychodynamic understanding remains useful, but only if applied in a focused way and combined with an emphasis on learning the behaviors of abstinence (Zweben, 1993). (These issues are elaborated on in the section on establishing abstinence.) As the period of abstinence lengthens and lifestyle changes occur, insight-oriented therapy becomes increasingly useful, improving the quality of sobriety substantially. However, probing anxiety-provoking issues prematurely often results in a resumption of AOD use, stalling the therapy, and perhaps resulting in dropout. Thus, the therapist who is able to make the appropriate shifts, drawing on both cognitive–behavioral and insight-oriented techniques, has the best prospects of a successful outcome.

The Therapeutic Process

We begin by focusing extensively on the condition in which many therapists find themselves: The patient is drinking or using, the effects of this behavior are unclear, and the patient is at best ambivalent about making changes in this area:

> Marsha, a single parent, came to treatment struggling with depression and loneliness and coping with raising her two children who exhibited behavior problems since her marriage broke up. She reported smoking marijuana nightly to relax and expressed reluctance to give it up because it was her most reliable friend.

The therapist considers the possibility that her marijuana smoking exacerbates her depression (which it appears to do in some, but not all people), undermines her stamina and ability to be consistent in her dealings with her children, and promotes social withdrawal. How can the therapist present this to the patient in a manner that will be acceptable?

We review the motivational enhancement strategies on which there is now an extensive published literature and discuss psychodynamic reasons for wanting to resist an abstinence commitment. Once an abstinence commitment has been secured from patients, we describe some of the cognitive–behavioral strategies used to achieve abstinence and how to formulate goals with respect to coexisting disorders for patients at this stage. We then discuss the tasks of later stages of recovery, particularly that of consolidating abstinence and creating a satisfying alcohol- and drug-free lifestyle. We also describe some of those issues; in chapter 9 we focus more extensively on relapse.

Developing a Commitment to Abstinence

AOD use can produce such a wide array of symptoms that there is no reliable way to quickly determine how great an influence it has (S. Brown, Irwin, & Schuckit, 1991; S. Brown & Schuckit, 1988; Schuckit, 1995). The therapist does not need to "prove" that alcohol and drugs are the source of the patient's distress but can suggest a period of abstinence to explore this issue productively. Ideally, this period will extend past the 2–4 weeks needed for the withdrawal symptoms to subside and expand into the longer period needed for the body to readjust to the absence of drugs. Usually, AOD use makes the patient appear to be more pathological than he or she will look after a period of abstinence (see Ries, 1994). Although the patient will often continue to experience periods of depression, irritability, and other forms of distress, he or she will normally show signs of healthier functioning and better resources to bring to bear on the problems that inevitably emerge.

It is not necessary to convince the patient that he or she is an alcoholic or addict to justify abstinence from mood-altering drugs. These labels are highly stigmatized and generate unnecessary resistance. The therapist can suggest that because alcohol and other drugs, even in moderation, can exacerbate distress, a moratorium allows the patient and the therapist to examine the ways in which they are woven into the patient's life and how they influence symptoms. There is no attempt to prove that they are causing symptoms, only an effort to engage the patient in a time-limited "experiment with abstinence," also called "sobriety sampling" (W. R. Miller & Page, 1991), to observe what changes occur when intoxicants are eliminated. This approach helps the therapist avoid power struggles around issues such as how much wine with dinner is "too much" and eliminates the pressure to probe frequently to determine whether the patient is minimizing use. The concept of "attachment" also is a useful, less stigmatizing way to discuss the issues. The therapist can take the stance that most people have attachments that are stronger than they realize until they try to give them up; hence, the exercise is fruitful. The choice of time period for the experiment with abstinence is an opportunity for exploration. Patients are hard-pressed to explain why a several-month "holiday" from drinking and using drugs is objectionable if they are not addicted; hence, this strategy often precipitates recognition of their own resistance. In practical terms, the therapist should aim for 1–3 months of abstinence, although this is often negotiated in shorter, more manageable time units.

Strategies for Enhancing Motivation

Five principles. An abundant research literature on motivation has yielded principles and applications shown to be fruitful in a variety of clinical situations. In contrast to the view that patients only become ready to change once they have accumulated sufficient negative consequences of their alcohol and drug behavior, this approach seeks to accelerate the proces of deciding to change in a more gentle manner.

Once the therapist has identified where the patient is located on the continuum of readiness to change described in chapter 3, Miller and colleagues (W. R. Miller & Rollnick, 1991; W. R. Miller, Zweben, DiClemente, & Rychtarik, 1994) offered specific motivational techniques designed to move the patient along the continuum of motivation for change and thus enhance readiness for treatment. This work is based on extensive empirical research, then translated into materials for practicing clinicians. They discussed five principles applicable to substance abuse issues. The first principle is to express empathy. W. R. Miller and Rollnick pointed out that by using accurate empathy, the patient develops a sense of acceptance that seems to free them to change, whereas non-acceptance often feeds resistance. The patient's ambivalence about maintaining sobriety is framed as a normal part of human experience rather than as a lack of motivation for change or a lack or seriousness about the therapeutic process.

The second principle is to develop discrepancy; the therapist notes the gap between where the patient is and where he or she wants to be. In developing discrepancy it is important for the therapist to realize that the patients themselves must be able to voice their concerns. The therapist should be sensitive to those statements that reflect an awareness of a discrepancy between the patient's achievements and goals. For example, in adolescents, an awareness of how substance abuse may have affected school performance, family relationships, and even peer interactions can often be a starting point for developing discrepancy. As W. R. Miller and Rollnick (1991) pointed out, "a goal of motivational interviewing is to develop discrepancy, to make use of it, increase it and amplify it until it overrides attachment to the present behavior" (p. 57).

The third principle is to avoid arguments. When resistance is encountered, the therapist must be prepared to shift strategies. Arguments over the label of *alcoholic* or *addict* are particularly fruitless. Fighting against patients detracts from the goal of motivating them for change.

A fourth principle involves rolling with the resistance. When the therapist encounters defensiveness or resistance, he or she is encouraged to retreat and then approach the problem from a slightly different perspective. Turning questions back to patients and allowing them to struggle with their own answers is particularly effective. As the therapist watches the patient struggle, he or she becomes a participant with the patient to support but never directly oppose his or her view of the situation. It is assumed that the patient is capable of developing insight and moving in a healthy direction (W. R. Miller & Rollnick, 1991).

The fifth concept is to support self-efficacy. Self-efficacy is the patient's confidence in his or her ability to cope with or manage a specific challenge. The patient who sees the possibility of achieving sobriety is more likely to achieve that goal than the patient who sees no hope for this outcome. Providing the patient with specific skills such as assertiveness training or stress reduction techniques can support self-efficacy. Also linking the patient up with community support groups can enhance self-efficacy by helping the patient to identify individuals who are successfully recovering from alcohol and drug abuse problems.

Intervention. Intervention, used in the formal sense, is a structured confrontation involving the family and significant others designed to precipitate a treatment attempt. It can sometimes be beneficial in motivating the patient to move through the stages of change, but it also can be misused in an overly confrontational manner. When used correctly, however, a formal intervention can be a caring and empathic event that dramatically highlights the concerns that the family and significant others have about the patient's behavior.

An intervention involves a gathering of family members and significant others who are encouraged to express their concerns directly to the patient. The goal of the intervention is not for the patient to enter a treatment program but to simply express those concerns and to offer treatment both for the patient and the entire family. The intervention is most likely to be successful when certain factors apply. These factors include the following: (a) Overly confrontational, judgmental, or blaming statements should be avoided. The statements should focus on specific behaviors and areas of concern that are couched in a caring, empathic tone. (b) The intervention should be planned and rehearsed in advance. Family members and significant others are encouraged to present their concerns in a structured manner. Concerns should be written down rather than given extemporaneously. (c) Family members and significant others are encouraged to avoid arguments. They are instructed to state their concerns as simply and straightforwardly as possible. (d) A specific treatment plan is offered to the individual. When these conditions are met, an intervention can be an effective motivating technique.

It is best to remember, however, that a formal intervention should be a last resort. Other, less dramatic attempts at motivating the patient should be used before initiating a formal intervention. Currently, many interventionists invite the identified patient to attend at whatever point in the process he or she is willing to join. It is common for family members or significant others to seek help before the user is ready to acknowledge a problem. Regular meetings to examine how they cope with their situation allow the therapist to identify collusive behaviors and help generate alternatives. It is common to find that once those people surrounding the user begin to change behavior, the user's situation becomes more difficult and acceptance of a treatment attempt becomes more likely. It is this development that often leads the identified patient to join the process without a formal confrontation.

Psychodynamic factors to explore. Understanding the emotional elements in resistance is crucial to moving the patient toward a commitment to abstinence. As long as the therapist maintains focus on both dynamics and behavior, exploration can be highly productive. One of the most common reasons to resist an abstinence commitment is fear of failure. A thorough assessment includes a review of past efforts to stop using, how long they lasted, and what worked and what did not. Detailed inquiry usually reveals flaws in the patient's strategy (e.g., hanging out in the bar trying to "be strong" instead of staying out of the bar in the first place). The therapist can use such flaws to lift morale: "You made a good effort, but you didn't have very good coaching." The therapist then offers to educate the patient about effective strategies for stopping.

Fear of withdrawal from alcohol or drugs is a related problem. It is a mistake to assume that the most important force behind the resistance to abstinence is the patient's continuing desire to get high. Motives and reinforcers change as people move from being naive (new) to chronic users, and much continuing use is perpetuated by fear-of-withdrawal discomfort. For the heroin user, this can be violent nausea; for the cocaine user, severe depression; and for the alcoholic, unmanageable anxiety. Describing an appropriate psychosocial and medical detoxification structure can be reassuring and can help build motivation to tackle the task of becoming abstinent.

A second reason to resist an abstinence commitment has to do with AOD use in the family of origin, or in the current household. Complex dynamics come into play here, and it is important to maintain focus on motivational goals while exploring these obstacles. If there was AOD use in the family of origin, it is common for family functioning to be organized around such use in a myriad of ways family members are unaware of and do not discuss (S. Brown, 1988). Alcohol use often is a way of "belonging," as is evident in family rituals organized around drinking. For many men, drinking with daddy is both a pubertal initiation ritual and an ingredient in ongoing bonding experiences. Marijuana may be a key element in socializing. Giving up alcohol and drugs can be felt as "being orphaned" because the patient correctly realizes entering a recovery process puts him or her in uncharted territory. The fears usually are not clearly articulated and are worth the time needed to elicit a fuller picture of the nature of the apprehension and the patient's picture of what his or her life would be like without alcohol and drugs. A related reason may be survivor guilt, leaving significant others behind and possibly becoming more successful as a result.

A third common reason is the belief that alcohol and drugs constitute effective self-medication (Khantzian, 1981, 1982, 1985b; Khantzian, Halliday, & McAuliffe, 1990). Here again, people may have legitimate reasons to believe that they are effectively medicating a disorder without realizing that their attempts to cope are actually exacerbating their disorder and undermining them in other ways. For example, many stimulant users cite depression as an impetus without appreciating that chronic stimulant use exacerbates depression by depleting key neurotransmitters (Gold, 1992). Patients need to be reassured that not only will their withdrawal discomforts be appropriately attended to but that if sustained abstinence does not result in improvement, other effective approaches (including medication) can be tried.

People with a history of traumatic experiences pose difficult challenges in this regard because unlike many others, they often feel considerably worse when they attempt to abstain from alcohol and drugs. In such cases, a firm safety structure and patience in working toward abstinence goals is crucial (Evans & Sullivan, 1994; Sullivan & Evans, 1994). Therapist refusal to work with patients who are actively drinking and using is particularly untenable at this point. Patients with histories of severe trauma will often never get to abstinence unless the therapist is able to move them in this direction while working to reduce the frequency and destructiveness of drinking and using episodes.

Establishing Abstinence

Psychosocial intervention issues. It is widely agreed that for substance-dependent individuals, abstinence from alcohol and drugs is the foundation for therapeutic progress on other issues. When possible, it should be the primary goal. This does not mean that other issues are ignored but that the therapist maintains focus on the task, addressing content from the perspective of the tasks of the recovering individual. For example, if a wife reports that conflict with her husband is her main trigger to drink, the therapist could ask how she might cope with this situation without drinking (e.g., call a friend, go to a meeting, go out walking). Couples' work on conflict resolution is usually too emotion laden to be successful if one member of the couple is struggling to establish abstinence. Psychodynamic and interpersonal issues should be explored to understand how to create a structure that will support abstinence without the expectation that issues can be resolved at this stage. Insight-oriented therapists frequently neglect to make the bridge between understanding and action, assuming that application of insight will occur on its own. Individuals in early recovery need simplicity and structure. They do not necessarily draw obvious implications, no matter how intelligent and educated they are. Therapists often underestimate the distress and vulnerability of patients struggling with establishing abstinence, particularly if the patient is highly articulate and appears to function well.

Cognitive–behavioral strategies have long been a key ingredient in the effort to establish abstinence. Helping the patient to formulate a sound action plan is one of the therapist's most important tasks. The Matrix Center's handouts in Appendix B illustrate materials used in this approach. The patient is helped to focus on behaviors that sustain the addiction or break the cycle. The recovery checklist helps the patient identify specific behaviors that will promote successful outcome and, in the process, identify obvious gaps. The material on the triggers sheet helps the patient to gain a conceptual understanding of how conditioning operates to produce craving and to identify his or her specific triggers to allow coping strategies to be generated. Thought-stopping techniques are tools for breaking the cycle that leads from trigger, to thought, to continued thoughts, followed by cravings and use.

In the early stages of recovery, emphasis is on avoiding hazardous situations when possible, devising ways to reduce the risk when it is not, and engaging in activities that promote recovery. The therapist can work with the patient to identify internal and external triggers (see Appendix B) and make a plan. He or she can challenge assumptions that keep the patient in high-risk situations. Patients at this stage often attempt to stop drinking and using without changing much else (e.g., continuing to go on fishing trips with their hard-drinking buddies). They may need support for the idea that avoidance is honorable and necessary in the early stages and perhaps for longer periods as well:

Brian came to treatment when his wife made it clear she would leave him if he did not stop his heavy drinking, during which time he had begun to threaten her with harm. He was troubled by his own behavior, agreed that it always took place when he was intoxicated, and reluctantly agreed to a trial period of abstinence. He agreed to stay out of bars, but refused to attend AA. He was adamant that he could socialize with his old drinking buddies and withstand temptation. He continued to participate in one of their favorite rituals, deep-sea fishing trips. He proposed that he would be "safe" if he brought nonalcoholic drinks for himself. On the first such trip, he did not drink, although he was shaken by how difficult it was. Emboldened, he planned another and did not drink then. By this time he had been abstinent for 10 weeks, the longest he could remember since age 17. On the third such expedition, he persuaded himself that one beer was okay to celebrate their splendid catch. Two days later, he drank to intoxication and had another ugly scene with his wife.

Brian had prematurely assumed that he had mastered an important trigger when he participated in two fishing expeditions without drinking. His unwillingness to participate in recovery-related activities other than his individual sessions and to change most of his social habits, at least temporarily, made him vulnerable. He also failed to understand that a conditioned trigger, such as years of fishing and drinking with his buddies, could have a delayed effect; he was misled by his ability to confine himself to one beer after the third fishing trip. These events provided an opportunity to deepen his understanding of his addiction as well as to reconsider which behavioral tools he was willing to use.

Specialized knowledge about addiction and recovery, and a fund of information about the intoxication and withdrawal effects of various drugs is, invaluable at this point. A fund of practical information that can be used to support and motivate is acquired gradually through reading, discussion, and experience. Through the psychoeducational stance, the therapist provides support, reassurance, and information that helps the patient understand and endure what he or she is experiencing. Detailed knowledge of the distinctive characteristics of various drugs of abuse helps guide the patient through the immediate difficulties and to anticipate and plan for likely ones. Education also provides the foundation from which resistance can be interpreted; if the patient is uninformed, one must start there. As described earlier, the therapist should first consider the possibility of lack of information before concluding that denial is operating. A common example is the need to abstain from all intoxicants, not just the drug of choice. Patients and their significant others often assume that the use of another drug is less serious or even acceptable. In fact, abstinence needs to be applied to all intoxicants. Long clinical observation and more recent empirical data (Rawson, 1994) indicate that those who retain or resume use of other drugs relapse at much higher rates than those who do not. Most assume that if a drug, for example, alcohol, was not a problem before cocaine use, one may return to drinking once abstinence from cocaine is well established. In fact, cocaine users are often engaged in more serious alcohol abuse than they recognize. They have a high vulnerability to substituting alcohol, or to relapsing to cocaine, independent of whether they were demonstrably alcoholic before or during the period of their cocaine use (Rawson, Obert, McCann, Smith, & Ling, 1990). This topic remains a challenging clinical issue throughout treatment. In the early stage, it is important to introduce the concept and make sure all parties involved in the treatment understand it.

Psychoeducational sessions should always allow enough time for discussion of material after information is presented. In addition to providing a forum for participants to apply the information to their own situations, it is common to find charged issues raised in a veiled form. Thus, these activities provide an opportunity for participants to "get their feet wet" in the less threatening "classroom" format.

Withdrawal and detoxification. The educational process should include a review of the intoxication and withdrawal effects of the drugs the patient has been using (see Schuckit, 1995). Defining an approximate time frame, particularly the length of time serious discomfort usually lasts, gives comfort and a framework within which to plan extra support activities. Many people assume the greatest dangers manifest early in the withdrawal period and are caught off guard by hazards that typically occur later. For example, the greatest danger of withdrawal seizures from Valium (a benzodiazepine) occurs in the 5–8 days after cessation of use (Wesson, Smith, & Seymour, 1992). Staff working in one of the many types of nonmedical settings may be completely unprepared for such an event. Those abstaining from cocaine often experience a period of anhedonia or loss of the capacity for pleasure after acute withdrawal phenomena have subsided (Rawson et al., 1990). They underestimate the danger of this anhedonia because it is less dramatic than the acute misery after recent cocaine cessation. However, the boredom and joylessness frequently trigger resumption of drug use.

It is useful to consider two main bodily processes: the process of the drug clearing the body and the process by which a new equilibrium or homeostasis is established. The former is usually what is referred to as the *detoxification* stage or *withdrawal* stage and may be appropriate to manage with medication (Wesson, 1995). The second takes place over a long time and can include specific upsurges of withdrawal symptoms referred to as a *protracted abstinence syndrome*. It also is highly variable in individuals, influenced by genetics, medical condition, nutrition, exercise, living environment, strength of recovery program, and other factors. Because many people assume that a relapse after a period of abstinence merely indicates weakening motivation, it is important to understand that complex biological processes as well as psychosocial factors may be influential.

Some drugs can be discontinued abruptly without health threat, although there may be great discomfort. Opiates (e.g., heroin, morphine, codeine) are an example of such drugs. However, the stress of withdrawal may precipitate a crisis due to other health conditions, such as heart problems. Cocaine and marijuana generally pose no problem to stop abruptly. However, alcohol, benzodiazepines, and barbiturates should always involve physician screening or protocol to determine what level of care is needed. Alcohol withdrawal is often uncomplicated, but it can result in seizures or delerium tremens, both of which can be fatal (Goodwin, 1992). Seizures cannot be predicted, and the signals of ongoing delerium tremens can be missed if there is no monitoring of vital signs. Medical monitoring (e.g., temperature and blood pressure checks of someone withdrawing from alcohol) can identify indications of an impending medical crisis. Detoxification can occur in a residential-type setting in which there is adequate medical backup in case of problems. This option is currently much less available to those who need it than would be the case in an appropriately designed treatment system. Medical screening and management (i.e., physician observation, medication) is needed for benzodiazepine and barbiturate withdrawal. Patients also combine drugs, both prescribed and illegally obtained, in ways that increase the need for physician collaboration. Major medical problems can pose a complicating factor. A more complete description of detoxification procedures and considerations can be found in *Detoxification From Alcohol and Other Drugs* (Wesson, 1995). It is advisable for outpatient clinics and private practitioners to have clear screening criteria and protocols for problems requiring medical attention.

Routine toxicology screens on admission can prevent many problems (Verebey, 1992). It is common for patients to focus on their primary drug of abuse and ignore or minimize other drug use. Drug screens reveal the presence of such drugs and thus indicate when physician consultation or intervention is necessary. It also identifies issues that patients with the best of intentions might have overlooked. Given the prevalence of AOD use in all clinical populations, it can be presented as a routine part of the intake process. By normalizing it, the stage is set for further toxicology screening if signs and symptoms warrant it.

Nonphysicians are wise to establish a relationship with a physician familiar with addiction medicine and collaborate whenever there are medical issues. The American Society of Addiction Medicine is a specialty society (see Appendix C) through which one can identify physicians with an interest or certification in addiction medicine. This provides some assurance that the physician is familiar with the specific needs of alcohol and drug users, particularly some of the prescribing hazards with this population. State chapters also may be a source of additional referrals and consultants.

Patients may prefer to see their own physician. If possible, it is good to assess the physician's familiarity with addiction medicine, because there is wide variation in the training of physicians in addiction-related matters. Patients expressing preference for their regular physician should be asked if they are willing to be completely candid about alcohol and drug use; otherwise, a referral is in order to someone with whom patients are willing to be honest.

There is no consistent relationship between managing withdrawal and long-term abstinence. However, doing so provides a window of intervention that allows for enhancing motivation and laying the groundwork to sustain a recovery process. Making a patient more comfortable certainly contributes to a positive attitude toward treatment. Unrealistic expectations for what medically managed withdrawal could accomplish, however, may lead to disappointment and reductions in funding that might make it less accessible than would be desirable. If medical management is combined with efforts to connect the individual to an ongoing recovery process, it can play an important role because it contributes to the longer retention that is associated with positive treatment outcome.

Other psychosocial interventions. The specific elements previously discussed should be woven into a treatment plan that maximizes structure in the early months of recovery. Patients at this stage do not plan and manage their time well and can benefit from attention to mundane details, such as regular eating, sleeping, and exercise patterns. Many programs use a monthly calendar in which the patient can enter specific activities and indicate days of abstinence. The therapist should be attentive to whether the patient has scheduled too little or too much. Unstructured time, particularly evenings, weekends, or other periods when drugs were used regularly, is a definite hazard. Overambitious plans also are risky. Solitude is often a problem. Outpatient AOD programs usually offer a menu of activities designed to address these problems. The private practitioner has the task of assembling a program from various elements available in the community.

Drug cravings and drug dreams are often a problem at this stage. Many patients do not experience cravings in the sense of a distinct drug hunger they can identify. Cocaine users are more likely to experience distinctive urges, but, for users of other drugs, the experience can be more ambiguous. For some, craving emerges in fantasies of using or in related fantasies such as musings about how to access money without a spouse's knowledge. For others it manifests itself as irritability, often a withdrawal symptom not recognized as a manifestation of craving. Patients need to be taught to identify and manage these states. They often interpret them to mean a failure of motivation or progress and need to be reassured they are often merely physiological states, signs that the brain is healing. Drug dreams can be highly distressing, particularly when patients awake unsure of whether they actually drank or used. In the early stages of treatment, dream interpretation should be kept simple and oriented to the present. For example, patients can be asked to explore a drug dream from the perspective of its message about how they need to augment their support system to reduce their vulnerability. A more complete discussion of the use of dreams can be found in Flowers and Zweben (1996).

Initiating 12-step program participation is invaluable at this point (Zweben, 1995). (Specific resistances and suggestions for handling them can be found in chap. 8 in this book.) In most urban communities, an extensive selection of meetings makes it possible to fill the vacuum left by eliminating AOD use with meetings and related activities. Thus, it is possible to quickly access a subculture that supports recovery and does not have financial barriers. The therapist's vigorous efforts to connect the patient with the 12-step system will greatly increase the chances of success at establishing and sustaining abstinence. Resistance to attending should not be met with ultimatums (e.g.,"I won't see you unless you go") but an insistence that the patient who feels strongly opposed to going needs to identify and commit to alternatives that will provide support and a learning structure offered within this system. Some therapists assume that regular participation in a self-help group constitutes addressing the addiction and they need not become involved with the issue. However, self-help groups do not give the kind of systematic attention to issues central to the individual patient that the therapist can be expected to provide.

Early and Ongoing Recovery Issues

Once abstinence is well established, many changes must occur to sustain gains. Time frames are hard to specify because of the considerable variation in individuals, but, in general, 3 months of continuous abstinence from all intoxicants is a frequent marker for moving into the second but still early stage of recovery. During this period, coping strategies need to be devised or strengthened to replace alcohol and drugs as a way of managing life difficulties and challenges. The abstinent individual is in a better position to acknowledge existing problems and address them, but the magnitude of this task can be daunting. Relationships are often damaged. Work performance may be affected. Old developmental issues, including traumatic experiences, become more visible. The therapist needs to help the patient prioritize these issues from the perspective of sustaining and building on the recovery achievements to date. The manner in which an issue can be addressed in someone with 4 months of sobriety is much different from what is possible after 2 years. Through all this, a deeper change is hopefully under way. S. Brown (1985) described in detail the identity transformation that takes place in recovery, emphasizing that behavior change is only the beginning of a process that will greatly affect self-concept, thinking, and behavior.

Accepting the identity of a recovering individual is an important achievement at this point. It is unfortunate that the media has focused on some examples in which this identity is dominated by self-disparagement, and it is certainly appropriate to examine ways in which "person in recovery" is a negative identity. The desirable end point is to integrate "recovering person" as a central (but not sole) dimension, accepted comfortably and without shame, as an element that brings awareness of the need for ongoing self-care. This includes the recognition that "I am an addict/alcoholic; I cannot drink/use" (S. Brown, 1985, p. 106). It also involves attention to stress management, health practices, and relationship issues that could constitute relapse hazards. A recovering individual who has done the inner work often exemplifies a level of personal awareness and honesty comparable to what is considered a "good" psychotherapy patient. Certainly, recovering people involved in 12-step programs make excellent psychotherapy participants because the processes are so complementary.

A patient who resists integrating the identity of recovering individual may terminate treatment or recovery-related activities prematurely. Several months of complete abstinence leaves most patients feeling a great deal better, and it is tempting to view alcohol and drugs as "the problem I used to have" and withdraw energy from the recovery process. The desire to avoid the stigma associated with being an addict or alcoholic can also influence their desire to disconnect. Wishing to believe that as long as they do not drink or use, they do not have to remain attentive to this area of their lives, they reduce or eliminate recovery-related activities. This makes them vulnerable to being taken by surprise by the many risk factors that emerge.

Euphoric recall, in which users remember only the glories of their drug experience, is common among stimulant users and occurs with others as well (Rawson et al., 1990; Washton & Stone-Washton, 1990). Painful negative consequences fade in memory, a cloud of denial settles in as the individual begins to have fantasies of the pleasures of using. "I feel better now; I'm together in a way I wasn't before. I can handle it," they muse. It is important that the therapist create a climate in which the patient can share these fantasies of drinking and using when they occur. Therapists need to be firm in their recommendations of abstinence while conveying a realistic acknowledgment that people have given up something they like very much and will have urges or even try to convince themselves that they can drink or use again. The therapist must make these a part of the discussion without making them the focus of a power struggle. A common error at this point is to attempt to deal with the issue by elaborating at length on the disease model rather than by clinical exploration to clarify the nature of the current issues. Education provides the basis for interpreting resistance early in treatment, and basic tenets do need to be repeated; however, if the clinician is not clear what the issues are, interventions can fall on deaf ears.

Instead, the therapist needs to determine what factors operate to increase the patient's interest in drinking or using drugs. These can range from growing anxiety over emerging psychological or interpersonal problems; social pressure or feelings about "not being normal, like people who drink"; unidentified triggers, such as approaching celebrations or vacations; and feelings of deserving a reward "for being so good." While exploring these issues, the therapist should encourage the patient to strengthen his or her behavioral supports for abstinence such as good self-care, self-help meeting attendance, and so on.

At this point in the process, the use of other intoxicants frequently becomes an issue. Patients will state that they are not in danger because "I never had a problem with alcohol before I used cocaine" or "I don't like benzos as much as I like drinking, the effect is not at all the same, so I don't see how it can become a problem." In fact, both clinical observation and empirical data indicate two major risks: substitution of another drug, which quickly or gradually becomes a problem, and use of another intoxicant as a precursor to relapse to the primary drug of abuse. In the case of the former, the substitution of a drug in the same or a related class as the primary choice (e.g., the alcoholic patient on Antabuse who develops a need for antianxiety medication, such as Xanax) is an obvious danger, but it also is common for other substitutions to become problematic. For example, a former cocaine user who, after 2 years of abstinence, begins to drink wine with dinner may not appear to have an alcohol problem for some time. Problems with alcohol typically develop over a longer time frame, and it would not be unusual for such individuals to appear to drink "normally" for several years and then gradually escalate their drinking.

In the case of the use of another intoxicant as a precursor to relapse, there are several possible scenarios. Most users will readily acknowledge that if they have consumed even a small amount of a psychoactive substance (e.g., alcohol), their chances of navigating successfully should their primary preference mysteriously appear (e.g., someone in the bar producing cocaine) is small. Thus, the idea that the use of another intoxicant is an immediate risk factor does not meet with much resistance. However, it is also common when one reconstructs an episode of relapse to the primary drug of abuse to find the use of another intoxicant occurred within a month or two before the relapse. One can speculate that this is part of the psychological setup for relapse (e.g., the desire to get high) or that the use of another intoxicant stimulates hunger in the brain for the primary drug of abuse; it is likely that a combination of factors is in operation. As in the first example of drug substitution, negative consequences removed in time are difficult for patients to connect. Thus, they downplay the role of the beer with the baseball game in the relapse 3 weeks later. However, this occurs so regularly that therapists should take the use of any intoxicant as an important warning sign. These issues are by no means easy to settle; the therapist should prepare for extended observation and discussion.

Another major task in ongoing recovery is to reconfigure the social networks to support abstinence. Over time, people modify their social behavior to conform to their AOD use patterns. For example, they invest more in relationships with those who drink at the same level they do and often leave nondrinking friends behind. Once sustained abstinence is the goal, they find themselves uncomfortable in many familiar social situations. Some attempt to learn to fit in anyway rather than face the intimidating task of starting anew. Ultimately, however, that is the more productive approach. Many can reconnect with friends who do not drink at all or not heavily; avoiding illicit drug use is usually easier, except for indigent individuals. Others need to regenerate their social network, which is not a welcome task in adulthood. For adolescents, this issue is especially important because peer influence is often the primary trigger for relapse. Therapist support and direction is important here, affirming that the task is crucial to consolidating gains.

Coping with feelings and ambiguity is another potential focus of work in ongoing recovery. Alcohol and drug users come to lean heavily on substances to manage unpleasant feeling states, and recovery often demands developing new capacities and learning new skills. As described earlier in detail in chapter 2, Khantzian (1981, 1982, 1985a, 1997; Khantzian et al., 1990) has written at length about how those with long histories of chemical use are often underdeveloped in their ability to identify their feelings and express themselves appropriately. Khantzian described four types of self-regulatory impairments that must be addressed throughout the recovery process but that are a particular focus of work in ongoing recovery: impairments in self-care, vulnerabilities in self-development and self-esteem, troubled self–object relations, and deficits in affect tolerance. Impairments in self-care are particularly evident from early abstinence on, as the patient looks for coping methods to fill the vacuum left by alcohol and drugs. Ongoing recovery permits more thorough examination of underlying issues. Vulnerabilities in self-development and self-esteem as well as troubled object relations, certainly not unique to substance users, also are best examined in depth once abstinence is solid. Affect tolerance can be addressed in a variety of ways. AOD use represents an attempt to prevent being overwhelmed by terrifying affect; particular drugs are chosen for their specific psychopharmacological action. For example, stimulants are attractive to women with eating disorders because they enhance feelings of powerfulness and suppress appetite. Once abstinence is established, these other issues come sharply into focus. Here again, a firm basis in abstinence is especially important as a foundation for anxiety-provoking explorations.

Tools such as those used in gestalt therapy can aid patients in learning to notice, track, and express their feelings appropriately. Focusing on learning to simply tolerate an experience, rather than forcibly changing it with a drug, can be valuable at this point. Ambiguity tolerance also can be a focus because the all-or-none thinking characteristic of alcohol and drug users can persist for long periods into recovery. These kinds of process variables can be more elusive than content areas, but they are important elements in the inner transformation that solidifies recovery. Patients with a strong 12-step connection will be exposed to a variety of people with long-term recovery who are active in working with these issues and elaborate on them in meetings. This provides support, encouragement, and insight to enhance the therapeutic process.

Later recovery also is the period when developmental issues, trauma history, and similar problems can be addressed in more depth. In the process of doing this, it is extremely important to maintain a focus on the alcohol–drug axis (S. Brown, 1985). This means periodic inquiry, even of someone with long-term abstinence, and encouragement to revive behavioral strategies (e.g., more meetings; attention to sleep, diet, and exercise) during periods of emotional upheaval. Although the therapeutic work at this point is primarily that of conventional psychotherapy, the therapist should never underestimate the relapse risk and should maintain awareness of relapse dynamics.

Conclusion

Therapists in private practice can make important interventions in the area of alcohol and drug use, particularly if they are connected to the collaborative networks that permit them to augment their own activities with resources beyond what can be provided in the dyadic therapy situation. Patients rarely embrace the need for abstinence without considerable turmoil, and the therapist can accelerate this process so it occurs before major psychological and social advantages are lost. For example, alcohol and drug use exacerbates mood disturbances, and it is advantageous to intervene as early in the process as possible. Basic clinical skills prepare the therapist well for developing the patient's motivation to change and exploring obstacles that emerge in the course of the recovery process. Sensitivity to the specific issues that regularly emerge in recovery will greatly enhance the success of the overall effort.

Family Therapy

Family therapy is an important modality in the treatment of addictions. Some clinicians view family therapy as an adjunctive modality in the treatment of addictions. Clinicians such as Edward Kaufman view family therapy not as a stand-alone treatment but as "a valuable and often necessary adjunct to treatment particularly when integrated into a comprehensive program" (Kaufman, 1994, p. 331). Other clinicians such as Timothy O'Farrell and Nathan Azrin have developed family therapy protocols that are stand-alone treatments for abusive drinking and drug problems (O'Farrell, 1993). In this chapter we examine some of the reasons for the increasing popularity of family therapy and discuss the etiology of alcohol and other drug (AOD) problems from a family perspective. The main body of the chapter focuses on specific tasks of the family therapist: joining, stabilization, behavioral contracting, education, family systems and structural analyses, development of alternative coping strategies, and relapse prevention.

Reasons for Popularity

Whether one views family therapy as a component of a comprehensive treatment program for addictions or as a stand-alone treatment, this modality has assumed a popular and significant role in the treatment of addictions during the past two decades:

> Twenty-five years ago families were by and large ignored by alcoholism clinicians ... one is now hard pressed to find a credible alcoholism treatment program that does not at least give lip service to the importance of including family members in the treatment plan. (Steinglass, 1994, p. 315)

Clinical Experience Supports

There are several reasons why family therapy has assumed an increasingly important role. First, the preponderance of clinical experience supports the view that including family members enhances the total treatment experience and improves outcomes. Over the past 40 years, there has been a growing awareness that family dynamics can help to explain both the initiation of substance abuse problems as well as their course and eventual outcome. Clinicians realize that treating the alcohol- or drug-addicted individual without treating the structural and systemic problems that contribute to the disorder may well lead to continued problems of daily functioning as well as increased relapse behavior.

Clinicians now realize that the impact of years of drinking and drug-using behavior on the family structure can devastate the normal patterns of family life. The dysfunction that is seen by many therapists in the "nonpatient" family members results from years of living in a stressful, crisis-centered environment in which daily living requires that individual needs be set aside in order to attend to the crises resulting from the alcoholic's drinking or drug addict's drug-using behavior. Children raised in alcoholic and addicted families grow up with a variety of affective and interpersonal disorders that, in and of themselves, require treatment. Through a total family recovery program, these dysfunctions can be addressed and individual family members can return to a more normal state of functionality (S. Brown & Lewis, 1995).

Growth of Al-Anon and Codependence

In addition to clinical observation, the growth of popular self-help programs such as Al-Anon and the codependence movement also has increased pressure for inclusion of family members in the treatment process. S. Brown (1995) noted that Joan Jackson in the 1950s and 1960s outlined developmental stages for the spouse and family members of the alcoholic. In conjunction with Jackson's work, the Al-Anon movement, a self-help 12-step recovery program for family members of alcoholics, emerged. The Al-Anon movement "provided instruction in how to detach and disengage from maladaptive and unhealthy reactions to the alcoholic" (S. Brown, 1995, p. 280). This was the first attempt to look at the progression of alcoholism in the context of the family and especially the unhealthy interactional patterns that developed within the family in response to alcoholism. This concept that unhealthy interpersonal and emotional reactions to alcoholism and addiction arise as a normal part of the overall addictive syndrome later developed into the concept of the *coalcoholic* or *codependent* individual. The codependency movement, which was popularized in the 1980s (Beattie, 1987; Woititz, 1983), may have overstated the dimensions of this syndrome, but it did serve to highlight the interactional and interpersonal dysfunctions that arise in addicted families. These movements in turn placed increasing pressures on treatment centers and clinicians to respond to the needs of family members who had previously been ignored in more traditional chemical dependency treatment programs.

Research Supports

The third reason why family therapy has become increasingly popular is that family therapy approaches have been shown to be clinically effective in a wide variety of studies. McCrady and Epstein (1996), in a review of family therapy theories, concluded that "a rich body of empirical literature provides strong support for family-based models and for the effectiveness of treatments based on these models" (p. 137).

Likewise, Steinglass (1994) concluded that family therapy has been shown to be efficacious in a variety of studies. Steinglass's review of the literature revealed three conclusions: (a) Although no specific family treatment model dominates the field, a wide variety of theoretical models have data-based research support for their efficacy; (b) involvement of the nonalcoholic spouse in the treatment process increases the participation, retention, and compliance of the alcoholic spouse in the treatment plan; and (c) treatment providers have been slow to incorporate sophisticated family treatment models into existing 12-step programs. Steinglass argued for more individualized programs that incorporate data-based treatment protocols into existing programs. Although research-based family therapy programs have proved to be efficacious, "few treatment programs seem cognizant of these research based clinical treatment models, preferring instead to impose standardized programs on families independent of the heterogeneity of this clinical population" (Steinglass, 1994, p. 327).

Family Therapy View of Etiology

As the field of family therapy has evolved, the overall approach has become more integrative and less reductionistic. There is a move away from viewing the family dynamics as playing a major etiological role in the development of alcoholism and drug addiction. Fifteen to 20 years ago, family systems theorists emphasized the adaptive function that AOD played in family interactions. According to this view, AOD problems were a response to dysfunctional family dynamics and served to stabilize the family system. The family's striving for stability or homeostasis was thought to be a necessary and sufficient condition to explain the continuation of the substance abuse problem.

Over the years, this view has become considerably broader. Dysfunctional family behavior is now viewed as being either the result of alcohol and drug abuse problems or one of many etiological factors (Steinglass, 1994). In many cases, the stresses associated with years of chronic abuse of substances creates a family dysfunction rather than vice versa. Steinglass (1994) went on to state that,

> as this new view has come to dominate thinking in the alcoholism/family field, the concept of the alcoholism prone family is no longer thought to be credible. Instead most family researchers are comfortable with multi-factorial models of alcoholism that acknowledge predisposing factors (e.g., genetic transmission), but also include a focus on the family environment as significantly affecting the clinical course of these conditions. (p. 316)

Tasks of the Family Therapist

There are several different models or theories of family psychotherapy as they pertain to substance abuse patients, and each has its own set of etiological assumptions and intervention strategies. Although there are significant differences between these schools, there also are surprising similarities. Most family therapists, regardless of their theoretical orientation, place much importance on the establishment of abstinence before meaningful therapeutic work can be undertaken. O'Farrell (1993) viewed abstinence as a prerequisite for participation in his behavioral marriage therapy, a form of family therapy for alcoholic patients that derives from a learning theory model. All participants in this program must accept abstinence as the preferred treatment goal. Moderate drinking is not acceptable as a goal:

> The therapist must structure treatment so that the control of the alcohol abuse is the first priority before attempting to help the couple with other problems ... [since] the hope that reduction in marital distress will lead to improvement in the drinking is rarely fulfilled. (p. 172)

Likewise, Steinglass (1994) and Kaufman (1994) also insisted on abstinence as a prerequisite for effective family ther-

apy intervention. Both therapists emphasized the need to negotiate an abstinence contract in the early stages of therapy.
Steinglass (1994) recommended an abstinence contract involving "family level detoxification" (p. 323); he advocated
an alcohol-free environment for all family members. Kaufman (1994) also believed that a therapeutic contract for abstinence is the appropriate way to begin the move toward a
healthy family system. Although he preferred to maintain
treatment with the family of a resistant patient, Kaufman did
suggest that, under some circumstances, discontinuing treatment of the whole family if there is repeated, continued AOD
use:

> It should be reemphasized that whenever the therapist
> maintains therapy with a family where serious drug use
> continues, he or she has the responsibility of not main-
> taining the illusion that a family is resolving problems
> when in fact they are really enforcing them. (Kaufman,
> 1994, p. 335)

Clinicians from other models such as the developmental
model (S. Brown & Lewis, 1995) and the community reinforcement model (Sisson & Azrin, 1993) also emphasize the
necessity of achieving abstinence as a prerequisite for meaningful therapeutic change.

Thus, there is overlap among different theoretical models
when it comes to specific intervention strategies regarding
the issue of abstinence as well as a variety of other issues. In
the remainder of this chapter we focus on an integrated
model that attempts to define this consensus by focusing on
the tasks of the family therapist who is working with substance-abusing patients. The model is derived from a consideration of salient clinical issues that face the practitioner who
works with AOD patients regardless of their theoretical orientation.

Joining

The therapist working with AOD patients, like the therapist
who works with other disorders, is joining. The term *joining*

refers to the process of the therapist affiliating with each individual family member. The therapist must be willing to carefully listen and convey that he or she is interested in what the family members have to say. The therapist also must attempt to understand each individual's viewpoint and to address each individual's concerns.

Initially, it is important for the therapist to respect rather than to challenge the defensiveness of the family. These families often have led lives centered on the frequent crises created by the behavior of the identified patient (the alcoholic or addict). It sometimes seems to the family as if the drinking or drug use is the source of the entire problem. Therapists often hear "If only he or she would stop drinking then our lives would be fine!"

There are several points that need to be challenged about this assumption. First, when the alcoholic stops drinking, life is often initially more chaotic and more confrontational. The drinker who has relied on alcohol as a coping mechanism for many years must undergo a difficult transition when he or she stops drinking and often becomes increasingly depressed, irritable, anxious, and so on when alcohol is removed from the picture. Second, emotions and feelings that have been medicated through the use of alcohol for many years rise to the surface after alcohol has been removed. Family tensions and underlying conflicts that may have contributed to the disorder in the first place are revisited after the alcoholic achieves sobriety.

It is important for the therapist to realize, however, that now is not the time to confront this simplistic view of the situation. Rather, now is the time to acknowledge that the family has a valid point. Drinking has certainly taken its toll on the entire family, and the therapist sympathizes with the family's concern over the continued drinking of the identified patient. In short, the therapist needs to communicate that he or she intends to take this issue seriously by making it a major focus of the therapeutic endeavor. The therapist can say "Given the involvement of the entire family, including the identified patient, we can jointly develop a plan to address this issue."

Another common misconception poses a greater challenge for the therapist: the notion that alcohol or drugs is not the problem. The following is an example of this clinical presentation in the family in whom the identified patient is a teenage boy presenting with all the signs of an emerging substance abuse problem:

His grades have been declining for the past several years. For the past 6 months he has been staying out late, either missing curfew or sneaking out late at night. He has become increasingly isolated, spending more time in his room. He has a new peer group of adolescents who have either had difficulties with juvenile authorities or have dropped out of school.

The precipitating event that led to the therapy appointment was his arrest at a party where alcohol and marijuana were present. The police determined that he had been drinking. Rolling papers but no actual drugs were found in his possession. The young man's story is that he was drinking for the first time and the rolling papers belonged to a friend.

The parents begin the session by assuring the therapist that it is not a substance abuse problem. Each parent has a somewhat different perspective on the problem. The mother believes that the father is a workaholic who pays no attention to the children and this is the source of the problem. She says, "A teenage boy needs a father to keep him in line." She continues, "When he does come home he is often too tired to bother with the children. He is moody and irritable and has only negative things to say. He puts the boy down all the time." The father, on the other hand, thinks that the mother is too soft with the kids. "She is always making excuses for them and never holds them accountable," he explains. "Of course I am irritable," he says. "When I try to intervene and discipline the kids she is always there to undermine what I am doing. She can't stop protecting them for one minute," he states. Both parents are united on only one point. They insist that the problem is not drugs and that they do not want alcohol or drugs to be the focus of the intervention. They begin by stating that they took their son

to one of those treatment centers where they were told
that he might have an addiction problem. They immediately left and took their son to see the clinician who
would understand that their son is struggling with issues
of self-esteem.

Here, the therapist is in a bind. The parents have presented a clinical picture that suggests substance abuse
but at the same time have given the therapist a clear
warning that this topic is off limits and should not be
the focus of the therapeutic efforts. In a somewhat controlling way, they have let the therapist know that the
last therapist who tried to focus on the substance abuse
issue was fired and if the therapist wants to continue
working with this family, it would be unwise to head
down the same road. The bind, then, is how to join with
this family and acknowledge their concerns without to-
tally accepting the directive to defocus from the teenager's abusive substances. The underlying family rule is
clear, "Don't talk about the substance abuse problem."
Perhaps mother comes from an alcoholic family in which
there is tremendous family disruption (constant crisis,
chaos, physical and verbal abuse, etc.) and in which a
negative outcome ensued (death, institutionalization,
etc.). Perhaps father has a moral or judgmental view of
people with substance abuse problems and cannot tolerate the idea that this problem exists within his family.
Perhaps both parents have overwhelming fear that their
son could turn out to be a "druggie" and that this would
be unthinkable. Whatever the underlying issues, the family is warning the therapist that this is a brittle, sensitive
issue that should not be confronted right away and must
be dealt with in a sensitive and caring manner only after
a trusting bond has been established.

In that instance, the therapist must acknowledge the fears
that both parents have. Sneaking out at night, declining
school grades, and the other symptoms mentioned are all
important. The therapist must look at the underlying reasons
and try to develop a plan to address the problem. The therapist also would be remiss, however, if he or she did not
raise the issue of the importance of the teenager remaining

free from alcohol and drugs as a prerequisite for addressing these other issues. Most parents are willing to support the concept of an alcohol- and drug-free life for their teenager as a positive goal. Requesting the parents' assistance in monitoring this through alcohol and drug screens and emphasizing that this is a routine part of the procedure in such cases is often received as a positive, affirming step even by families with such a rigid defense structure. In this way, the notion of substance abuse as a possible confounding variable in the overall symptom or problem pattern is introduced without identifying substance abuse as the source of the problem. Later, an examination of the family's particular sensitivities about substance abuse issues can be undertaken and perhaps addressed more directly. Also, depending on the outcome of the monitoring process through alcohol and drug screens, the true nature of the problem may become more apparent.

In this regard, the family therapist does not directly challenge the family rules early in therapy. Instead, the therapist works within existing family structures and supports areas of family strength, especially for the family members who are most threatened. Kaufman (1994) referred to this technique as "maintenance." Kaufman also suggested mimesis or using the family's preferred adaptive mode and styles of communication as a way to join with the family. In the example of the teenage boy, for instance, when speaking to the father, the therapist might state in a more authoritative voice, "Yes, I agree rules are important. One of the things we are going to try to do in here is to set up reasonable rules and make sure that they are consistently applied." In speaking to the mother, on the other hand, the therapist might say in a somewhat softer, comforting voice, "We must also look at self-esteem. It is important not only for Johnny to learn how to feel good about himself but for the whole family to learn how to feel good about this family unit." In this way, the therapist has supported each of the parents without undermining the other. The degree to which the family uses humor or physical touching are other areas in which the therapist can mimic the style of family members and enhance the joining process (Kaufman, 1994).

Stabilization

The next task of the family therapist who works with AOD patients is stabilization. The term *stabilization* refers to a set of intervention strategies that are designed to assist the patient in either abstaining from mood-altering chemicals completely or, when appropriate, reducing AOD use to the point at which the patient's functioning is not impaired. Stabilization is the task that is most often overlooked by both beginning and experienced therapists who are unaccustomed to working with this population. In many ways, traditional psychotherapy training seems to work against therapists in this endeavor: The psychodynamically trained therapist wants to look for underlying causes; the systems-structural therapist wants to rearrange dysfunctional structural patterns within the family; and the learning theorist wants to begin teaching more adaptive coping skills. All these interventions have their place with the AOD patient; however, they are not likely to be effective until the drinking and drug using is stabilized. In most cases, stabilization means attaining abstinence.

Loss of control. Having abstinence as the central goal for the family in the early stages should never be done in a heavy-handed way (e.g., labeling the identified patient as an alcoholic and refusing to talk about anything except sobriety). It should be done in a way that acknowledges the very real concerns of each family member while at the same time begins to link the presenting problems with the drinking and drug use. The job of the therapist is to focus on these connections and to highlight the loss of control that ensues when the identified patient is drinking or using drugs.

In many cases, however, this focus is the opposite direction from the one in which the family wishes to proceed. The family members have often joined with the alcoholic or drug addict in rigidly maintaining the existence of alternative explanations for the identified patient's problems. Thus, the source of the problem is not the husband's drinking but the stress of his job or perhaps the death of his father 2 years earlier. In the clinical example presented earlier about the adolescent the source of the problem from the mother's perspective is not the AOD use but the father's parenting; from the father's perspective, it is the mother's enabling behavior that creates the difficulties. When these explanations are in danger of breaking down, other explanations can be added or substituted. Therapists frequently hear parents say, "He failed the algebra class because of the bad teacher" or "She drinks because she is under tremendous pressure from her peers."

Faced with these rigid defenses, the therapist's job is to gently but firmly shift the focus back to the drinking and drug use. Fortunately, cracks begin to appear in the defense structure over time. The therapist highlights these cracks, notes the discrepancies, and focuses the family on the meaning of these episodes. Thus, the adolescent skips school; drinks or uses drugs; and, as a result, misses a test and drops a full letter grade. This event shows her loss of control over AOD use. The therapist needs to highlight the loss of control and define it for what it is: an example of AOD use behavior that needs to be stabilized. By keeping the focus on the drinking and drug use, by highlighting episodes that illustrate loss of control, and by interpreting the meaning of these episodes, the therapist accelerates the process by which the family's defense structure implodes on itself. The reality of the AOD use becomes too blatant to ignore.

The final realization may come in the form of information provided from the therapist to the parents, "Mrs. Smith, Johnny's drug screen is positive for marijuana and cocaine." Or it may come from the parents to the therapist, "Dr. Jones, Johnny ran away last night after we grounded him and we found him early this morning passed out drunk in the woods."

Behavioral contracting: abstinence contracts. Behavioral contracting is a specific method in which the therapist can help maintain the focus on AOD use. The contract is often for a period of abstinence. The abstinence contract needs to be long enough to allow the physical and psychological realities of not drinking and using drugs to impinge on the identified patient. These realities include not only the physical withdrawal phase, which can often be endured through willpower alone, but also the waves of psychological craving that are sure to follow. A contract should be at least 30 days; 60 or 90 days are preferable.

Establishing an abstinence contract allows the therapist to experience the impact of sobriety not only on the identified patient but also on the other family members. In the early stages of abstinence, the identified patient often becomes increasingly moody, depressed, and irritable in response to the removal of his or her major coping mechanism. Other family members may insist that the situation has worsened. In some cases, wives have actually suggested that the husbands return to drinking because they were more likable the old way. Still other family members may find themselves feeling surprisingly empty and lost because the crisis-centered nature of their existence has slowed down. If their role has been that of the rescuer or the enabler, family members may feel as if their main function in life has been usurped. Most important, during the abstinence contract period, the identified patient has the opportunity to examine feelings that arise secondary to sobriety. He or she can focus on the dreams, feelings, and thoughts about AOD use that are indicators of how attached the individual was to the substance.

Behavioral goals. Although an abstinence contract is desirable in most cases, it is not always achievable in the early stages of therapy. Fortunately, two other important components of the contract can help to move the patient closer toward achieving an abstinence contract. The first component is to focus on behavioral goals jointly set by the therapist, the family members, and the identified patient. For the adolescent, these goals might include going to school, passing courses, and coming in on time. For the adult, they might include enhanced performance at work, accepting responsibility at home, and increased involvement with the children.

Therapeutic regimen. A second component of the contract includes compliance with a specific therapeutic regimen such as taking Antabuse for the heavy drinker, agreeing to attend group therapy, or going to a certain number of self-help meetings per week. Establishing a contract allows for the imposition of structure on a previously chaotic existence. It allows the family members and the identified patient to set specific goals by which progress can be measured. Setting specific goals and measuring progress on a weekly basis can help the resistant individual to understand how out of control their life has become and the need to move in a different direction. Likewise, contracting for a specific therapeutic regimen also can help to reinforce the need for structure in the lives of the patient and family members. If the patient agrees to attend five self-help meetings a week and the family members agree to do the same, it soon becomes clear when these goals are not getting met. When the patient, for example, misses meetings on a regular basis, this becomes grist for the mill to explore resistance by discussing unpleasant feelings or reactions to the meeting environment.

Steinglass. A variety of clinicians working from different models endorse the idea of behavioral contracting as a useful adjunct to treatment (Kaufman, 1994; O'Farrell, 1993; Sisson & Azrin, 1993; Steinglass, 1994). Steinglass (1994) recommended "family level detoxification" (p. 323), the establishment of a written contract that emphasizes an alcohol-free environment for all family members. Initially, Steinglass advocated that no drinking occur at home and that the house is alcohol free. The contract eventually is extended to the larger social network and the environment of the family. He stressed the use of certain techniques to maximize the effectiveness of the contract, including (a) making the terms of the contract public so that friends and relatives are aware of the situation and (b) the use of rehearsal to anticipate problems that might arise when implementing the contract (Steinglass, 1994, p. 324).

O'Farrell. O'Farrell (1993) operated from the perspective of a learning theory model and also advocated strongly for abstinence contracting. Initially, identified patients entering O'Farrell's behavioral marital therapy (BMT) program agree on an Antabuse (disulfiram) contract. Antabuse is a medication that causes an individual to become violently ill with nausea and vomiting if he or she drinks. It is frequently used in alcohol and treatment programs. In O'Farrell's contract, the alcoholic agrees to take Antabuse daily and the spouse agrees to monitor the person taking Antabuse. They agree to report any violation of the contract to the therapist. O'Farrell also had the partners negotiate specific methods of handling continued AOD use as well as specific commitments for participating in the therapy process.

Sisson and Azrin. Sisson and Azrin (1993) developed a model of family therapy referred to as the *community reinforcement approach* (CRA). Sissin and Azrin also insisted on an Antabuse contract for their alcoholic patients. The identified patient takes the Antabuse dispensed by the spouse. The spouse receives specific instructions about dissolving the Antabuse in a cup of water and then giving it to the identified patient. They agree on a set time and place to take the Antabuse and rehearse procedures for when and if the alcoholic patient refuses to take it. In the CRA, family members not only negotiate an Antabuse contract but also commit to reciprocity counseling and a variety of other behavioral goals (Sisson & Azrin, 1993, p. 50).

Behavioral contracting is a vital part of the overall stabilization process and is endorsed by family therapists from a variety of competing models. Once stabilization is achieved, however, the work of the family therapist has only just begun. At this point the family may enter a true crisis stage. The identified patient often finds himself or herself in the uncomfortable position of having stopped drinking but having absolutely no coping mechanisms. Physical violence, suicide attempts, and other forms of acting out are not uncommon. The therapist must be prepared to intervene with other strategies to provide support, reassurance, and guidance for the patient and family members once the drinking and drug using has stopped.

Education

As stated previously, the goal of stabilization is a movement toward abstinence or, when appropriate, a reduction in the substance abuse. In addition, behavioral contracting assists the identified patient and family members in forming a more realistic picture of the nature of the substance abuse problem.

They are more in touch with issues such as loss of control and more aware of the destabilizing role that AOD use has played in the overall family problems. As this awareness emerges and behaviors begin to change, the patient is left without access to his or her primary coping mechanism, AOD use. An underlying sense of panic often emerges. The patient may become more irritable, moody, depressed, and isolated.

Sequencing and expectations. This set of behaviors can be troubling and disturbing for the family and can create a ripple effect. For years the family may have had the illusion that the cessation of drinking would bring improvement; instead, the reverse is the case. Education can be extremely helpful in the therapeutic process at this stage. To be helpful, however, the education must be based on knowledge of the dynamics of addiction and the normal developmental sequence that ensues as the patient moves from drinking or using drugs into a recovery mode. For a thorough discussion of these developmental phases, see *Treating the Alcoholic* (S. Brown, 1985) and *Treating Alcoholism* (S. Brown, 1995).

It is extremely important to normalize for the family the behaviors that the identified patient is exhibiting. The regression in behavior occurs as part of a normal sequence of recovery. What is motivating this behavior is the nature of addictive craving itself. Discussing addictive craving directly with patients and family members is often beneficial, comparing it to a primary drive state (see chap. 2, this volume). The family members who have never experienced this craving for themselves are encouraged to think how they would react if they had had nothing to eat for many days and were suddenly denied access to food. Is it not possible that their behaviors would be similar to those of the identified patient?

Other family members, especially parents of adolescents, often become concerned because the patient is not performing up to their expectations. "Sure he is sober, but he still doesn't bring home any books from school. He never studies and he seems disinterested in playing sports like he used to," is a common refrain. The father of an adolescent patient exclaimed angrily, "He needs to get on with his life. It's his senior year in high school and he has football; he has academics; he has college applications. Why is he so disinterested in all of this?" At this point, family members need to be encouraged to scale back expectations and to keep focused on the target.

In the early days, sobriety is a full-time job. Although patients need to be encouraged to immerse themselves in a recovery program, the family members need to be encouraged to step back and allow this process to happen, supporting it when they can, but certainly not obstructing it. Family members, especially spouses, may become jealous of the time that the husband or wife spends going to self-help meetings. "He spends more time with them than he spends with me," is often heard by therapists. Family members may feel that the identified patient has become addicted to the program itself. "Why is he so obsessed with this recovery program?" many family members want to know. Unfortunately, more than a few psychotherapists support the family's misguided line of thinking about "an addiction to Alcoholics Anonymous" (AA).

The patients' reality in the early days of sobriety is that they are hanging on for dear life, trying not to use but not having many recovery skills of their own. They are attracted to a support group precisely because they are so desperate. They see others at these meetings who seem happy but who also understand their own reality, the craving that they are experiencing. These recovering people do not judge or analyze the situation; rather, they provide support and give the patient concrete tools for staying sober "one day at a time." The patient slowly learns how to structure leisure hours previously devoted to drinking and using drugs. They learn how to call their sponsor or contact person in times of crisis. They learn the soothing effects of daily meditation and reading literature that relates to their experience. Forming new relationships and new behavior patterns makes it easier to let go of the old patterns. This process is the full-time job of recovery.

At this stage in the process, the therapist's knowledge of addiction and recovery stages is vital to the family. They are desperate for information, especially knowledge about the sequencing of recovery-related behaviors and knowledge about what they can expect in the future. They want to know how long before they are themselves again. The patients want to know how long before they will not wake up in the middle of the night dreaming about using. Parents want to know whether their child can return to the old school environment or whether he or she must be transferred to another one. All family members want to know what it is safe to talk about at home. Will they trigger a relapse if they say the wrong thing? The therapist must be prepared to respond to these questions with factual information based on experience.

Also especially valuable at this point is referring family members to self-help meetings of their own, such as Al-Anon. This rapidly accelerates the learning curve because they are immediately exposed to other family members who have progressed farther through the process and can provide knowledge and support for them. Family members soon begin to resent the patients' time at self-help meetings less because they are deriving nourishment and support from their own recovery programs.

The therapist also must be prepared to address the underlying emotion of fear, which is expressed by the questions, "Will they ever get better?" "Will they survive?" "Will they ever be normal?" The family is seeking reassurance at this point, and some should be forthcoming. Of course, the patients can get better and there is no reason why they should not. Millions of others have gone before them and have recovered, so they can, too. By the same token, it also provides an opportunity for education. If they are truly AOD dependent, recovery is closely tied to remaining abstinent from all mood-altering chemicals. Both patients and family members need to know this principle early in the process.

Rebuilding trust. Aside from questions about sequencing and expectations, another series of questions is often posed by family members. These questions involve the process of rebuilding trust. Parents wonder, "How can we ever believe anything our child says again?" Parents often will say, "He used drugs for years right under our noses. We are afraid of being burned again." Although their fear is real, the therapist needs to remind the parents that they are now more educated about this topic than they were in the past. Most appropriately, the therapist can review the warning signs that the family saw but perhaps ignored in the past.

The patient is afraid of relapsing, whereas the family is afraid of returning to the chaos and crisis that permeated their lives for so many years. A frank discussion of this issue is in order. The therapist should support the family members at this point by saying something like, "You should never have to return to that type of chaos. Let's develop a plan for dealing with it should it arise." A statement of this type can effectively lead into a discussion of a relapse prevention plan. It is often appropriate at this point for the patient to state what he or she plans to do in the event of a relapse and what are some ways of regaining sobriety.

Rather than a rigid plan such as going to long-term treatment on relapse, a more flexible plan is preferable, such as "In the event of a relapse we [the patient and family members] agree to contact you [the therapist] immediately and jointly develop a set of strategies and recommendations." These recommendations might include increasing frequency of meeting attendance, increasing frequency of therapy sessions, or attending a special group for assertiveness training. Another recommendation, based on the nature of the relapse, might be long-term treatment.

The essential point is that the therapist and the family members as well as the patient are not locked into a predetermined plan that might not be appropriate given the nature of the regression. All relapses are not equal, and therefore it is impossible to specify in advance an appropriate intervention for a given relapse. Once again, these issues are educational points that need to be emphasized to the patient and family members at some point during the early stages of the recovery process.

Other questions that family members ask involve signs of knowing when the patient is not doing well. The answers to these questions revolve around three essential warning signs. The first warning sign of not doing well is the use of any psychoactive chemicals. The patient whose drug of choice is cocaine and whose abuse has progressed to the level of dependency cannot drink alcohol and expect to be successful. Therefore, the patient who attempts to use any psychoactive chemical on a responsible basis should be considered to be in relapse.

Although many therapists distinguish among relapses, lapses, and slips, with each carrying a progressively lesser connotation of severity, in our experience these distinctions are not helpful. They inevitably lead to arguments about whether a particular set of using behaviors is a slip, a lapse, or a relapse. It is more effective to say that any use at all constitutes a relapse while at the same time acknowledging that, as stated previously, not all relapses are equal.

The second sign that the patient is not doing well is a failure to comply with the therapeutic plan. The patient may stop attending recovery meetings, refuse to take medication as prescribed, or refuse to attend scheduled psychotherapy sessions. Of particular significance are situations in which a patient does not show up for appointments, refuses to be monitored by drug and alcohol screens that had previously been agreed on, or both.

The third major warning sign of relapse behavior is a return to old habits and patterns. For adults, the signs may be staying out late, becoming isolated from the family, experiencing increased irritability and moodiness, as well as failing to fulfill responsible duties in the family (e.g., parenting duties, chores around the house). For adolescents, the signs may be falling school grades, running away, sneaking out at night, and a diminishing interest in extracurricular activities. For both adults and adolescents, returning to old friends who use AOD and frequenting old places where AOD are used sends a strong signal of increased relapse potential.

There is a certain sense of relief and satisfaction on the part of both the patient and the family members when these warning signs are discussed openly. Patients sometimes describe it as feeling as if a safety net has been erected. Although they tend to protest (especially adolescents), they know that those who love and care for them will never again be so easily manipulated. They know that their conning and deceiving is not likely to go unnoticed. As one alcoholic put it, "If I ever relapse again, I hope someone will stop me."

For the family members, knowing the warning signs can sometimes free them to let go of trying to control the patient so much. "If he is using, we are all going to know about it sooner rather than later" is a therapeutic statement that relieves some of the family's and patient's anxieties.

Although these interventions are described as educational in nature, they also serve a psychotherapeutic purpose. They address underlying insecurities, anxieties, trust issues, and fears that are common to family members and patients alike. They begin to help the family members and patients feel a sense of control over a previously unmanageable situation.

Note that although these tasks such as stabilization and education are presented as if they are sequential in nature, in reality they are intertwined. The therapist may often go back and forth between education and stabilization interventions within the course of the single session. Likewise, it is not uncommon to be educating the family members and the patient in the midst of the first session. It also is not uncommon to be engaged in stabilization efforts months or even years into the therapeutic process.

Family Systems and Structural Analysis

The fifth task of the family therapist working with AOD abuse families is an analysis of the family system and structures that are dysfunctional and contributing to the problem. In some cases, the family dysfunction precedes the initiation of AOD abuse; in other cases, the dysfunction arises in response to the destabilizing effects of the substance abuse. In either case, however, the family therapist must help the family members see how their own dysfunctional behavior has contributed and sustained the substance abuse problem.

Steinglass, Bennett, Wolin, and Reiss (1987) pointed to the development of an alcoholic family system in which alcohol plays an increasingly dominant role in the lives of the identified patient and other family members. As the drinking progresses, alcohol slowly begins to dominate the lives of all family members. Family daily routines are changed in order for some semblance of normal family life to proceed. Family routines such as sleep–wake cycles, mealtimes, and shopping all may be altered to accommodate the alcoholic's drinking (Steinglass et al., 1987, p. 63).

Family rituals also are altered over time. The alcoholic who is drinking may disrupt family vacations. As a result, the family plans vacations that are less stressful to the alcoholic. Thanksgiving dinner may be eaten at home rather than at a relative's house so that the alcoholic can be brought to the table at least for a few minutes to participate in the family ritual. Over time, as the family changes its rituals to accommodate the drinking, the value of the rituals decreases for the family members: "Alcoholic behavior has in this case taken precedence over the performance of the ritual. This disruption of an existing family ritual furthers the reinforcement of the alcoholic identity" (Steinglass et al., 1987, p. 73).

Furthermore, the alcoholic family becomes increasingly desperate to maintain order at any cost. Family problem solving is affected. Reactions to problems are often disproportionate and overly aggressive relative to the magnitude of the problem (Steinglass et al., 1987, p. 69). A certain rigidity in family rules and problem solving emerges. In some families, the expression of certain behaviors (e.g., expression of affect) occurs only in the presence of intoxication. Other behaviors may occur only in the presence of sobriety. Thus, alcoholism further distorts the family's expression of problem-solving capabilities.

Over time, the patient's drinking or drug use becomes the central organizing principle of family functioning. Steinglass et al. (1987) noted that a common reaction of alcoholic families is to accommodate to the condition because they fear that addressing the problem head-on will result in a total disintegration of the family. In this case, accommodation is preferable to disintegration as homeostatic mechanisms attempt to preserve the structure of the family at all costs: "Here regulatory behaviors are adjusted, altered or completely restructured to prevent a showdown. Unsure of what the consequences of such a showdown might be, the family reactively adjusts its behaviors enough to establish internal stability" (Steinglass et al., 1987, p. 72). Although these modifications may be subtle at first, eventually the changes are profound.

Steinglass et al. (1987) noted that the family regulatory behaviors become invaded by alcohol:

> The direction of this modification is one that makes it more rather than less likely that alcoholism will continue to thrive. Hence the family system has been modified in a direction supportive of chronic alcoholism and is now a system organized to maintain the constancy of its internal environment in the face of what was previously a destabilizing force—chronic alcoholism. (p. 73)

The task of the family therapist at this point is first to help the family members see how alcohol has invaded the family routines and rituals and then to help the family restructure daily functioning so as to not reinforce drinking and drug-using behavior. This point is a difficult one in the therapeutic process because the suggestions made by the therapist usually are exactly the types of problem-solving strategies that the family has already considered and rejected. For example, the therapist may suggest a variety of restructuring behaviors that are designed to allow the substance-abusing patient to experience the consequences of his or her behavior as well as to restore a sense of normalcy to family functioning. Examples of these types of behaviors might include a wife allowing her husband to sleep on the floor after he has passed out drunk or not calling his boss in the morning to make excuses when he is unable to get to work on time. For an adolescent, this restructuring might involve allowing the adolescent to experience the consequences of the juvenile court system when he or she has been arrested for possession of marijuana.

The family members might view these suggestions with astonishment, thinking that the therapist has taken leave of his or her senses. Sometimes it helps to start with small steps such as encouraging the family to plan a night out together. The therapist might reinforce the notion that this outing is to take place with or without the participation of the identified patient.

Once again, it is often helpful for the family members to meet and talk with other families of recovering alcoholics or addicts. Such a contact usually is accomplished through support groups such as Al-Anon or Nar-Anon. By contact with other "recovering" family members, individual family members can begin to see their problems in a different light. Family members often note the remarkable similarity between their issues and those that are highlighted during the meetings. They begin to see the role that AOD abuse has played in organizing family life. They hear about concepts such as "enabling," "codependence," and "detachment." They learn that by not allowing the alcoholic or drug addict to experience the consequences of their behavior, they are enabling the process to continue. They learn that allowing the substance-abusing individual to "hit bottom" provides the best hope for positive outcomes. They also learn that by allowing patients to experience the consequences, the family members are constructing a "higher bottom" for the addict so that the patient will ask for help sooner.

They learn that as addiction progresses, family members often alter their behavior to accommodate the addiction and develop their own disorder known as codependence. Codependent individuals live a reactive lifestyle in which they are enmeshed in the daily activities of the addict. "As a result of this emotional enmeshment, the codependent tends to lose all sense of 'self' or identity, and to become emotionally dependent upon the addict. The addict's mood dictates the codependent's mood. In a sense the codependent becomes an appendage to the addict and the substance abuse" (Thombs, 1994, p. 161). The codependent is encouraged to develop a sense of detachment. To "detach with love" is the way out of the trap. Detachment comes by acknowledging one's powerlessness over the behavior of the addicted individual and by stopping the controlling and enabling behavior patterns.

Family members often initially view all of this advice and

new learning with skepticism because it runs so contrary to their thinking. Through support, sharing, and confrontation by other group members, the family members begin to see the value of this new behavior. They then become more amenable to the restructuring suggestions of the therapist. Because both the therapist and the support group are giving a consistent message, the strength of that message assumes greater power. The family slowly begins to change behavior patterns and with great fearfulness awaits the results.

The therapist now must be willing to provide extra support. Telephone calls after hours are common because family members need to be reassured that they are doing the right thing. In one particular situation, the mother of a substance-abusing young adult who refused to stop using eventually asked the young man to leave the home. Over the next 6 months, this young man would periodically appear at the mother's doorstep and request readmission to the family. As the weather turned colder, his requests were more urgent and forceful. The advice to the mother was always the same: Offer the young man treatment and tell him that he could return home after 1 month's sobriety in a halfway house. The mother called each time the young man appeared at the door and asked the same question, "Is it okay to do the same thing and stick with the plan?" The answer was always in the affirmative, and the mother would say, "Thanks. I just needed to hear that." After 6 months the young man entered treatment. The therapist must be able to openly acknowledge the fears of the family members as they move toward new ways of dealing with the patient's drinking or drug using. At the same time, the therapist must stay firm in the resolve that the family "stay the course" even when it looks as if things might not work out.

Family therapists from a variety of different theoretical models emphasize the restructuring of family systems so as to alter behavior patterns which inadvertently reinforce the drinking or drug using behavior. The CRA, developed by Sisson and Azrin (1993), acknowledges this point using the language of a learning theory model: "CRA acknowledges the powerful role of environmental contingencies in encouraging or discouraging drinking, and attempts to rearrange these contingencies such that sober behavior is more rewarding than drinking behavior" (J. E. Smith & Meyers, 1995, p. 251). The initial stages of the CRA program focus on identifying and altering behaviors of the spouse or other family member through specific behavior change strategies in order to increase the probability that the identified patient will seek help. As Sisson and Azrin (1993) noted, "if family members can be trained to recognize the relationship between their behavior and the alcoholic's drinking behavior, they may be able to obtain the desired reduction or elimination of the alcoholic's drinking" (p. 35). Like Nar-Anon, the CRA method teaches spouses to stop reinforcing the drinking behavior and to develop alternative leisure activities so that they can develop a life of their own.

Likewise, theorists from a developmental model approach discuss the necessity for restructuring family dynamics such that enabling behaviors are eliminated and the addicted individual is allowed to hit bottom. S. Brown and Lewis (1995) explained that during the initial stages of therapeutic work, it is often necessary for the alcoholic and the family to both hit bottom and thus allow the alcoholic system to collapse. As this process proceeds, the therapist must work with each family member to shift focus away from the identified patient and toward a personal program of recovery. The family members "must disengage from their unhealthy addictive attachment to the alcoholic and focus on themselves" (S. Brown & Lewis, 1995, p. 295). The therapist must work closely with the entire family to help them tolerate the separation of different recovery programs and to support their ongoing involvement in this process.

Families nearly always experience this stage of recovery as a destabilizing time. Once enabling behaviors have been reduced or stopped and the alcoholic or addicted individuals are allowed to hit bottom, the work of the family therapist is to help the family tolerate the stress. The introduction of sobriety into the lifestyle of the family is expected to be positive but rarely is. The therapist now begins the next task, helping the family to develop new coping mechanisms that will better serve them in their new lifestyles.

Alternative Coping Strategies

The next stage in the therapeutic process involves helping the patient and the family tolerate the anxiety that inevitably goes with change. The next stage involves the development of new coping strategies such as enhanced communication skills and dealing with conflict to sustain the therapeutic gains that they have fought so hard to achieve.

One of the first coping skills that the family needs to learn is how to explore and talk about affective material. Although uncovering affective material is an important part of therapy with addicts as with other psychiatric disorders, timing is of the essence with AOD patients. S. Brown and Lewis (1995) explained the importance of timing in the use of psychodynamic concepts in the treatment of addicts and alcoholics. They observed that the uncovering of deep-seated affective material too early in the treatment of alcoholics can often lead to relapse (S. Brown & Lewis, 1995). If too much painful affective material is uncovered, it can trigger overwhelming anxiety and depression for the alcoholic in the early stages of recovery. Because these individuals usually have no coping skills other than the use of alcohol and drugs, they are likely to drink or use drugs to blot out the painful affective experience.

Family members of addicted patients also are often threatened by the emergence of affective material too soon in the therapeutic process. In many instances, alcoholic families have developed rigid boundaries with inflexible rules. These rules typically include prohibitions against speaking about affectively laden material. The family often believes that talking about conflicts could trigger more drinking or drug using by the addicted patient. As the family accommodates itself to the invasion of alcohol (Steinglass et al., 1987), they attempt to completely dampen or suppress affective material. Thus, painful feelings fester beneath the surface for years.

For these reasons, the therapist should uncover affective

material gingerly at first. Inevitably, painful feelings and discussions of traumatic events emerge as the patient and the
family move toward greater recovery. In the early stages of
family therapy, however, the focus is not on an in-depth discussion of traumatic events or deep exploration of affective
material but on how these issues are likely to affect abstinence and the recovery programs of the other family members. The therapist encourages the family to keep on course
and to push ahead with their individual personal programs
of recovery. The emphasis is on the maintenance of therapeutic gains (e.g., abstinence for the patient and a personal
program of recovery for all family members).

Of course, issues of abuse, abandonment, or other painful
affective topics do emerge during family therapy sessions.
The skilled therapist knows how threatened the patient
and family members can become by the emergence of
this material. At the end of a difficult therapy session, the
therapist might state, "I know this has been a difficult
time for family. Sometimes this may trigger cravings or a
desire to use. Let's talk about how we can address these cravings if they should occur." The individuals might sustain
themselves and handle the cravings by increasing the frequency of self-help meetings and sponsor contact. In this
way, self-help meetings and family psychotherapy work in
conjunction with each other to support the family's ongoing
process of recovery. One adolescent patient told the following
story:

> This young man had been dealing with the reality that
> his parents were on the verge of divorce. Even as the
> adolescent was progressing through treatment and get-
> ting sober, the parents were planning to separate. At the
> time of the session, the parents were still living together
> and tension was high at home. The patient was attempt-
> ing to deal with his sadness and frustration over the di-
> vorce by isolating himself in his room. The patient's
> mother, a recovering alcoholic with 10 years of sobriety,
> went to see him in his room and encouraged him to go
> to a meeting. The patient and his mother went to the

meeting together. By talking in the meeting, the patient gained support and came home feeling more relieved and relaxed. Through this simple experience the boy realized for the first time that he could relieve his feelings of sadness and frustration without the use of chemicals. He began to see feelings more like waves that would pass over him rather than like a permanent fixture that needed to be blotted out through pharmacological means. With experiences such as these, it becomes safer to begin exploring affective material in a more meaningful way.

As therapy progresses into later stages, abstinence becomes more secure. The therapist can then begin the work of traditional psychodynamic uncovering because the family no longer views this work as a threat to recovery.

In addition to the uncovering of painful affective material and the working through of traumatic family events, the family psychotherapist can offer other specific skills to family members to help them cope with the stresses of living a sober lifestyle. Many of these interventions, such as communication skills and stress reduction mechanisms, originate from behavioral or learning theory models of family psychotherapy.

O'Farrell (1993) developed BMT, a form of couples therapy that incorporates many of these strategies. In BMT, couples participate in 10 weekly group therapy sessions. During these sessions they learn a variety of skills. Couples engage in pleasing behaviors that enhance their awareness of the benefits that they derive from their relationship. These skills include noticing, which entails having each spouse be responsible for recording a caring behavior of the other spouse each day. Group leaders model acknowledging caring behaviors, and couples are assigned homework sessions to practice acknowledging these behaviors. Later, couples are encouraged to spontaneously initiate caring behaviors. Couples are then encouraged to engage in shared rewarding activities, and these activities are planned and carried out in between group sessions.

In BMT, couples also work on communication skills training. Group leaders teach and model the basic principles of effective communication. Couples practice these communication skills in between group therapy sessions, beginning slowly with 2- to 5-min daily sessions and working up to longer sessions. Through modeling and extensive role playing, they learn techniques of active listening, how to take responsibility for their feelings, and how to use "I" statements. They learn to be direct in their communications and to begin sentences with "What I heard you say was ..."

The couples also learn how to make specific behavior change agreements using positive specific requests as a prerequisite for these behavior change agreements. First, the couple presents the change requests in the group sessions. The group members give them feedback and help in the phrasing of the requests. Both partners specify and agree on behavior changes that they are willing to implement during the following week. Even if one partner does not keep the agreement, the other partner is to continue to fulfill his or her part of the agreement (O'Farrell, 1993, pp. 183–189).

Other programs teach similar behavioral skills to enhance marital satisfaction and decrease the probability that the identified patient will return to drinking or drug use. Noel and McCrady (1993) and Sisson and Azrin (1993) have also developed programs that focus on the learning of communication and stress reduction techniques that help the early-stage recovering person.

Although O'Farrell's (1993) techniques are used in his couples program, many of these techniques can be altered and used in a more traditional individual family psychotherapy setting. The therapist who wishes to work with AOD patients should become familiar with these techniques as a means of enhancing effectiveness with this population. The therapist who is most effective in working with addicted families is generally not locked into one ideological model (e.g., the disease model, social learning model, or psychodynamic model) but knows and uses an assortment of tools to achieve the desired outcome.

Relapse Prevention

The final task of the family therapist who works with AOD patients is to assist the family in formulating and implementing a relapse prevention strategy. On a basic level, a relapse prevention plan addresses how each family member, including the identified patient, intends to address relapse if and when it occurs. On a more complex level, the plan should identify what steps the identified patient and the family members can take to prevent relapse from occurring in the first place. The plan should address not only what to do once the relapse has occurred but also what concrete steps can be undertaken to prevent the relapse.

For the purposes of the plan, the definition of relapse is expanded to include not only the use of psychoactive chemicals by the identified patient but also the return to dysfunctional behaviors by the individual family members. These dysfunctional behaviors signal a regression of the family toward more primitive, dysfunctional coping strategies. For example, after having worked a recovery program successfully for several months, a wife may find herself returning to controlling behaviors such as searching through her husband's car and possessions to find evidence that perhaps he has returned to drinking. These behaviors sometimes reappear at the very point at which the identified patient is beginning to make real therapeutic gains. Many family members feel threatened by these gains, especially when the identified patient begins to behave more autonomously. Perhaps an adolescent girl is beginning to develop new friendships within the recovering community. She wants to go on a weekend camping trip to the mountains. She will go with her new recovering friends, and the trip will be properly supervised by adults. Unfortunately, the parents associate this type of fun with using behaviors and become increasingly suspicious. "Why does she want to go camping? What are they doing out in the woods? Can they be trusted? Will there be girls and boys together?" As they become increasingly suspicious, the parents move to reassert control. They cancel the plans for the camping trip, thus undermining the adolescent's attempts to bond with other recovering peers. The family therapist should identify and address these behaviors as relapse behaviors. Although the fears of the parents must be validated, it is important to identify for the parents how they have allowed their fears to propel them into relapse behavior. In this case, however, relapse is defined not as the use of psychoactive chemicals but as a regression out of recovery and into dysfunctional, controlling behavior patterns.

Thus, the relapse plan needs to begin to focus on the dysfunctional behaviors that often precede relapse for the identified patient and for the family members. Often a good place to start with the relapse prevention plan is to discuss triggers for the identified patient. For adult patients, the most common relapse triggers include negative affect states. For adolescent patients, the most common triggers involve peer interactions. The therapist can assist the patient and family members to identify triggers, the obvious triggers such as returning to old using friends or frequenting places where using occurred, and the unanticipated situations and events. For example, major life changes such as moving to another city or a change of jobs are potential triggers.

A move to another city involves establishing a new support network, a new therapist, and new outside support meetings. These situations involve a large amount of planning. Contacting a new therapist before the move is an important step. Perhaps the family can make contact with existing self-help support groups while visiting the city in advance so that the process of bonding with a new group can begin before the move actually occurs. Changing jobs may mean that the patient's meeting schedule is disrupted. In addition, the new environment may be less conducive to recovery (e.g., coworkers who frequent bars after work). The therapist also should discuss the timing of these changes. Is it wise to undertake a change of jobs early in the recovery process? Probably not.

Some triggers cannot be avoided. These would include serious illnesses or deaths. Although it is impossible to develop specific plans for unforeseen catastrophes, it is often important to mention that they are a possibility and to underscore the necessity of the patient connecting with his or her sponsor, therapists, and other support systems in time of crisis.

In addition to a discussion of triggers, the therapist should openly discuss the nature of cravings and how the patient intends to handle them. Craving is normal for addicts and alcoholics. To deny the existence of craving is to ask the patient to suppress powerful urges and feelings and thus to shut down communication within the family. Although it is scary for family members to hear that the patient is craving, it is an important realization that needs to be acknowledged and validated by the therapist. The relapse plan helps because it gives the therapist and family members specific tasks to do when cravings occur and gives them a sense of mastery over the situation. The patient can call his or her sponsor or can go to a meeting. The family can assist the patient by providing transportation or taking over responsibilities, thus freeing the patient to deal with the cravings in a healthy way.

Another goal of the relapse prevention plan is to specify specific behaviors that the family members can practice that will minimize the possibility of a relapse for each family member. Family members and patients may commit to practicing daily stress reduction techniques such as exercise, meditation, or breathing exercises. The therapist can remind the family members of the new communication patterns that they have developed and incorporate them into the relapse prevention plan.

The therapist should encourage the family to commit to handling troubling new situations and issues by reengaging in the therapeutic process. Frequently sexual issues emerge after some months of sobriety. As these issues emerge, the couple needs to reengage with the therapist to resolve them as part of the relapse plan.

O'Farrell (1993) discovered, after developing a 10-session BMT protocol, that although patients often reported increased marital satisfaction a year later, their rates of relapse did not differ significantly between the BMT group and the control group. After adding a 12-month relapse prevention component to his program, drinking outcomes improved considerably.

O'Farrell's (1993) relapse prevention component consists of 15 couples sessions over the course of a year with a gradually decreasing frequency. There are basically three goals to the relapse prevention component. The first goal is to help the couple maintain the gains achieved in the BMT group during the initial phase of the program. The couple is asked to list the specific goals that were achieved and to examine any problems that might arise with regard to maintaining these goals. The couple is encouraged to develop a written plan that involves specific therapeutic interventions such as continuing with Antabuse, attending AA and Al-Anon meetings, and implementing new coping strategies such as improved communication skills.

A second goal of the relapse prevention phase is to deal with unresolved issues that emerge during the first year of recovery. O'Farrell (1993) noted that often difficulty arises when the identified patient attempts to assume a more assertive or dominant role in the family after having been labeled the "sick" person for so long. Other issues include substance abuse by other family members and sexual issues. Couples are encouraged to apply the communication and coping skills that they were taught during the initial phase of the program.

A third goal of the relapse prevention phase is to develop and rehearse cognitive–behavioral strategies for dealing with relapse. The strategies involve a framework or method for discussing relapse, identification of high-risk situations and early warning signs, plans for preventing drinking, and plans for minimizing the intensity and duration of any relapse occurrence. Identified patient and spouse are encouraged to specify what they will do if they encounter high-risk situations and how they will deal with any drinking that might occur.

After the 15 sessions over the course of a year, couples also participate in quarterly follow-up visits either in the clinic or at home for an additional 18 months. As stated previously, the outcomes regarding drinking were significantly improved and marital satisfaction remained high after the implementation of the relapse prevention plan. O'Farrell's

(1993) program is an example of one specific relapse prevention plan or program within the context of family or couples therapy. More general discussions of relapse prevention and relapse plans can be found in Marlatt and Gordon (1985) and Gorski (1989).

Although a formal relapse prevention plan including contracts and agreements is an essential component of the relapse prevention process, the therapist's attitude and skill in keeping the family focused around sobriety and recovery-related issues is of paramount importance in helping to prevent relapse. Good psychotherapy with AOD patients, whether in a family, individual, or group context, involves a focus on recovery alternating with a focus on interpersonal and psychodynamic issues. S. Brown (1985) described this process of shifting between an alcohol–drug–recovery focus and a psychodynamic or cognitive–behavioral focus as "cyclotherapy" (p. 271).

The question that beginning therapists ask is "When is it safe to shift to a psychodynamic or interpersonally oriented focus and move away from the abstinence or recovery focus?" The answer is never. The skilled therapist who works with AOD patients realizes that relapse behavior can be and often is just on the horizon regardless of the length of sobriety achieved by the patient. As painful affective material is uncovered, the risk of relapse, or at least craving, increases.

The patient views such questions as "So how are things with your recovery program?" as a sign of caring and an indication that the therapist is sensitive to the ever-present daily struggle with sobriety. Returning to this line of questioning periodically is always a good idea. Staying in touch with the patient's recovery focus allows the therapist to be sensitive to the ebb and flow of the patient's inner process. It helps to remind patients that they need to maintain this same sensitivity. Of all the specific relapse prevention skills that a therapist can bring to the process, this focus is perhaps the most important. Although the tasks discussed in this chapter are common to all forms of family therapy, they are altered and enriched by an understanding of addiction-related dynamics.

Conclusion

Family therapy techniques have added a new richness and depth to the treatment of substance-abusing patients. For years clinicians have stated that returning addicts to dysfunctional families sets them up for relapse. Although they acknowledged the importance of family dynamics for several decades, it was not until the family therapy movement became popular in the 1980s that family therapists developed the structured family therapy programs that support and reinforce this view. Since then, substantial research indicates that family therapy enhances treatment outcomes in terms of both sobriety and overall life satisfaction for addicts and family members.

8

Group Therapy and Self-Help Groups

Group treatment and other activities such as self-help group participation are viewed by most addiction treatment practitioners as being the primary element in treatment. This practice arose for historical reasons, such as the heritage from Alcoholics Anonymous (AA) and from the therapeutic community model, in which the group or the community is the agent of change. In many addiction treatment settings, individual sessions are seen as unnecessary or potentially detrimental if they undermine attachment to key reference groups. For example, individual therapists sometimes minimize the importance of self-help group participation and concentrate dependency on themselves. Our clinical experience indicates that connection to a subculture that supports recovery is important to produce enduring gains. Although individual psychotherapy work has an important place, it is essential for the therapist to understand the significance and purpose of group activities and be prepared to facilitate participation if not conduct such activities themselves. The existence of well-developed group interventions has permitted the addiction treatment system to handle greater numbers of clients than would be the case if individual sessions were the norm. Indeed, this feature has allowed practitioners to negotiate for extended lengths of stay in outpatient treatment in some managed care and health maintenance organizations, obtaining a duration of treatment more likely to produce positive outcomes.

An important factor in the wide acceptance of group activities is the recognition that a culture that promotes recovery is an essential element in successful outcome. Although the concept of the community as the change agent is perhaps best articulated by therapeutic community proponents (De Leon, 1994a, 1994b), similar elements are evident in self-help groups, recovery groups, and other affiliative activities. Yalom (1995) and Vannicelli (1992) enumerated the therapeutic factors that also are common to other group activities: reducing the sense of isolation, instilling hope, acquiring information, learning by watching others, learning socializing techniques, altering distorted self-concepts, and having an opportunity for a reparative family experience. These forces operate both in treatment and in self-help groups, and the treatment outcome literature suggests that long-term immersion is associated with a positive outcome (De Leon, 1993; Gerstein & Harwood, 1990).

In this chapter we describe various forms of groups in addiction treatment, discussing their commonalties and differences. We also explore some of the controversial areas of group work, such as phase models and the role of confrontation. We do not provide a comprehensive overview of all aspects of group functioning but instead select certain issues that are routinely discussed in case conferences and supervision (see Flores, 1988; Khantzian et al., 1990; Vannicelli, 1992; and Washton, 1992, for more comprehensive coverage). We offer recommendations for facilitating the use of self-help groups and describe a process for creating a network of concerned others who can support an individual's recovery process.

Groups Led by Professionals

A variety of professionally led groups are available for people in and out of addiction treatment. These include motivational enhancement groups, recovery groups, network therapy, and harm reduction groups. We review them from the perspective of the stages of recovery, looking at how they facilitate addressing the tasks of the patient. Newer group activities outside abstinence-oriented models also are described.

Motivational Enhancement Strategies

As it becomes more widely appreciated that untreated alcohol and other drug (AOD) use is expensive, activities designed to enhance motivation are becoming more common. As described in chapter 3, it is possible to identify patient position along a continuum of readiness for change and design interventions accordingly (Prochaska, DiClemente, & Norcross, 1992). Programs geared for compliant patients willing to commit to action about their AOD use are taking a second look as they come to recognize the high cost of untreated AOD users in the larger health care system. For example, some treatment programs within health maintenance organizations have extensive requirements for participation and may rapidly discharge those unable or unwilling to meet program expectations. Washton (1995b) analyzed the difficulty as a mismatch between the program and what the client is willing to accept. The client is at fault (e.g., "unmotivated, not ready yet"). Reliance on the denial concept to describe client behavior allows clinicians to justify hostile and rejecting behavior that promotes dropout rather than encouraging them to analyze what happened to alienate the client. Washton reframed the task as assessing the client's readiness for change and strengthening the commitment to change.

It is becoming apparent that those who refuse treatment or who drop out early go on to use more costly medical services, as do their family members (McLellan, Metzger, et al., 1995). Thus, increasing attention is being paid to equipping practitioners who have a relationship with the patient (e.g., primary care physician, therapist) to prepare the patient to address AOD use. In this context, group activities for the skeptical or unwilling are becoming more common. These groups are referred to in a variety of ways: transition groups, early intervention groups, pretreatment groups, or step zero groups (Washton & Stone-Washton, 1991). Their purpose is to provide an opportunity for patients to explore their concerns without pressure to label themselves or commit to action on the program's timetable. As Washton and Stone-Washton described it, such groups provide an arena for patients to take a closer look at their relationship with whatever mood-altering substances or behaviors are causing them trouble or inconvenience. It is a common clinical trap to attempt to convince the patient that he or she is an addict or alcoholic as a means of securing an abstinence commitment; however, this is by no means necessary to begin (W. R. Miller & Page, 1991; W. R. Miller & Rollnick, 1991; Zweben, 1989). In these groups, participants take a new look at their situation, work on achieving greater clarity, explore convictions that change is not possible for them, build a vision of an alternative lifestyle, and take action. In later work, they will have to address the issues that emerge with abstinence, typically a theme of recovery groups. Washton recommended a duration of 8–12 sessions, to remain a catalyst for movement, rather than a substitute.

Recovery Groups

We use the term *recovery groups* to describe the wide variety of abstinence-oriented forms of group therapy that can be found both in institutional and private practice settings. We consider how basic principles of group psychotherapy are adapted to meet the needs of AOD-using patients. We do not attempt to provide a comprehensive overview of group therapy but focus instead on issues specific to AOD-using patients. We initially assume abstinence-based treatment models and then discuss harm reduction groups that are not primarily abstinence based.

Phase models. Larger programs have the option of offering phase models, in which participants are grouped according to stages of recovery. For example, the program may offer transition groups for those who are actively using and are on a waiting list for treatment; Phase 1 groups for those in the process of establishing abstinence; and Phase 2 groups for those in later stages of recovery. This stratification offers the advantage of composing groups of individuals struggling with similar issues and of providing tangible markers of progress as individuals complete a phase. The groups themselves can be ongoing, with patients leaving and joining according to specific program criteria. For example, a patient can graduate from Phase 1 after reaching 90 days of continuous abstinence and attending a prescribed number of education groups and self-help meetings. A Phase 1 group typically focuses on strategies for achieving abstinence and exploring other issues in a focused manner as related to that goal. Later-stage recovery groups deal with a wider range of issues in more depth, as required by the recovery tasks of such stages: repairing interpersonal relationships and forming new ones, working to resolve trauma issues, learning new ways of managing stress, and so on. Although relapse issues certainly arise, the Phase 2 group as a whole does not focus primarily on AOD use but on broader issues. Although phase programs have their advocates, a significant disadvantage is resistance of members to leaving a group with which they have bonded. Given that this cohesion and bonding is a powerful force for change, it is appropriate to ask whether the trade-offs of phase programs are worth the disruption, particularly for members who do not easily adapt to new groups.

Mixed-phase group models are more feasible for the private practitioner or small program. In a mixed-group model, the group can be open-ended, and members arrive when there is an opening and terminate according to goals in their individual treatment plans (i.e., they stay as long as participating is productive). Group members in early recovery are exposed to role models of other members with longer term sobriety. Members with sustained abstinence report it is useful to be reminded of the life circumstances of someone who is struggling with using, particularly if this period of their lives seems so remote that they become overconfident and begin taking risks. No matter how long the period of sustained abstinence, the issues of someone who has relapsed are similar to those of the newcomer, with variations depending on the severity of the regression evident in the relapse pattern. Also, people in recovery move at such different tempos it is difficult to select any particular marker and obtain homogeneity on an issue. Two people, each with a year's sobriety, may have much different levels of personal and life-style transformation.

Inasmuch as there is no empirical evidence that either model is superior to the other, considerations are largely practical: what best meets the needs of the patient population and is possible within the treatment setting.

Screening and orientation. An interview before placing an individual in group is used to assess appropriateness for group, to elicit the prospective patient's concerns and hopes, and to orient him or her to expectations and requirements. Individuals who are still actively using may exhibit such sporadic attendance at other treatment activities that it is doubtful he or she is ready to maintain consistent participation in recovery group. Indeed, this is one of the most difficult issues. Dropout from substance abuse treatment is greatest in the first 30 days, and new group members who attend several sessions and disappear have a demoralizing effect on a group. On the other hand, it is often the support of savvy group members that facilitates establishing abstinence. In the screening process, the group leader should attempt to determine whether the prospective member is capable of consistent attendance. If not, transition groups (in which there is no expectation of stable composition) or individual work can help stabilize a patient and create readiness for other activities.

The screening interview also is the place to review the specifics of the individual's treatment plan and orient him or her about how to use group to achieve personal goals. For example, a woman whose ability to remain abstinent is undermined by her partner's drug use can be encouraged to use the group as a laboratory for practicing assertion. New members may see the group mainly as a place to obtain help by getting feedback on the content of their issues and may not be aware of other advantages offered by the group format. It also is common for patients to be concerned about being subjected to aggressive confrontation (discussed later in this chapter). The group leader can then reassure the prospective member that the leaders work to ensure that there is a healthy feedback process that is not assaultive.

Another important issue to clarify in screening is how the group process in 12-step programs is different from recovery group. Patients who are active in 12-step programs can be a great asset in recovery groups, particularly if they are actively working the steps. The group leader, however, needs to clarify the distinctions between recovery groups and 12-step meetings. The most important distinction is that the "no cross-talk" rule (i.e., no feedback or interactive discussion by others in the meeting) does not apply to therapy groups; in fact, the feedback process, guided by the leader, is one of the great benefits of a professionally led group. There are other differences, such as the expectation of regular attendance and active participation (discussed further later in this chapter). Prospective members should be helped to see professional groups as being complementary to 12-step groups, not substitutes.

The abstinence commitment. It is important that group members have a common understanding that the goal of treatment is abstinence from all intoxicants. Group members can struggle for many months to achieve abstinence and be highly ambivalent about this goal, but if the patient is truly uncommitted to abstinence for extended periods of time, there will be a negative impact on other group members. Resistance and ambivalence should be viewed as the focus of the clinician's work, just as it is with other issues. It is widely accepted among addiction specialists that there is a population in the community who is able to stop using alcohol, tobacco, and illicit drugs with no intervention from professionals. Professionals working in treatment settings see a subgroup that, for a variety of reasons, finds it difficult to stop without help. Resistance and ambivalence are a given. Professionals are there to help people deal with their inner and outer obstacles, but there must be a fundamental understanding of the importance of complete abstinence as the goal of treatment. This can be a difficult matter to determine, particularly if the therapist is committed to encouraging the patient to verbalize ambivalence openly. A patient who is floundering but showing signs of progress is different from one who continues to attend but shows no signs of change:

> Janice came to recovery group having recognized that her long period of dependence on a variety of prescription drugs was becoming hazardous as her use of them escalated. Frightened by recent events, she openly and insightfully grappled with her ambivalence about considering herself an addict. She successfully eliminated the regular use of opioids (obtained for pain) and benzodiazepines (for anxiety) but refused to consider eliminating alcohol ("I don't drink regularly, and it's not my preferred drug anyway") and used the opioids and benzodiazepines episodically. Her psychotropic medication could be better fine tuned in the absence of regular drug use, she felt better, and her life had more stability. As this occurred, she realized that improvement made it easier for her to downplay the seriousness of her addictive behavior. Group members had varying reactions to her ambivalence, as she verbalized familiar thought patterns that they recognized in themselves and found threatening. Many productive discussions ensued.

If the group is working productively, the members will zero in on this issue and often read it more accurately than a nonrecovering professional. At that point, the leader can decide (with input from group members) to remove the individual from the group and work individually until commitment to common goals is more dependable. In the previous example, the group members considered Janice an integral part of the group and were clear that they did not want her to leave despite the apprehension evoked by many of the group discussions of her issues.

Group structure. Many therapists prefer that group members meet only for therapeutic purposes and discourage contact at other times. This is impractical with AOD-using populations. Members have often had previous or current contact in settings where they drank and used drugs, at work sites,

Exhibit 1

Group Rules and Expectations

Our groups are one of the most lively and powerful parts of our program, but to keep them working well, we ask certain commitments:

1) Come on time.

2) Do not come intoxicated.

3) Notify your group leader if you will be absent or you know you will be late. Other group members are usually concerned about those missing.

4) Keep the identities of the members in strictest confidence. You can share anything you like about what *you* experience in the group, but not about others.

5) Be open to looking at yourself and your behavior and to giving and receiving feedback. It is especially important to discuss any alcohol or drug use in the group.

6) Although contact with other group members outside group can be beneficial, please do not become involved in *any* relationship outside group that would interfere with your ability to be honest and explore issues in the group. Romantic or sexual relationships with other group members is an obvious example but not the only type of relationship that can be an impediment.

7) A minimum of 3 months' participation is needed to learn to use the group, more to receive full benefits. Please give 1 month's notice if you plan to terminate the group.

8) There is a list of group members' names and telephone numbers because we think you are an important support system for one another. This list must be kept strictly confidential.

I give/do *not* give (circle one) permission to have my name on the group list given to members. (First names only on the list.)

I have read and agree to the above rules and guidelines:

Name:_____ Date:_____

Note. From Joan E. Zweben. This form can be used or reproduced without permission from the publisher or the authors. For republication, a source citation is appreciated.

in homeless shelters, treatment programs, and self-help meetings. The norms of the latter are for members to provide ongoing help to one another outside meeting times, and a therapist's attempt to discourage such contact is likely to be viewed with surprise and skepticism. It is more useful to review the hazards of such contacts and create a climate in which relationships outside the group are discussed freely in the group. Exhibit 1, Group Rules and Expectations, provides an example that can be used or adapted for particular settings.

This handout can be modified to cover fee issues and other program requirements. Prospective group members can be given the handout at screening and asked to sign it when they commit to joining the group.

It is useful to have an initial check-in process that explicitly refers to the patient's status with respect to AOD use. Check-in is a process that allows both leaders and members to hear briefly from each person about the significant events in their week, and allows members to explicitly ask for time to discuss a specific issue. It provides an overview of issues and encourages more reticent members to participate. In a recovery group, check-in should include a statement about whether there has been any alcohol or drug use (including prescription drug misuse) since the last session. Like the statement "I am an addict or alcoholic" in 12-step meetings, this is an opportunity to disclose and is a process that disrupts denial. Although some patients will lie, this structure creates a confrontation with the self over behavior that otherwise may be minimized more easily. Ries (1996), who dealt with severely mentally ill substance-abusing clients, also added the following elements: "when I last was offered a drug," "when I last offered someone else a drug," "my psychiatric diagnosis," and "the medication I am on." This addresses the tendency toward denial in the area of the patient's mental illness and reveals other significant issues in the person's life situation.

Confrontation. Substance abuse treatment is widely viewed as favoring aggressive confrontation. In this practice, challenging comments are given with the intent of heightening awareness and disrupting complacency. This practice originated in Synanon, which at the time it was launched offered the only effective intervention for heroin addiction. The founder, Charles Dederich, viewed addicts as having a "character armor" that had to be penetrated to launch a meaningful change process (Deitch & Zweben, 1981). Individuals emerging from Synanon formed the leadership in proliferating therapeutic communities and to some extent in developing the 28-day inpatient hospital programs.

In some programs, harsh confrontation was promoted as a dominant feature, which we would argue created more casualties than successes. In addition, the successes occurred despite this practice because of the presence of other positive elements. The practice was perpetuated by the fact that in the early days, programs were staffed by recovering people with no clinical training, so there were few alternatives available to the counselors, many of whom were troubled by the practice. By the mid-1970s, alternative interventions were being taught in addiction treatment programs, but the stereotype has persisted and is defended by some. De Leon noted that follow-up research indicates therapeutic community clients view confrontation groups as perhaps the most significant treatment component in the therapeutic community. He summarized current objectives with respect to this dimension as follows: "confrontation, properly implemented and balanced by other elements such as support, responsible concern and affirmation, is a useful element of group and individual therapy, at least for certain subgroups of clients and at particular stages of recovery" (De Leon, personal communication, July 25, 1997).

Clinical supervisors should keep in mind that many counselors who wish to renounce harsh practices nonetheless repeat them because their early models and experiences have become so ingrained. Both didactic and experiential (e.g., role-playing alternatives) are necessary to move counselors beyond reliance on the "tough" style. Individuals exposed to this in the course of their treatment attempts may be decidedly reluctant to enter groups. It is important that the therapist respect their concerns and be vigilant to foster a feedback process that is forthright without being assaultive. Those supervising noncredentialed staff should be aware that basic clinical skills such as active listening and skilled inquiry go a long way toward reducing reliance on heavy confrontation. Motivational interviewing techniques (see chap. 6 in this book) have been enthusiastically welcomed by counselors in need of a broader repertoire.

Dealing with the intoxicated patient. A member who comes to group intoxicated can provide a difficult challenge for the therapist, particularly if the patient's state is not apparent until after the group is under way. Such members are often unable to follow what is going on in the group, interrupt impulsively, launch conversations while others are talking, and in some cases threaten violence if confronted. If the intoxication is clear at the outset, the patient can be sent home, with provisions made for traveling safely if needed. If the question emerges during the group, the therapist can comment on specific behaviors that are inappropriate and suggest that the patient take a break for a few minutes and return when able to exercise restraint. Although some clinicians take the position that intoxicated individuals should be immediately removed from group, a rigid policy has its disadvantages, particularly if there is no immediate way to verify intoxication. The therapist can base that decision on the patient's ability to cease being disruptive and can ask the patient to be an observer (the practice in AA meetings) and not speak up during that particular session. Because newcomers are more likely to have problems abstaining, this approach is less likely to exacerbate shame and create obstacles to returning to group.

A most difficult problem is the faint smell of alcohol in the room. It is unwise to avoid mention of this, as others may have noticed and the leader should not model ignoring an issue that is obvious. Also, recovering individuals are much more sensitive to the signs of intoxication than nonrecovering therapists. It is useful to introduce the issue by commenting on a faint smell that could be alcohol and asking for group members' reactions. "Proving" the existence of a smell is usually impossible, but even in the event that no others detect such an odor, a discussion of whether members would comment openly if they had suspicions is productive for clarifying work norms in the group. Members often worry about "being right" or being too intrusive; hence, it is necessary to emphasize the value of open discussion of topics usually taboo.

The patient in individual therapy. Several possible arrangements occur for combined individual and group therapy. The patient in an addiction treatment program may participate in both if the resources of the program permit. For example, patients in methadone programs are often required by regulation and clinic policy to participate in individual counseling and attend groups as well. Some therapeutic communities also include individual sessions, particularly for those with severe psychiatric conditions. Managed care organizations are often unenthusiastic about providing individual sessions within addiction programs, so insured populations usually have to pay out of pocket if such service is desired. It is not unusual to find individual therapists in the community sending patients to recovery groups by specialist practitioners or addiction treatment programs, as the following vignette illustrates:

> Jerry was referred to recovery group for crack-cocaine use by his psychodynamically oriented individual therapist. He had recently remarried, and at age 45 was eager to break out of his decades-long, highly destructive pattern of binge use. Sexual concerns and activities were a key element in his cocaine use. The therapists remained in regular communication, as Jerry's gradually lengthening periods of sobriety continued to be followed by 3- to 4-day cocaine binges. Discussion of his sexual issues provoked great anxiety and stimulated urges to use cocaine but could not be avoided because of the salience of this issue as a trigger in the absence of discussion. He explored this issue first in individual therapy and was encouraged to bring it to group. On other occasions, the group members appeared to be the lesser threat. After a relapse, he would sometimes find it easier to overcome his shame with group members who shared his addictive

problems and thus find his way back to his individual therapist.

Therapist collaboration was a key element in retaining this man in both forms of treatment and gradually making progress. Such collaboration requires bridging the gap between practitioners of differing orientations and establishing an understanding about communication in routine as well as urgent situations.

Network Therapy

Network therapy is an approach that addresses the all-important task of developing a support system to promote recovery. Formulated by Galanter (1993, 1994), a physician specializing in addiction medicine, it brings together family members and relevant significant others in a team and coaches them on how to help the patient achieve abstinence and a satisfying drug-free adaptation. It gathers those who are part of the patient's natural support system and guides their activity so they can be effective in promoting treatment goals. In contrast to participants in couples' or family therapy, members of the network are not the focus of treatment and are not invited to use network meetings to work toward goals for themselves. Similarly, exploring past or current areas of conflict is avoided as potentially disruptive to the main task. The therapist functions as a coach to keep the team focused. Galanter (1993) offered the following recommendations for forming and working with the network:

1. Select significant others who are trusted and have a long-standing relationship with the patient.
2. Avoid active AOD users because they are often ambivalent and unreliable.
3. Avoid superiors and subordinates at work because their interests may potentially conflict.
4. Select for balance in age, gender, and type of relationship.
5. Promote a focus on areas of necessary cooperation;

avoid areas of conflict and other sources of negative exchanges.

6. Schedule meetings as frequently as necessary to facilitate achieving abstinence and as often as needed after that to accomplish specific goals (e.g., relapse prevention).

Specific agenda items for network discussion can include securing a stable and drug-free residence, avoidance of substance-using friends, compliance with medication regimens (e.g., Antabuse, psychotropic medication), attendance at self-help programs, and any other items relevant to the individual. There should be a common understanding that network members will contact the therapist at any time they feel the patient is vulnerable to relapse, and the therapist can summon network members as well. Thus, this approach has the potential to accelerate the development of a healthy support system and fill in the gaps felt by the private practitioner working with addicted patients on an outpatient basis.

Harm Reduction Group Activities

Public health concerns, intensified by the AIDS epidemic, has brought increasing attention to harm reduction strategies. The term *harm reduction* is defined as "a set of strategies that encourage substance users and service providers to reduce the harm done to drug users, their loved ones and communities by their licit and illicit drug use" (Harm Reduction Working Group and Coalition, 1995, p. 2). This approach begins from the position that abstinence should not be the only objective of services to drug users because it excludes a large proportion of the people who are involved in long-term drug use. Although abstinence is envisioned as a possibility and for some a final goal, commitment to it is not a prerequisite for participating in activities or obtaining services. Proponents note the alienation that occurs when users seek help from abstinence-oriented programs and stress the importance of creating alternatives. In their view, the most effective way of getting people to minimize the harmful effects of their drug use is to provide user-friendly services that encourage contact and empower them to change their behavior toward a suitable intermediate objective. This approach is increasingly used to address HIV issues in community settings, particularly because treatment capacity is inadequate even when individuals are motivated to pursue it and other approaches have been documented to have a beneficial public health impact (Rhodes, 1993; Weibel, 1993).

These groups usually use a psychoeducational model, in which information is shared and participants have an opportunity to explore issues. They focus on increasing safety in a variety of ways, such as identifying the dangers of particular use patterns (e.g., sharing needles) or sexual practices. Participants list their own hazardous behaviors and discuss ways to reduce their risk. The educational component covers ways in which using alcohol and drugs increases vulnerability to victimization through violence, participating in unsafe sex, accidents, and acting out negative moods (e.g., exacerbating depression). They address how to reduce HIV transmission by using clean needles and practicing safer sex. Reducing the frequency and amount of drugs used is a valid safety strategy, as is attention to using in safe environments.

There are other examples of harm reduction strategies, either as an end in themselves or as a stepping stone to an abstinence-oriented treatment. Ries (1996) described an outpatient program for mentally ill chemical abusers in which the prephase component of the program offers groups illustrating harm reduction principles. Patients in this component are relatively unengaged in treatment and are unstable in either their behavioral or substance abuse disorder. They are not ready for interactive groups or many structured activities. However, on referral from their case manager, they may attend "Club Med," a 1-hr morning group that meets daily, in which they receive coffee and snacks and take their medication in front of a staff member. At the end of the session, they receive a small amount of spending money. The group encourages routine daily activity, promotes medication compliance, and provides a structure to budget funds on a daily basis (and reduces the amount available at one time to spend on drugs). This low-demand group activity begins to stabilize patients and prepare them to take advantage of other treatment opportunities.

Self-Help Groups

Self-help group participation is widely viewed as a key element in successful recovery because it provides several essential ingredients. These groups provide access to a culture that supports the recovery process from which participants can begin to rebuild social networks that are not organized around AOD use. They also offer a process for personal development that has no financial barriers. The rapid proliferation and wide variety of groups makes it possible to find a good match within most urban communities and many rural ones. We review some of the basic characteristics of self-help groups and suggest strategies for fostering effective use.

Self-help groups usually strive to maintain the least amount of hierarchy and structure necessary for smooth functioning and the safety of participants. They generally emphasize the voluntary nature of participation (e.g., "a program of attraction") and tolerate a wide range of commitment and participation. Some confusion is evident among professionals and the public about the similarities and differences between self-help groups and treatment, especially when there are close links between them. For example, 12-step programs are different from treatment programs based on 12-step principles; however, these distinctions are sometimes unclear in discussion and in the literature.

There are important differences between self-help groups and professional treatment, with each having strengths and limits. At their best, self-help groups offer a powerful sense of belonging (exemplified by the term *fellowship*) that generates hope and enthusiasm, in addition to the beneficial effects of the activities offered. Meetings or members may be available any time of the day or night and provide forms of support not possible outside of residential or inpatient treatment. Professional treatment offers the possibility of much greater accountability and structure. It is possible to track whether and how well individuals participate in a treatment plan usually formulated by an interdisciplinary team. Although various procedures have been devised to monitor attendance at self-help meetings, by the very nature of such meetings there is minimal or no formal hierarchy; hence, there is no objective means of holding the patient accountable. Treatment programs, employers, and probation officers can mandate attendance, but this gives a false sense of accountability that is in some ways worse than none at all. In addition, many meetings have been disrupted by the negative behavior of those mandated to attend.

If a patient becomes involved with a self-help group, the therapist will see evidence of learning and application of new concepts. Reliable monitoring is usually not possible; hence, the therapist is better off investing effort elsewhere. Although self-help groups have a definite structure, they do not necessarily accomplish what the therapist may need at a particular point in time. For example, anyone attending regularly will learn a great deal about alcohol and drugs and about the process of recovery. However, they will not get the kind of systematic presentation that allows the clinician and patient to arrive at a meaningful treatment plan on an appropriate time schedule. Family members beginning to attend Al-Anon may go to an entire meeting and never hear the word *alcohol*, although over time they will learn a great deal about alcoholism and be exposed to many coping strategies. Thus, the clinician hoping to build a foundation quickly needs to fill these gaps with other treatment activities, such as education classes. The combination is particularly powerful because a basic conceptual framework usually enables participants to derive much more benefit from self-help meetings.

The clinician's role is to facilitate self-help participation through encouragement, sharing information, and exploring resistance. Attitudes and feelings about attendance are a mirror of feelings about being addicted or in recovery. Focus on the nature of the patient's resistance clarifies the obstacles to attendance. Eliciting the patient's picture of what goes on in meetings often reveals areas of misinformation as well as charged issues. For example, being exposed to others in the group situation challenges denial and intensifies the shame many feel about their addiction. A common initial resistance is "I'm afraid someone will recognize me." Thus, meeting attendance is often a perfect metaphor to talk about these other issues. It is useful to stress that resistance or ambivalence does not preclude benefit. In AA lore, "Bring the body, the mind will follow." It is common for patients to report that it took great effort to overcome the desire to stay home, but once present they felt better during or after the meeting even when they disliked being there. Thus, the therapist seeks a balance of focus between feelings and behavior, understanding that action that is less than wholehearted nonetheless produces benefits.

Practical supports also are important. Stranger anxiety is certainly a major obstacle, and many participate enthusiastically once they have found a group in which they feel at home. Therapist encouragement and facilitation by connecting the patient with others who attend can go a long way to help surmount this obstacle. The camaraderie (as reflected in the term *fellowship*) that ultimately becomes a powerful force for change can be a deterrent at the outset for those who are shy, sensitive about being rejected, or sensitive about being the outsider. Firm encouragement to "give it a fair try" and coaching about how to make use of the process often results in a connection that greatly augments the treatment process. As S. Brown (1996) noted in response to a query about what to do when a patient says "I don't want to go": "I never met *anyone* who wanted to go to an AA meeting. But I've met hundreds who managed to find a way to make use of AA."

12-Step Programs

"Twelve-step programs" is the generic name for the many descendants of AA, which formulated the principles and traditions on which these groups are based. Founded in 1935, these groups, 96,000 worldwide, now constitute the largest self-help system in the world (Alcoholics Anonymous, 1996), and for this reason they are a major staple of addiction treatment. In the most recent survey (Alcoholics Anonymous, 1996), members indicated the major factors responsible for them coming to AA were self-motivation, other AA members, treatment facility, and family influences, in that order. More than 60% of respondents received some type of treatment or counseling, and, of this group, 77% said it played an important part in directing them to AA. After coming to AA, 62% of the members received some type of treatment, and 85% said it played an important part in their recovery. These results suggest that the partnership between AA and treatment is improving and that the negative attitudes toward professional treatment, including psychotherapy, are diminishing. However, it is important for therapists to understand that a long history of professionals failing to appropriately address alcoholism and addiction left a legacy of deep mistrust that is, unfortunately, often well founded. The situation improves steadily as more and more professionals become proficient at handling addiction issues and more and more 12-step program members recognize the value of addressing their coexisting disorders through psychotherapy, medication, and other professional services.

Twelve-step programs have a group process that shares some characteristics with therapy groups and has some important differences. It is useful to consider the strengths and limits of each approach. The policy of "no cross-talk" emphasizes that helping occurs through learning from the experiences of others and is widely viewed as a safety feature important in a leaderless group. Participants are not to inquire, confront, or otherwise disrupt another's "share." This fosters an atmosphere of acceptance and offers some protection against aggressive interrogation and other forms of invasiveness. Therapists are typically troubled by the fact that a person in great distress may not receive an immediate response, but usually support is offered once the meeting is over. The constraint on confrontation also may make it difficult to control members whose behavior is disruptive. However, the "no cross-talk" feature is widely viewed by members as providing protection and wide latitude to progress at their own pace. The therapy group, by contrast, offers the benefits of interaction and feedback under the guidance of a trained leader. When 12-step program members come to therapy groups, they may need assistance in distinguishing between the norms of the meetings and those of the therapy group, and the leader's job is to keep the process productive. Some are so conditioned to avoid comment on what others say that they do not engage in the kinds of interaction that makes therapy groups useful.

Patients and therapists often wonder which 12-step program would be best: AA, Narcotics Anonymous, or some other variant. In general, it is useful to pick a place to begin, looking for meetings composed of people from a similar socioeconomic group in the neighborhood of home or work. For those starting out, however, there is an advantage to selecting a group organized around their drug of choice (e.g., Cocaine Anonymous, Marijuana Anonymous). Rapid engagement is useful, and patients report being able to identify more readily when they hear "their story" in meetings. They can and should be encouraged to "shop" until they find a "home" meeting, one in which they feel comfortable and are willing to return regularly. Once they select one or more of such meetings, they can begin to use them to develop social relationships, increasing understanding and support for the process of recovery, and building a support system that is compatible with a satisfying abstinent lifestyle.

Initial resistance frequently centers on the first step, "We admitted we were powerless over alcohol—that our lives had become unmanageable." Members of various disempowered groups, such as women and minorities, find the concepts of admitting powerlessness and surrender to be painfully close to their ongoing life experience and do not see its relevance to healing. The empowering feature of this concept is usually better appreciated after a period of abstinence. The therapist working with this early form of resistance can reframe the issue, emphasizing how the patient gains control over his or her life by abandoning efforts to engage in controlled alcohol and drug use. Many patients report that relinquishing the struggle to control AOD use frees enormous energy to devote to other things.

Selecting a sponsor is a key element in successful engagement and fruitful participation. A sponsor is an experienced, recovering member who acts as an advisor, guide, or teacher on how to work a program of recovery (Alcoholics Anonymous, 1983). Although there are no formal rules for selecting a sponsor, newcomers are encouraged to find someone with a year or more of sobriety who "has something you want." It should be someone who appears to be enjoying sobriety and is not an object of sexual or other interest that would detract from the primary purpose of the relationship. Sponsors can be short or long term; members are encouraged to change them as their needs evolve in recovery. For the therapist, the sponsor relationship can provide a challenge, especially if the sponsor disparages professional treatment. S. Brown (1985) described ways in which therapists and sponsors can develop difficult conflicts and made recommendations for a productive partnership in which AA involvement, in all its aspects, is complementary to psychotherapy.

Discomfort with the spiritual component is a common form of resistance that can often be reduced by exploration and providing information. Inquiry into how the patient understands the spiritual focus often yields misconceptions; it is intended to be a nondenominational element, with participants identifying their own "Higher Power" wherever they find it (Alcoholics Anonymous, 1976). In some regions of the country, groups tend to reflect the religious affiliation of that region (e.g., Christian fundamentalist), and churches, where meetings are often held, may be uncomfortable for some. However, many communities have meetings available in hospitals, community centers, mental health centers, and other settings.

On a psychodynamic level, several experiences can contribute to discomfort with the spiritual dimension. Negative experiences with institutionalized religion in childhood is a common source of resistance. Another is the projection of harsh, punitive features onto God or the Higher Power, which is then seen as a force to be avoided. Self-esteem issues, such as "I don't deserve anything good," also may be involved. All these issues are amenable to modification. In addition, reminders to "Take what you need and leave the rest" can encourage patients to select what is useful, use therapy to air their negative feelings and otherwise avoid dwelling on elements they dislike.

Newer Self-Help Groups

A variety of discomforts and objections have led to the development of other self-help groups, offering an advantage for clinicians working with those unable to make a 12-step connection. The sheer number and variety of 12-step meetings is an asset; however, there are many who do not use this system and seek alternatives. The clinician encouraging this path should remain mindful of the need for a readily available support structure. If the patient selects a self-help group that meets only once a week, other activities will be needed to fill the gaps. Rational Recovery (RR) is a program based on rational–emotive therapy, originally developed by Albert Ellis, and adapted for alcoholics by Jack Trimpey (Trimpey, 1988). Addictive voice recognition techniques, the self-examination of irrational beliefs, permits mastery of vulnerabilities to drinking and using. These compulsive thoughts are termed *The Beast*. Members use a "sobriety spreadsheet," on which they list the irrational thoughts that activate the desire to drink or use. An RR coordinator leads the groups, which meet once or twice a week for 90 min. Each coordinator maintains contact with a mental health professional, a person familiar with RR who serves as an advisor. Meetings are interactive, but supportive exchanges and phone calls between meetings are not encouraged (Galanter & Jaffe, 1995). These meetings appear beneficial to those with an affinity for the cognitive–behavioral orientation. A major limitation is the relative scarcity of groups in most communities, but the organization is young. More groups presumably will continue to form.

Cultural adaptations of 12-step and other self-help group

principles are becoming increasingly common as communities develop their own variations and invigorate them with new rituals. Reverend Cecil Williams, of Glide Methodist Church in San Francisco, has developed a recovery program that he thinks is more compatible with African American cultural values (D. E. Smith, Buxton, Bilal, & Seymour, 1993; Williams, 1992). He offered the Terms of Resistance, repeated at recovery meetings:

Terms of Resistance

1. I will gain control over my life.
2. I will stop lying.
3. I will be honest with myself.
4. I will accept who I am.
5. I will feel my real feelings.
6. I will feel my pain.
7. I will forgive myself and forgive others.
8. I will rebirth a new life.
9. I will live my spirituality.
10. I will support my brothers and sisters.

Glide meetings are magnetic, attracting a wide range of ethnic and cultural groups. Many other activities are offered through the church, making it an excellent example of a vital community that supports recovery.

Therapist Field Trip

Familiarity with self-help meetings in the community increases effectiveness in facilitating participation. Visiting meetings is an excellent way to understand what actually goes on in meetings and increases the ability to neutralize resistance. The following assignment is offered to students and new staff members (see Exhibit 2):

Conclusion

In summary, in this chapter we have described a variety of group activities that facilitate recovery. Therapists primarily

Exhibit 2

Understanding 12-Step Programs and Other Self-Help Groups

A good understanding of 12-step programs (the generic term for all the descendants of AA) is crucial for anyone working in the addiction field. These programs offer a wealth of resources at every stage of the recovery process and have no financial barriers. One of the most important jobs of the therapist or counselor is to help the client make a good connection with these programs and learn to use them effectively. This is a complex task.

To increase your effectiveness, it is important that you have some familiarity with the meetings in your community. Please look up the telephone number of Central Office in your telephone book (you can start with AA) and select 2 meetings in your area. These can be an AA meeting, or Al-Anon, Narcotics Anonymous, Cocaine Anonymous, or anything else you prefer. If you are not in recovery yourself, check to be sure you have selected an open meeting (i.e., people who do not consider themselves addicts or alcoholics can attend). You also can ask for a nonsmoking meeting. If you are not recovering, you can introduce yourself only by first name, or you can give your name and identify yourself as a guest, therapist, or counselor. Within 24 hours of your visit, please make some notes (journal style) on the following issues:

1. What you felt in anticipation of going (avoidances, resistances, etc.).

2. What you felt on arriving, throughout the meeting, and afterward.

3. Your observations on the group process (both the standard rituals, like introductions, and the informal aspects), its advantages and limitations.

Please distinguish between your feelings, observations, and analyses and include all three.

Those who wish to attend Rational Recovery or other self-help groups are encouraged to do so. Staff and students who are in recovery and familiar with meetings should visit a type of meeting they are not familiar with (e.g., Overeaters Anonymous, Sex and Love Addicts Anonymous). This "assignment" typically generates strong feelings and often clarifies attitudes about addiction; hence, a forum for discussion is enormously useful.

Note. From Joan E. Zweben. This handout can be used or reproduced without permission from the publisher or the authors. For republication, a source citation is appreciated.

engaged in doing individual work need to develop an appreciation for the many essential ingredients provided by group activities. Indeed, for the addiction specialist, individual work plays an adjunct role among a variety of treatment settings where patients will find additional comfort, education, and encouragement. The most powerful and enduring forces for change are activities in which peers in the patient's community create an expectation and provide assistance in making the lifestyle transition that is needed to promote recovery. To the extent that the therapist assists in fashioning such a support system, or connecting the patient to an existing support system, treatment effectiveness will be enhanced.

Relapse Prevention

The term *relapse prevention* refers to a set of strategies and specific interventions designed to forestall a resumption of alcohol and other drug (AOD) use. Although often discussed as a separate component, these strategies and interventions are embedded in good treatment. In this chapter we focus on the relapse prevention element, separating it out for purpose of discussion.

Alan Marlatt is regarded as the father of relapse prevention, and he and his colleagues (Marlatt & Gordon, 1985) developed a set of interventions based on the premise that the behaviors necessary to initiate abstinence are different from those needed to maintain it. Before the appearance of Marlatt's work, the possibility of relapse was not a focus of attention, partly because of reluctance to suggest that an individual (or program) might fail. With the advent of a conceptual framework from which intervention strategies flowed, research proliferated and materials were developed for patients with a range of educational levels.

Identifying Relapse Precipitants

The first step was to understand relapse precipitants. Focusing on events that triggered relapse, their research indicated that most precipitants fell into three categories: (a) negative mood states, such as boredom or depression; (b) interpersonal conflict; and (c) social pressure. Other factors (less dominant) include physical discomfort, pleasant emotions or pleasant times with others, testing personal control, and urges or temptations to drink.

Annis and colleagues (Annis, 1982, 1987; Annis & Graham, 1988, 1995; Annis, Graham, & Davis, 1988) have developed the Inventory of Drinking Situations, an instrument designed to identify specific patterns of vulnerability for each patient (i.e., whether the patient has a generalized relapse profile or is susceptible in specific areas). Its 100 items are organized into categories based on Marlatt and Gordon's (1985) classification system. These categories are as follows: unpleasant emotions, testing personal control, urges and temptations, conflict with others, social pressure to drink, and pleasant times with others (Annis & Graham, 1995). This instrument, which can be used as part of an initial workup or during ongoing treatment, has been used to define relapse profiles and identify effective interventions. It allows the therapist to prioritize the clinical issues.

Previous periods of abstinence ending in relapse provide information about important relapse prevention issues. The therapist needs to verify that the patient was indeed abstinent and did not make exceptions such as for marijuana ("It's natural" or "It's so mild it doesn't count") or alcohol ("It wasn't a problem before I found cocaine" or "It's legal, so not a problem") or prescription drug misuse. The quality of that sobriety, and detailed inquiry about what happened to end it, sheds light on untreated coexisting disorders or hidden issues that need to be addressed. For example, long periods of sobriety characterized by persistent dysphoria may indicate untreated depression, a common occurrence among chronic relapsers. Empirical evidence indicates that relapse rates decrease once such disorders are properly addressed (Gallant, 1988).

Careful, detailed inquiry focuses attention on psychological or interpersonal issues that need attention. Conflict in intimate relationships or significant losses are common factors.

Patients also need to be alerted to periodic occurrences that constitute hazards, such as holidays, birthdays, celebrations, and anniversaries (e.g., sobriety dates). Increased stress is often a component. The Alcoholics Anonymous (AA) maxim to be especially watchful when one is hungry, angry, lonely, tired, or sad is a practical tactic that can guide the development of new coping skills.

Gorski (1988a, 1988b) was among the first to provide materials for recovering people to use in identifying and addressing their own relapse vulnerabilities. He noted that relapse is a state of mind that precedes actual use and offered ways to take inventory of those shifts:

Internal Warning Signs

Difficulty in thinking clearly
Difficulty in managing feelings and emotions
Difficulty in remembering things
Difficulty in managing stress
Daydreaming and wishful thinking
Feeling hopeless
Irritability

Behavioral Warning Signs

Irregular sleep or eating habits
Loss of daily structure; routine becomes haphazard
Irregular attendance at AA and treatment activities
Episodes of anger, frustration, resentment
Lying, manipulation

These and other aids (such as found in the Matrix [1995] manual; see Appendix B) can help the therapist become familiar with early warning signs and intervene accordingly. It is common for patients to conceal slips and relapses to avoid being confronted or disappointing the therapist. A concealed relapse breeds many taboo topics, ultimately causing the therapeutic process to stagnate, so it is crucial for therapists to be attentive and vigorous in efforts to address this issue.

Familiarity with experiential techniques, such as role-plays, is invaluable. Many of the effective relapse prevention strategies focus on the development of new coping skills for high-risk situations, and active learning strategies are essential. Several manuals are available for therapists to use in formulating tasks for individual or group sessions or for the patient to use as a workbook (Gorski, 1988a, 1988b, 1990; Kadden et al., 1994; Monti et al., 1989). Drink refusal skills are one example of how attention to specific details of each patient's situation can build skills, strengthen self-confidence, and bring psychological and interpersonal issues into focus. Using behavioral strategies may reveal psychodynamic issues because issues emerge in the course of the role-plays and other exercises that otherwise remain hidden or more ambiguous:

> Sam was a construction worker with a high investment in the tough, independent male stance. He was introduced to cocaine at his work site and rapidly began to develop problems. In working on a role-play in which he refused cocaine and extricated himself from the situation in which he was offered it, he began to become aware of the extent to which he was influenced by a strong need for his coworkers' approval. He wondered aloud why he so badly wanted to belong to a clique engaged in self-destructive behavior. This evoked memories of a childhood situation in which he abandoned the effort to maintain his excellent school performance when he was recruited into a peer group with antisocial propensities. These issues were tagged for later exploration. He was encouraged to view the refusal of cocaine and aloofness from the group as a sign of great strength in a difficult situation.

In thinking about the timing of relapse, it is useful to distinguish between a failure to establish abstinence and a resumption of AOD use after a period of time. Washton and Stone-Washton (1990) noted that the former may reflect ambivalence about the abstinence commitment or simply the struggle to establish it. For these early-stage events, it is often useful for the therapist to focus initially on the motivational status of the patient before focusing on behavioral strategies that might be useful. Adequate discussion of relapse prevention strategies followed by repeated failure to apply them is also a tipoff that motivation, not behavior, is the first issue to consider. Faced with a patient who continues to use episodically in the early stages, some clinicians will expend considerable energy on behavioral strategies, becoming frustrated when this does not yield success. Focusing on the ambivalence and working to enhance motivation is likely to be more fruitful. Once progress is made in these areas, behavioral strategies are used more readily.

Washton and Stone-Washton (1990) used the term *jump* to describe deliberate, sometimes preplanned instances of drug use. These patients may be committed to reducing rather than eliminating drug use and may defend the behavior on the grounds that some progress has been made. By contrast, a "slip" is an occasion of use, often seen as accidental, to which the patient responds with concern and remorse and a renewal of effort to achieve abstinence. In this situation, emphasis can be placed on behavioral strategies to promote success.

Circumscribed episodes of use should be distinguished from a resumption of ongoing use. The pattern of recurrence of use can vary from a single recurrence (a slip or lapse), to a time-limited episode (a binge), and a return to the frequency and pattern of use before abstinence (a full-blown relapse.) De Leon (1990–1991) noted that even if a full relapse occurs, it is important to distinguish between individuals who seek help at that point and those who return to the behavior and attitudes characteristic of a drug-abusing lifestyle. The deeper the regression, the more difficult to reverse the relapse.

Specific Relapse Factors and Strategies

Despite the drama of media focus on cocaine, and in earlier times heroin, research indicates that there are similarities in treatment issues and outcomes for opiate, cocaine, and alcohol users. Greater severity of AOD use at admission was the main predictor of substance use at follow-up (McLellan et al., 1994). Demographic characteristics and other patient factors did not predict alcohol and drug use after treatment. Psychosocial adjustment factors, however, have long been agreed to be related to relapse and are thus a focus of most treatment efforts. Measures generally focus on employment, criminal behavior, medical (including psychiatric) status, and family functioning. Severe psychiatric, employment, and family problems at admission were associated with worse adjustment in these areas after treatment. However, treatment services targeted specifically to those areas were associated with improved social adjustment scores. McLellan et al. have demonstrated that treatment that is truly individualized and disciplined with respect to providing activities relevant to the individual's areas of difficulty as identified by their Addiction Severity Index profile (see chap. 3 in this book) improves functioning in areas related to relapse vulnerability. This is referred to as problem–service matching (as discussed in chap. 5 in this book).

Left to their own devices, clinicians do not necessarily use readily available intake data to implement an individualized plan. McLellan and his colleagues (McLellan et al., 1997) demonstrate that even when adequate data are in the chart, clinicians implemented a more focused treatment plan when an employee assistance program representative constructed a tailored treatment plan requiring the provision of at least three professional sessions in any of the three areas (i.e., psychiatric, family, employment) indicated as problematic at the time of admission. Although all patients improved, those who were not under the specific problem–service matching protocol tended to drop out of treatment earlier and their outcomes were somewhat less positive. Thus, clinicians in a supervisory role, particularly in a managed care environment, need to attend to the specificity with which the patient's needs are being addressed.

Tradition has granted wide latitude to experienced licensed clinicians, most of whom are unaccustomed to having their clinical work closely scrutinized. However, this may not produce the best outcome for the patient in addiction treatment.

For example, most therapists are not usually highly skilled in the area of vocational counseling, so the patient with strong needs in that area may not even receive a well-chosen referral. Therapists with a preference for individual sessions will reconceptualize family problems to be amenable to intervention in an individual-session format. Although this is successful for some, it is less effective to tailor treatment to the preferences, skills, and limitations of the individual therapist rather than the needs of the patient.

The outpatient therapist. If the patient is in outpatient psychodynamically oriented psychotherapy, and not involved in an addiction treatment program, a variety of challenges can arise. Indeed, many therapists see recovering people who have been clean and sober for a long time and make a profound contribution to the quality of their sobriety. However, such therapists also may miss more subtle warning signs that usually signal problems to an addiction specialist: discontinuation of regular exercise, self-help meeting attendance, or other self-care activities without thought or discussion; a drift into daydreaming about the possibility of controlled use or experimentation with "lightweight" forms of a drug; and a growing rejection of the identity of a recovering person:

> Sara had been a methamphetamine user as an adolescent and had ended her first year in college in an inpatient chemical dependency program. She completed the program successfully, made a good connection with 12-step groups, and attended regularly for 3 years. After this, she gradually diminished her attendance but remained clean and sober for 7 years. During this time she entered graduate school, where her performance was stellar. While in graduate school, she ended a difficult long-term relationship and geared up reluctantly to face the "relationship marketplace." During this period, she resumed occasional drinking. Her therapist, impressed by her personal growth and professional accomplishments, did not raise questions about this practice. At a party, after two glasses of wine, an acquaintance offered her cocaine and she accepted.
>
> The therapist was surprised and unnerved by this ep-

isode and sought consultation from an addiction specialist. Careful review of the case revealed other precur-
sors to relapse, such as becoming "too busy" to maintain
a regular exercise schedule, falling into the unhealthy
eating habits characteristic of her professional group, and
becoming critical of people who dwell on their identity
as a recovering person. In the course of discussing these
issues, the patient recognized the elements in her relapse
drift and reconnected to some of her previous recovery
supports.

In a case such as this, the therapist has a variety of options.
One is to secure regular consultation from the addiction specialist for a period of time, until the patient has again been
stabilized. Another is to refer the patient to a recovery group
for the kind of exploration and feedback that benefits from
the keen eyes of a group of other recovering people. The
patient can and should be encouraged to reconnect with 12-
step programs that worked well for her in the past as well
as to resume the self-care practices that protect sobriety. The
extent to which specialized addiction treatment (including a
residential stay) is necessary is usually decided on the basis
of the duration of the relapse and the extent of the regression
to an earlier lifestyle. This assessment is best done in collaboration with an addiction specialist.

It would likely be beneficial for the individual therapist to
explore the patient's resistance to the identity of a recovering
person. Some therapists concur with the popular criticism
that this constitutes a form of self-disparagement, but the
desirable outcome is a comfortable integration of one's recovery status and an acceptance that one cannot safely use
intoxicants regardless of how much personal progress has
been achieved.

Patient relapse profiles. Treatment interventions can be
further tailored by focusing on actual relapse profile types.
Annis and colleagues (Annis, 1982; Annis & Graham, 1995;
Annis et al., 1988) developed and applied the Inventory of
Drinking Situations to define subgroups and match interven-
tions accordingly. Of particular interest are profiles of posi-

tive and negative emotions that describe the emotional states most likely to elevate risk. Positive-profile clients show significantly more heavy drinking on the subscales measuring pleasant emotions, social pressure to drink, and pleasant times with others. They show a social (rather than solitary) drinking style, fewer years of problem drinking, and lower consumption levels on drinking occasions. This finding is consistent with earlier stage drinking behavior and indicates they are appropriate for early intervention programs (Annis & Graham, 1995). Clients with a negative profile type show significantly more heavy drinking in response to negative emotions and conflict with others. They are more likely to be women, consistent with data in the literature on the high comorbidity of anxiety and depression in female alcoholics (Kessler et al., 1994). They also are more likely to have higher alcohol dependency scores and a solitary drinking style (Annis & Graham, 1995). Thus, the clinician can use this information to individualize counseling and formulate a relapse prevention plan with specific homework assignments.

Relapse factors: specific drugs. When developing relapse prevention plans, it is useful to look separately at the different drugs, especially at the distinctive features of each substance. Rawson (1995) examined this issue within his outpatient clinic system. Although relapse prevention strategies are generic to all the drugs, knowledge of some key differences can help the therapist attend to details that might otherwise seem insignificant. For alcohol, the key relapse factors were its widespread availability and social pressure to drink. Consistent with many studies in the literature, negative affect states also were important. Effective strategies included enhancing self-efficacy, developing skills to cope with emotional triggers, teaching techniques from social skills models, managing depression, and focusing on the role of relationships in relapse.

For stimulants such as cocaine or amphetamines, the distinctive factors identified are drug craving and external cues, sexual behavior as a stimulus, and alcohol use as a common antecedent. Effective relapse prevention strategies include creating structure, using information, identifying triggers, addressing the connection with sexual behavior, and reducing craving. The power of conditioned triggers seems especially great in working with cocaine users, presumably because of the unique manner in which it acts on the pleasure centers of the brain. Thus, a high level of structure and attention to specific triggers is essential, particularly in early recovery.

For opiate users, relapse factors include stressful events or periods of time, pain control, and related medical factors. Relapse prevention strategies include providing tools for dealing with protracted abstinence and relapse, using and complying with narcotic antagonists, teaching stress reduction techniques, and using behavioral and careful pharmacological measures for managing pain.

For benzodiazepine users, factors include rebound anxiety, symptom reemergence, or both. These are difficult to distinguish, particularly because withdrawal from these drugs is accompanied by a rebound that can last for long periods of time. As with any prescription drug abuse or misuse, physicians' offices or medical settings can be a trigger. Strategies include coping with insomnia, using physical exercise for anxiety reduction, and teaching progressive relaxation and thought-stopping procedures.

The Abstinence Violation Effect

Marlatt and Gordon (1985) made an excellent conceptual and clinical contribution by focusing on the abstinence violation effect, the impact on the individual of having failed to keep a behavioral commitment. Thus, the abstinence violation effect is assumed to occur when the individual is personally committed to an extended or indefinite period of abstinence and a lapse occurs during this period. The actual abstinence violation effect is a "cognitive-affective reaction to an initial slip that increases the probability that the lapse will be followed by an increased use of the substance or activity" (Marlatt & Gordon, 1985, p. 179). Thus, the greater the intensity of the reaction, the higher the probability of an exacerbation effect after a lapse. For example, it is common for patients to feel so ashamed and discouraged that they conclude, "Well,

I've already blown it; might as well go all the way." In Marlatt and Gordon's terms, however, when the individual perceives the cause of the lapse to include specific factors over which he or she potentially has control, the relapse can more easily be abbreviated. Within the patient's framework, perceived self-efficacy is of central importance. The patient who concludes he or she is powerless once a lapse has occurred is more likely to fall into a more serious behavioral regression. This has been a criticism of the 12-step program approach. The emphasis on powerlessness is seen as unhelpful in this situation. Resetting one's sobriety date is another example. For the patient with 20 years of abstinence who relapses, starting again from Day 1 is interpreted as invalidating the achievements of the two decades of sobriety. Although these are matters of understanding and interpretation, there is little question that many patients respond negatively to their perceived sense of failure and benefit from having previous accomplishments validated and being empowered to move forward.

It is important for the therapist to help the patient and his or her family or significant others develop a plan to interrupt a relapse:

> Dan complained bitterly to his individual therapist about his wife's return to episodic drinking after a period of extended sobriety. His antenna grew finely tuned to her increasing irritability, insomnia, and distractibility, which he had come to recognize as a harbinger of a drinking episode. When he tried to discuss this with her, she exploded and then cried, telling him she felt he was impossible to please. On the recommendation of his therapist, she agreed to short-term work with an addiction specialist, who reviewed the situation and helped them make a plan.

In the case of relapse warning signs, before actual drinking and using, agreements on how others can give constructive feedback on what they observe can reduce defensiveness and friction of such interactions. Similar action plans are useful once a relapse has occurred. Once elements in the buildup have been identified, preventive measures can be incorporated into a relapse prevention plan (Daley & Marlatt, 1992). Recovering partners or spouses can express their preferences about how constructive feedback can be offered once warning signs are noted. Other strategies include using constructive self-talk (e.g., from "I am a failure, I used" to "I can get a grip and build on what I have accomplished"), behaviors that have worked in the past (e.g., exercise regimens), and resumption of self-help group involvement. Reducing the extent to which the patient regresses to engagement in an AOD-using lifestyle and increasing the commitment to recovery-related behaviors is the main focus of psychosocial efforts.

Strategies for Early and Ongoing Recovery

In keeping with the conceptual framework of initiation versus maintenance strategies for change, Annis (1990) identified specific strategies for relapse prevention counseling. For those focused on initiating a change in behavior, making use of external supports is emphasized. Examples include avoidance of risk situations, coercion, hospitalization or residential care, protective drugs, involvement of spouse or collaterals, and a directive role on the part of the therapists. In the next phase, after a period of abstinence has been achieved, external aids are gradually withdrawn while activities that promote self-efficacy are emphasized. Annis used graduated real-life exposure to a hierarchy of risk situations, multiple homework tasks within each type of risk situation, gradually reducing the use of all external aids to performance, and design of homework tasks to promote self-attribution of control. Thus, the therapist and patient, working together, identify and prioritize the high-risk situations, and the patient develops coping skills in a step-by-step fashion. In this phase, it is important that the patient not attribute success to a drug, other external constraint, or the therapist but instead grows in confidence that he or she has mastered coping skills for the difficult situations.

Medication as a Tool

A variety of medications are useful in addressing relapse dangers. Taken alone, they are ineffective, but, combined with a full program of recovery, they can be invaluable. Medications can be used to treat acute withdrawal, provide deterrence by causing negative or unpleasant symptoms, block the effects of a drug, block craving, and treat comorbid disorders. Through all these means, medications can be used to address specific difficulties that precipitate relapse.

Treating Withdrawal

Treatment of acute withdrawal is primarily an issue of medical safety and makes the patient more comfortable. Neither of these things in themselves correlates with long-term abstinence, but the detoxification process should be viewed as an opportunity to engage the patient further in treatment, provide a "map" of the journey, and make the link to activities that constitute an appropriate next step. Although expectations for the detoxification process should be limited, omitting it can undermine efforts that might otherwise be effective. Abundant clinical experience suggests that failure to provide a medicated withdrawal often results in premature treatment dropout. For example, the high early dropout of heroin addicts from therapeutic communities could probably be reduced by increasing the accessibility of a methadone detoxification closely linked with the residential program to prevent attrition near the end when the detoxification dose gets low. The admission workup for a therapeutic community is typically extensive; hence, losing the patient quickly is a costly proposition. Brief medicated withdrawal of alcoholics permits better treatment participation by improving attention and concentration. Thus, medicated withdrawal should be considered as an adjunct in the process of establishing abstinence, an important component in a comprehensive treatment strategy. Wesson (1995) provided detailed descriptions of detoxification protocols for different drugs and discussed their unique issues.

Antabuse and Other Deterrents

The use of Antabuse (disulfiram) as a deterrent to impulsive drinking is perhaps the practice most widely recognized by those outside the addiction field. It is an alcohol-sensitizing drug that was introduced in 1948 as a treatment for alcoholism (Banys, 1988). Antabuse inhibits the oxidation of alcohol, causing a buildup of acetaldehdye, a breakdown product of alcohol that causes a toxic reaction. A person who drinks while taking Antabuse may vomit for several hours and may experience flushing, tachycardia, shortness of breath, sweating, and a fall in blood pressure. It is the specter of profound physical discomfort that provides the deterrent effect. Unlike other medications used in treatment, Antabuse itself has no direct drug effect; it "works" by putting the brakes on impulsivity and, as such, is useful for some patients.

The research literature on Antabuse fails to support the view that its addition to a treatment program improves the long-term abstinence outcome. This is partly because there are many conceptually and methodologically flawed studies, and clinicians support the proposition that there are subgroups of alcoholics for whom it can make an important difference. These subgroups include those who are older, relapse prone, uninsightful, compulsive, capable of tolerating a treatment relationship and following rules, and those who are court ordered. Other considerations are patients in early abstinence who are in crisis or are under severe stress and those with established sobriety who can benefit from support for anxiety-provoking explorations in individual or group psychotherapy (Banys, 1988).

Antabuse should be integrated into a comprehensive program of recovery, with collaboration between the prescribing physician and others involved in the treatment. It is all too common to find that Antabuse has been prescribed by a physician who is not connected to the overall recovery effort and gives little instruction about how to use it effectively and how to decide when to discontinue it. Thus, the therapist with a patient on Antabuse is advised to assume the coordinating role in this matter.

If the therapist or patient decides that Antabuse might be useful, collaboration with the prescribing physician is important. If the patient has had a recent contact with the physician, an actual visit may not be required; otherwise, laboratory work is usually done to rule out medical conditions (e.g., severe liver damage) that would contraindicate the use of Antabuse. Physicians will often prescribe when there is some liver damage because the risks of Antabuse are usually lower than those of drinking until the existing liver damage becomes too great. Patients can be encouraged to obtain a prescription even if they do not fill it because it may not be possible to obtain Antabuse quickly if a crisis occurs. The therapist should ask the physician to keep him or her informed of any changes and, if possible, to notify the therapist if the patient does not refill the prescription on the timetable that would be expected if the medication is taken as prescribed.

The therapist also should inquire periodically if the patient is taking the Antabuse, bearing in mind that "taking my Antabuse" can drift into taking it every 3 days, when the patient happens to remember. This is often part of the buildup to drinking. Antabuse is less useful for those who plan their drinking because they plan to discontinue their Antabuse more or less consciously. Monitored (observed) Antabuse use may be ordered by the criminal justice system or by employers as a condition of returning to work. Less formal practices include a husband taking his Antabuse in front of his wife, who notifies the therapist if days are missed (these practices are discussed in more detail in the section on community reinforcement strategies in chap. 7 in this book).

Many patients report that Antabuse brings enormous relief from the struggle to avoid drinking. "I only have to make the decision once a day, when I take the Antabuse" is a common reaction. Once the routine is established, the therapist should be attentive to whether the patient continues to make the behavior changes needed to achieve reliable abstinence. For some, the Antabuse provides safety, and the patient becomes more passive:

Mary began taking Antabuse after an episode with drinking that landed her in the emergency room in a life-threatening situation. She had a stormy relationship with her sister, also an alcoholic, who was still drinking. Before a planned visit, she asked her sister on the telephone to remove the alcohol from the refrigerator and other obvious places, and her sister agreed. When she arrived, she discovered an open bottle of wine in the refrigerator. She said to herself, "Oh well, I'm on Antabuse, I don't really need to worry" and did not raise the issue with her sister. Although she did not drink, she also missed an opportunity to develop the kind of assertion skills she will need to protect herself once she discontinues Antabuse.

Thus, Antabuse is most useful when the therapist integrates it into the rest of the work, monitoring medication compliance and determining whether the necessary behavior changes are occurring. The decision to go off Antabuse is one that is only given proper attention when the therapist brings it into the treatment. Exhibit 3 is a handout for patients that captures the issues.

Naltrexone (Trexan)

This opioid antagonist (blocker) was first developed for use with heroin addicts and was subsequently discovered to have benefits for alcoholics. It occupies the receptor sites and thus blocks the effects of opiates, such that if the person uses heroin he or she does not get high or readdicted. It blocks reinforcement of drug taking ("No point in spending the money if I'm not going to get anything out of it") and in the same manner protects the patient from readdiction. Naltrexone has been widely studied in opiate users of various socioeconomic strata and appears to be most useful for medical professionals seeking to retain their licenses, middle-class or suburban addicts, and those on probation (Brahen, Henderson, Capone, & Kordal, 1984; Greenstein, Fudala, & O'Brien, 1992; Ling & Wesson, 1984; Washton, Pottash, & Gold, 1984). Among others, the dropout rate is high. It is difficult for

Exhibit 3

Preparing to Go Off Antabuse

Antabuse is a valuable tool that can help you buy time while changing behavior patterns to support sobriety. Although it can provide security in the short run, it is important not to allow it to *substitute* for making needed changes.

1) Looking back over the period you have been taking Antabuse, what were the hazardous times in which you might have begun drinking had you not been on it? What were the key elements that made you vulnerable?

2) What old behavior patterns need to be changed to reduce your vulnerability? Pay particular attention to the areas of assertion and stress reduction. What specific changes do you need to make in order to be on more solid ground when you go off?

What criteria do you need to meet in order to set a date?

3) What are the difficult times you see during the 90 days after the date you propose for getting off? What changes or new supports would you need in order to weather them without Antabuse?

4) What would be warning signs that you need to resume Antabuse for at least a short period of time? (Use relapse prevention materials and identify *specific* signs.) How would you like your spouse or significant other to cooperate in this task? Have specific discussions with him or her to clarify the issues and come to an understanding about constructive actions.

5) Elicit input from others about how they decided to go off Antabuse, what worked and did not work, how they would have done things differently, and so on.

Note. From Joan E. Zweben. This handout can be used or reproduced without permission from the publisher or the authors. For republication, a source citation is appreciated.

street heroin addicts or patients on methadone maintenance to complete the detoxification and remain free long enough to be put on naltrexone, and, once on they do not continue to take it for long (Greenstein et al., 1992).

The use of naltrexone with alcoholics (in this context it is named "Revia") began in the early 1990s with the publication of several studies indicating decreased relapse rates when used with alcoholics in outpatient treatment (O'Malley et al., 1992; Swift, 1995; Volpicelli, Alterman, Hayashida, & O'Brien, 1992). Participants in the studies reported significantly less craving and less drinking. Although the neurobiological mechanisms by which naltrexone acts are under investigation, there is evidence that it modifies the reinforcing effects of alcohol (J. E. Smith & Meyers, 1995). Efforts are under way to identify subgroups of alcoholic patients most likely to benefit, with high levels of craving and somatic symptoms being two indicators (Volpicelli, Clay, Watson, & O'Brien, 1995). O'Malley et al. (1992) investigated the integration of naltrexone and psychosocial therapy in the treatment of both opioid and alcohol dependence (O'Malley et al., 1992), looking at both supportive and coping skills therapy in an effort to determine the best matching strategies. The optimal time frame for treating alcoholics with naltrexone is not presently known.

These and other issues will be clarified through studies in process and longer clinical experience. Several considerations emerge for the practicing clinician. New medications often generate an excitement that may enhance the placebo effect in patients treated by practitioners compared with those in carefully controlled research studies. Thus, they generally appear to be more effective for the first few years, before the "romance" wears off. Problems (e.g., new side effects) emerge after medications have been in use for a while. Motivational issues of the patient remain to be clarified. The patient who seeks naltrexone rather than Antabuse may prefer to preserve the option of drinking. There also is the danger of feeding the fantasy that the drug will magically make the patient not want to drink, and the commitment to do the work of recovery will diminish. These things remain to be seen as clinicians gain more experience with this drug. Thus, it is important for the clinician to emphasize that medications are only tools, not solutions.

Medication Issues for the Therapist

The use of medication is increasingly a part of integrated treatment. The temptation to use it as a substitute for psychosocial services is increasing as managed care organizations push for quicker, less costly solutions to complex problems. Frequently, however, the best outcome is obtained through the combination. Interdisciplinary collaboration is an important part of success (Zweben & Smith, 1989). In their comparison of addiction treatment outcome with three medical disorders characterized by frequent relapse (i.e., insulin-dependent diabetes, hypertension, and asthma), McLellan, Woody, et al. (1995) noted that poor medication compliance was a major relapse factor. This is well-known to be the case with psychiatric disorders. In fact, denial may increase as the patient feels better and this leads to discontinuing the medication.

The psychotherapist is in an excellent position to monitor and encourage medication compliance and to help the patient problem solve if difficulties arise. Many patients are too timid, confused, and distressed to ask their questions or talk openly with their psychiatrist about their concerns. Encouragement to tolerate transient initial side effects is important to promoting an adequate medication trial. The therapist also needs to address the patient's disappointment that most psychotropic medications do not produce the immediate relief to which alcohol and drug users are accustomed. Control issues are often salient: taking the medication as prescribed versus altering the physician's recommendation without discussion. This latter should be seen as a variant of an addictive pattern.

At the same time, recovering people who are highly motivated are keenly sensitive to the meaning of taking any pill to feel better. Side effects (e.g., feeling speedy from Prozac) may trigger cravings and conflict about taking medication. It is important that the psychotherapist is open to exploring these issues and is willing to assume an active role in working with the physician while coaching the patient to do the same. It is important for the therapist to remain as pragmatic as possible, basing recommendations on careful observation of the patient's status and changing needs. Some therapists turn to medication only as a last resort, but some conditions (e.g., depression) are more easily modified or arrested if they are addressed early.

Medications as Relapse Hazards

Benzodiazepines

Certain medications constitute serious relapse hazards and need to be carefully managed. Benzodiazepines are the sedative-hypnotic medications (also called *tranquilizers*) singled out for special caution in people with a personal or family history of alcoholism. Trade names include Xanax, Librium, Klonopin, Valium, Dalmane, Ativan, Serax, Restoril, and Halcion. A review of studies of humans indicated that benzodiazepines have reinforcing effects in people with a past or current history of AOD abuse (Griffiths & Roache, 1985). Clinicians and some studies also have concluded that parental alcoholism is a risk factor in benzodiazepine abuse (Ciraulo, Barnhill, Ciraulo, Greenblatt, & Shader, 1989; DuPont, 1990), perhaps because of an underlying genetic factor that produces an altered response to benzodiazepines as well as alcohol.

DuPont (1990) noted that patients who are not chemically dependent who are prescribed benzodiazepines for anxiety disorders use them at low and stable doses, with little physician supervision of their dose levels. They do not escalate their dose, do not exceed the usual dose prescribed for anxiety, and do not develop tolerance to the antianxiety properties even when they use them over a long period of time. In patients with a history of alcoholism, benzodiazepines can themselves be used abusively (with escalating doses) or can precipitate a relapse to alcohol, to whom it is a chemical cousin. There are unfortunate examples of patients who told their physician that they could not take Valium because they were in recovery, only to be prescribed Halcion instead. Thus, patients who are not sophisticated about members of this drug class can be placed at risk by careless prescribing. Others, however, deliberately seek benzodiazepines or develop an interest in it once they are on Antabuse. They may obtain a benzodiazepine for a specific stressful event and suggest they will not get in trouble with it because "It's nowhere near a similar experience." Monitoring over time can reveal that the occasions for the medication become more numerous or the patient begins to take it before making any attempt to master the difficult situation. Thus, collaboration with the prescribing physician is desirable. In many cases, however, tricyclic antidepressants, some of the selective serotonin reuptake inhibitors, and Buspar, as well as other medications, can be effectively used without the risks of benzodiazepines, and this is the common practice in addiction medicine. Acupuncture also is available in many addiction treatment programs. It has proved difficult to properly mask a controlled study (McLellan, Grossman, Blaine, & Haverkos, 1993), but patients consistently report regular acupuncture soothes anxiety and increases their stress tolerance. Behavioral techniques for managing anxiety also are documented to be effective. It is when these tools alone are not sufficiently effective that medication should be considered.

There are times when other medication options are exhausted and the patient is still struggling with debilitating anxiety, certainly a major relapse risk. Most practitioners within the addiction field may insist benzodiazepines can never be used. Others disagree, however, and note that they may sometimes be safely used in abstaining patients who are carefully selected and closely monitored (DuPont, 1990; Frances & Borg, 1993). Caution about the use of benzodiazepines is certainly well founded; however, clinicians should avoid the level of dogmatism that precludes problem solving in the exceptional case.

Wesson et al. (1992) noted the reluctance of psychodynamic

psychotherapists to use medication for anxiety out of the conviction that treatment is best focused on understanding and resolving the underlying issues that generate it. They noted an important pitfall in assuming that everyone's experience of anxiety is more or less the same, thus underestimating how disabling a true anxiety disorder can be: "Pharmacological Calvinism extracts a toll in terms of needless human suffering. Some people who could benefit ... do not seek medical treatment even when anxiety is disabling and alternatives to medication are not accessible" (p. 271). Thus, the task of the clinician working with someone in recovery is to maintain a balanced perspective that challenges the patient to master new coping skills for life's stressors without discouraging medical intervention when it can make the difference between steady progress and repeated relapse.

Pain Management

Medical conditions requiring pain medication can be an occasion for relapse, and it is important that the therapist be sensitive to a range of complex issues. Opioids are the most effective analgesics and are popular drugs of abuse as well. Patients with other drug preferences are still at risk because the use of another intoxicant elevates the risk of return to the primary drug of abuse. At the same time, inadequate pain management for acute illness prolongs physical recovery time and also may be a factor in relapse to alcohol or illicit drugs. In the case of chronic pain, the dilemmas are even more complex because maintenance on opioid drugs may be desirable. In this context, the distinction between physical dependence and addiction is important. Physical dependence is a pharmacological property of opioid drugs defined solely by the occurrence of an abstinence (withdrawal) syndrome after abrupt discontinuation. Addiction includes compulsive, escalating use despite adverse consequences (Portnoy & Payne, 1992). Clinicians (physicians as well as psychologists) are often confused about these distinctions, with important consequences for sensible and humane pain management. Thus, even the patient in recovery is well advised to use ad-

equate pain medication. For former opioid users or methadone patients, this will mean higher than the usual doses.
The elevated risk should be addressed by a review of safety
strategies and an increase in recovery-related activities for
several months (at least). For example, the patient who no
longer attends meetings can be encouraged to resume attendance for a while. A review of other self-care activities (e.g.,
diet, exercise, sleep) can suggest areas for improvement or
temporary enhancement. Some patients can succeed in sur-
viving medical or dental procedures without pain medications, and their anxious desire to do so should be treated with
great sensitivity. However, they should be helped to be realistic and to put energy into strategies that have worked in
the past if they find themselves in a situation more difficult
than they anticipated and decide they need pain medication.

Other Forms of Addictive Behaviors Associated With Relapse

Reciprocal Relapse Patterns

Eating disorders, gambling, compulsive sexual behavior, and
complusive spending are areas in which disturbed behavior
patterns resemble addiction so closely that the addiction
treatment model has been applied to develop intervention
strategies. Although there is controversy about whether these
are "true" addictions, there is no question that patient behaviors can display the characteristics of being compulsive,
out of control, and persistent despite adverse consequences.
Criteria from the fourth edition of the *Diagnostic and Statistical Manual of Mental Disorders* (*DSM–IV*) for substance
abuse can be applied to these behaviors, and descriptions of
the cycle of indulgence and its aftermath certainly seem to
have physical "intoxication" and withdrawal phenomena as
part of the experience. It is essential to identify these coexisting disturbances because it is common for them to remain
hidden and become a precipitant of relapse (Marlatt & Barrett, 1994). Many patients become trapped in what Washton

and Stone-Washton (1990) described as a reciprocal relapse pattern, in which the compulsive or disturbed behavior precipitates relapse to cocaine (or other drugs) and vice versa.

Eating Disorders

The relationship between eating disorders and substance abuse is a large and complex topic (Zweben, 1987). We address issues most germane to relapse here. An eating disorder is a severe disturbance in eating behavior that is consistently associated with a psychological or behavioral syndrome (American Psychiatric Association, 1994). Bulimia is the most common eating disorder and the one most frequently associated with substance abuse (Holderness, Brooks-Gunn, & Warren, 1994; Wiederman & Pryor, 1996). However, it is important to be attentive to eating behaviors even when they do not meet sufficient criteria to constitute a psychiatric disorder. Krahn, Kurth, Demitrack, and Drewnowski (1992) studied subthreshold levels of eating abnormalities and substance use and concluded that the relationship between eating disorders and substance abuse (including alcoholism) in clinical populations extends in a continuous graded manner to subthreshold levels of dieting and substance use behaviors. Thus, concerns about dieting can increase susceptibility to relapse, especially in young women.

There are many possible ways eating disorders can be related to substance abuse patterns. They may be present before the onset of substance use and may either be obscured by the substance-using behavior or quiescent during this period. They may coexist with AOD-using behaviors, serving similar ends. For example, there are striking parallels between a relapse state of mind and the thinking and behaviors associated with alcohol, drug, or food binges. Binge eating, like alcohol and drugs, can be a way to avoid rather than address emotional stresses and problems (Washton, 1989). Alcohol also can be used to suppress the shame and panic associated with bingeing and vomiting and then escalate in a further reaction to violating abstinence. Women with eating disorders, noted for their low self-esteem, are especially sus-

ceptible to cocaine, which makes them feel powerful and indifferent to eating. Cocaine users may be highly invested in
the thinness easily achieved and maintained while using.
Weight gain during abstinence may pose a serious relapse
risk. It also is a risk for patients on antidepressants, many of
whom cannot achieve or sustain abstinence unless their depression is effectively addressed. Thus, treating the psychiatric disorder to achieve abstinence carries a risk of triggering
an eating disorder, particularly if the latter has gone unnoticed during the assessment process.

It is more likely that inquiry about eating disorders will be
included in the assessment in adolescent treatment programs,
but eating problems also are widespread in adult women. In
fact, clinicians have noted that eating disorders may be more
common in substance-abusing men than the baseline rates in
epidemiological studies would indicate. Clinicians observe
gay men and middle-aged heterosexual men engage in eating
behaviors that qualify as disordered, but they are rarely the
subject of systematic inquiry:

> Steve, a gay man who was HIV-positive but medically
> stable, went through several years of stressful events and
> gradually lost weight, although he remained asympto-
> matic. His recovery group was alarmed at the deterio-
> ration and encouraged him to pursue other options be-
> sides the marijuana he lauded for enhancing his appetite.
> He was accepted into a study using growth hormones to
> address weight loss in HIV-positive patients and began
> to gain weight and improve in appearance. At about the
> point when he again began to look healthy, he panicked
> about "getting fat and becoming unmarketable" and dis-
> continued the medication.

It is important that basic interventions for eating disorders
be integrated into substance abuse treatment if the relapse
potential is to be effectively addressed. Specialized elements
(e.g., medical evaluation for problems known to be associated with substance abuse disorders, nutritional stabilization
strategies to stop aberrant eating) may need to be provided

by an eating disorders program, but substance abuse treatment must integrate assessment and other elements needed for an adequate relapse prevention plan. This involves having a clear understanding of the relationship between disturbed eating behaviors and the substance use pattern. Making food issues a routine part of discussion in educational sessions and therapy groups will go a long way toward ensuring that eating disorders do not become a concealed relapse risk.

Gambling

Pathological gambling is described in the *DSM–IV* (American Psychiatric Association, 1994) as persistent and recurrent gambling behavior that disrupts personal, family, or vocational pursuits in the absence of a manic episode. Lesieur, Blume, and colleagues (Lesieur & Blume, 1987, 1990; Lesieur, Blume, & Zoppa, 1986) developed a screening instrument to identify pathological gamblers and subsequently used it to determine the prevalence and characteristics of gamblers seeking treatment in a substance abuse treatment program. Of 458 patients interviewed, 9% were diagnosed as pathological gamblers (11.5% men and 2% women) and an additional 10% showed signs of problematic gambling. Parental gambling was an influential factor; fully 38% of the children of pathological gamblers were pathological gamblers themselves (Lesieur et al., 1986). In a later study of patients admitted to an acute adult psychiatric service, 7% were identified as pathological gamblers, with a demonstrable association between gambling in the parent and offspring. These pathological gamblers had a range of primary diagnoses, including schizoaffective disorder, paranoid schizophrenia, and major depression (Lesieur & Blume, 1990). A broad, statewide prevalence study in New York indicated that gamblers in the general population differed substantially from those in treatment. Previous research on treatment populations had indicated that pathological gambling affected primarily middle- and upper-middle-class White men in their 40s and 50s who were highly employable and had fairly

stable family lives until their gambling escalated. Those identified in the New York community sample were significantly
younger, were minority group members, and had a higher
proportion of women (Volberg & Steadman, 1988). This suggests that greater access to treatment is needed for disadvantaged populations.

Gambling operates as a relapse factor in several different
ways. Alcohol flows freely in gambling environments, and
cocaine and other drugs, although less conspicuous, also are
usually available. Gambling also is a strong conditioned trigger because it is usually associated with AOD use in those
with a substance abuse disorder. The patient's description of
the arousal and withdrawal phenomena is sometimes indistinguishable from a cocaine binge. For these reasons, it is
advisable to discourage gambling even if the patient does not
meet criteria for pathological gambling. Patients are often difficult to convince of the importance of abstaining from gambling, but engaging in this pursuit should be viewed as a
striking relapse warning sign.

Compulsive Sexual Behavior

Compulsive sexual behavior does not have its own formal
diagnostic category, but it is certainly a concern of an addiction specialist. There is controversy about whether the behavior is a separate entity or secondary to other diagnoses.
These behaviors are marked by a repetitive, compelling, or
driven quality that persists despite adverse consequences.
Travin (1995) offered four models for understanding compulsive sexual behavior: (a) obsessive–compulsive spectrum
disorder model; (b) compulsive sexual behaviors as an affect
disorder (particularly depression); (c) sexual addiction; and
(d) sexual impulsivity. He noted that some compulsive sexual
behaviors fit neatly into one of the models, whereas others
have features of two or more of them. Treatment can include
medication for the features of obsessive–compulsive disorder
or the affective disorder. Compulsive sexual behavior is particularly common among cocaine users, although it is also
observed in alcoholics and other drug users. Washton and

Stone-Washton (1990) noted that cocaine-related compulsive sexuality contributes to chronic relapse, treatment failure, and perpetuation of high-risk sexual behaviors that foster the spread of AIDS. They emphasized that undiagnosed and untreated compulsive sexuality is one of the most common preventable relapse factors. Rarely is this issue systematically addressed at intake. Washton and Stone-Washton (1990) recommended asking the following specific questions:

1. Does your cocaine use ever involve sexual thoughts, fantasies or behaviors?
2. If so, during what percentage of your drug use episodes does this happen?
3. Do you engage in any of the following behaviors while high on cocaine—compulsive masturbation, encounters with prostitutes, compulsive intercourse, compulsively viewing peep shows or pornographic movies, switching from heterosexual to homosexual sex, cross-dressing in clothing of the opposite sex or sadomasochistic sex? (p. 146)

Washton and Stone-Washton (1990) noted that this behavior is much more common among cocaine-dependent men than women, and more common among crack smokers than snorters. This addiction does not disappear when cocaine use stops; indeed, sexual feelings and fantasies often trigger cocaine craving. A reciprocal relapse pattern, in which compulsive sexual behavior precipitates relapse to cocaine and vice versa, is unfortunately common. Patients should be asked to refrain from all sexual activity for the first 30 days of treatment in order to give time to identify sexual relapse triggers and respond to them safely (Washton & Stone-Washton, 1990).

Conclusion

Relapse prevention strategies have evolved considerably in the past 10 years and include a variety of well-researched behavioral strategies, which, in selected cases, can be augmented in their effectiveness by pharmacological adjuncts. It is important to keep the resumption of AOD use in perspective. Although certainly an appropriate focus of intervention, it has been singled out as a clear indication of treatment failure, doubtless contributing to the public perception that "treatment doesn't work." In fact, when one considers improvement in one or more areas of psychosocial functioning and reduction of AOD use, the majority of those in treatment show positive benefits (Gerstein & Harwood, 1990; Hubbard et al., 1989; McLellan et al., 1994). In most cases, unless there is a complete regression to an earlier AOD-using lifestyle, other gains will likely remain. These gains in the areas of reduction of illicit drug use, reduction of crime, improvement in health and psychiatric status, employment, and family functioning are meaningful accomplishments even if complete abstinence cannot be sustained. This does not mean that therapists should espouse a permissive attitude or send the message that controlled use is an equally valid goal. Many patients have devoted decades of their lives to an effort to control their use, to the detriment of their relationships, health, and job performance. To avoid heightening the abstinence violation effect, however, relapse is best treated as a fact of life from which the patient can restore good functioning relatively quickly with the appropriate commitment and effort.

References

Abram, K. M., & Teplin, L. A. (1991). Co-occurring disorders among mentally ill jail detainees: Implications for public policy. *American Psychologist, 46,* 1036–1045.

Alcoholics Anonymous. (1976). *Alcoholics Anonymous* (3rd ed.). New York: Alcoholics Anonymous World Services.

Alcoholics Anonymous. (1983). *Questions and answers on sponsorship.* New York: Alcoholics Anonymous World Services.

Alcoholics Anonymous. (1996). *Alcoholics Anonymous: 1996 membership survey.* New York: Alcoholics Anonymous World Services.

American Psychiatric Association. (1987). *Diagnostic and statistical manual of mental disorders* (3rd ed., rev.). Washington, DC: Author.

American Psychiatric Association. (1994). *Diagnostic and statistical manual of mental disorders* (4th ed.). Washington, DC: Author.

American Society of Addiction Medicine. (1996). *Patient placement criteria for the treatment of substance-related disorders* (2nd ed.). Chevy Chase, MD: American Society of Addiction Medicine.

Amodeo, M. (1995). The therapist's role in the drinking stage. In S. Brown (Ed.), *Treating alcoholism* (pp. 95–132). San Francisco: Jossey-Bass.

Anglin, M. D., & Hser, Y.-I. (1991). Criminal justice and the drug-abusing offender: Policy issues of coerced treatment. *Behavioral Sciences and the Law, 9,* 243–267.

Annis, H. M. (1982). *Inventory of Drinking Situations (IDS-100).* Toronto: Addiction Research Foundation of Ontario.

Annis, H. M. (1987). *Situational Confidence Questionnaire.* Toronto: Addiction Research Foundation of Ontario.

Annis, H. M. (1990). Relapse to substance abuse: Empirical findings within a cognitive-social learning approach. *Journal of Psychoactive Drugs, 22,* 117–124.

Annis, H. M., & Graham, J. M. (1988). *Situational Confidence Questionnaire user's guide.* Toronto: Addiction Research Foundation of Ontario.

Annis, H. M., & Graham, J. M. (1995). Profile types on the Inventory of Drinking Situations: Implications for relapse prevention counseling. *Psychology of Addictive Behaviors, 9,* 176–182.

Annis, H. M., Graham, J. M., & Davis, C. S. (1988). *Inventory of Drinking Situations user's guide.* Toronto: Addiction Research Foundation of Ontario.

Ashley, M. (Speaker). (1996). The scientific basis for guidelines on moderate drinking (Cassette Recording No. Infomedix J134-ABCD). Garden Grove, CA: Infomedix.

Azrin, N. H., Sisson, R. W., Meyers, R., & Godley, M. (1982). Alcoholism treatment by disulfiram and community reinforcement therapy. *Journal of Behavior Therapy and Experimental Psychiatry, 13,* 105–112.

Ball, J. C., & Ross, A. (1991). *The effectiveness of methadone maintenance treatment*. New York: Springer-Verlag.

Bandura, A. (1977). *Social learning theory*. Englewood Cliffs, NJ: Prentice Hall.

Banys, P. (1988). The clinical use of disulfiram (Antabuse): A review. *Journal of Psychoactive Drugs, 20*, 243–261.

Beattie, M. (1987). *Co-dependent no more*. Center City, MN: Hazeldon.

Beck, A. T., Wright, F. D., Newman, C. F., & Liese, B. S. (1993). *Cognitive therapy of substance abuse*. New York: Guilford Press.

Becker, J. V., & Miller, P. M. (1976). Verbal and nonverbal marital interaction patterns of alcoholics. *Journal of Studies on Alcohol, 37*, 1616–1624.

Begleiter, H., & Kissin, B. (Eds.). (1995). *The genetics of alcoholism*. New York: Oxford University Press.

Bickel, W. K., & Kelly, T. H. (1988). The relationship of stimulus control to the treatment of substance abuse. In B. A. Ray (Ed.), *Learning factors in substance abuse* (NIDA Research Monograph Series No. 84, pp. 122–140). Rockville, MD: National Institute on Drug Abuse.

Blume, S. (1992). Alcohol and other drug problems in women. In J. H. Lowinson, P. Ruiz, & R. B. Millman (Eds.), *Substance abuse: A comprehensive textbook* (2nd ed., pp. 794–807). Baltimore: Williams & Wilkins.

Bohman, M. (1978). Some genetic aspects of alcoholism and criminality. *Archives of General Psychiatry, 35*, 269–276.

Brahen, L. S., Henderson, R. K., Capone, T., & Kordal, N. (1984). Naltrexone treatment in a jail work-release program. *Journal of Clinical Psychiatry, 45*, 49–52.

Brehm, N. M., & Khantzian, E. J. (1992). The psychology of substance abuse: A psychodynamic perspective. In J. H. Lowinson, P. Ruiz, & R. B. Millman (Eds.), *Substance abuse: A comprehensive textbook* (2nd ed., pp. 106–117). Baltimore: Williams & Wilkins.

Brown, B., & Ashery, R. S. (1979). Aftercare in drug abuse programming. In R. L. Dupont, A. Goldstein, & J. O'Donnell (Eds.), *Handbook on drug abuse* (pp. 165–173). Washington, DC: U.S. Government Printing Office.

Brown, S. (1985). *Treating the alcoholic: A developmental model of recovery*. New York: Wiley.

Brown, S. (1988). *Treating adult children of alcoholics: A developmental perspective*. New York: Wiley.

Brown, S. (Ed.). (1995). *Treating alcoholism*. San Francisco: Jossey-Bass.

Brown, S., Irwin, M., & Schuckit, M. (1991). Changes in anxiety in abstinent male alcoholics. *Journal of Studies on Alcohol, 52*, 55–61.

Brown, S., & Lewis, V. (1995). The alcoholic family: A developmental model of recovery. In S. Brown (Ed.), *Treating alcoholism* (pp. 279–315). San Francisco: Jossey-Bass.

Brown, S., & Schuckit, M. (1988). Changes in depression among abstinent alcoholics. *Journal of Studies on Alcohol, 49*, 412–417.

Brown, S. (1996, February). Title of Lecture. *Lecture presented at the meeting of the Los Angeles County Psychological Association*, Los Angeles, CA.

Bukstein, O. G. (1995). *Adolescent substance abuse: Assessment, prevention, and treatment*. New York: Wiley.

Campbell, R. J. (1989). *Psychiatric dictionary* (6th ed.). New York: Oxford University Press.

Center for Substance Abuse Treatment. (1997). *Treatment improvement exchange: Opioid addiction special topic* [On-line]. Available: http://www.samhsa.gov/csat/csat.htm

Childress, A. R., Ehrman, R., Rohsenow, D. R., Robbins, S. J., & O'Brien, C. P. (1992). Classically conditioned factors in drug dependence. In J. H. Lowinson, P. Ruiz, & R. B. Millman (Eds.), *Substance abuse: A comprehensive textbook* (2nd ed., pp. 56–69). Baltimore: Williams & Wilkins.

Childress, A. R., Hole, A. V., Ehrman, R. N., & Robbins, S. J. (1993). Cue reactivity and cue reactivity interventions in drug dependence. In L. S. Onken, J. D. Blaine, & J. J. Boren (Eds.), *Behavioral treatments for drug abuse and dependence* (NIDA Research Monograph Series No. 137, NIH Publication No. 93-3684). Rockville, MD: National Institute on Drug Abuse.

Childress, A. R., McLellan, A. T., & O'Brien, C. P. (1988). Classically conditioned responses in cocaine and opioid dependence: A role in relapse? In B. A. Ray (Ed.), *Learning factors in substance abuse* (NIDA Research Monograph Series No. 84, NIH Publication No. 90-1576). Rockville, MD: National Institute on Drug Abuse.

Ciraulo, D. A., Barnhill, J. G., Ciraulo, A. M., Greenblatt, D. J., & Shader, R. L. (1989). Parental alcoholism as a risk factor in benzodiazepine abuse: A pilot study. *American Journal of Psychiatry, 146*, 1333–1335.

Clark, W. D. (1981). Alcoholism: Blocks to diagnosis and treatment. *American Journal of Medicine, 71*, 275–285.

Cleary, P. D., Miller, M., & Bush, B. T. (1988). Prevalence and recognition of alcohol abuse in a primary care population. *American Journal of Medicine, 85*, 466–471.

Cloninger, C. R. (1983). Genetic and environmental factors in the development of alcoholism. *Journal of Psychiatric Treatment and Evaluation, 5*, 487–496.

Cloninger, C. R., Bohman, M., & Sigvardsson, S. (1981). Inheritance of alcohol abuse: Cross-fostering analysis of adopted men. *Archives of General Psychiatry, 38*, 861–868.

Daley, D. C., & Marlatt, G. A. (1992). Relapse prevention: Cognitive and behavioral interventions. In J. H. Lowinson, P. Ruiz, R. B. Millman, & J. G. Langrod (Eds.), *Substance abuse: A comprehensive textbook* (2nd ed., pp. 533–542). Baltimore: Williams & Wilkins.

Deitch, D. (1973). The treatment of drug abuse in the therapeutic community: Historical influences, current considerations, future outlook.

Drug use in America (Vol. 4, pp. 158–175). Rockville, MD: National Commission on Marijuana and Drug Abuse.

Deitch, D. A., & Zweben, J. E. (1981). Synanon: A pioneering response in drug abuse treatment and a signal for caution. In J. Lowinson & P. Ruiz (Eds.), *Substance abuse: Clinical problems and perspectives.* (pp. 289–302). Baltimore: Williams & Wilkins.

De Leon, G. (1990–1991). Aftercare in therapeutic communities. *International Journal of the Addictions, 25,* 1225–1237.

De Leon, G. (1993). What psychologists can learn from addiction treatment research. *Psychology of Addictive Behaviors, 7,* 103–109.

De Leon, G. (1994a). The therapeutic community: Toward a general theory and model. In F. M. Tims, G. De Leon, & N. Jainchill (Eds.), *Therapeutic community: Advances in research and application* (NIDA Research Monograph Series No. 144, NIH Publication No. 94–3633). Rockville, MD: National Institute on Drug Abuse.

De Leon, G. (1994b). Therapeutic communities. In M. Galanter & H. D. Kleber (Eds.), *Textbook of substance abuse treatment* (pp. 391–414). Washington, DC: American Psychiatric Press.

De Leon, G. (1995). Residential therapeutic communities in the mainstream: Diversity and issues. *Journal of Psychoactive Drugs, 27,* 3–15.

Dinwiddie, S. H., & Cloninger, C. R. (1989). Family and adoption studies of alcoholism. In H. W. Goedde & D. P. Agarwal (Eds.), *Alcoholism: Biomedical and genetic aspects* (pp. 259–276). Elmsford, NY: Pergamon Press.

Dodd, M. (1997). Social model of recovery: Origin, early features, changes and future. *Journal of Psychoactive Drugs, 29,* 133–140.

Dole, V. (1988). Implication of methadone maintenance for theories of narcotic addiction. *Journal of the American Medical Association, 260,* 3025–3029.

Donovan, D. M. (1995). Assessments to aid in the treatment planning process. In J. P. Allen & M. Columbus (Eds.), *Assessing alcohol problems: A guide for clinicians and researchers* (NIH Pub. No. 95-3745). Rockville, MD: National Association on Alcohol Abuse and Alcoholism.

DuPont, R. L. (1990). Benzodiazepines and chemical dependence: Guidelines for clinicians. *Substance Abuse, 11,* 232–236.

Ellis, A., McInerney, J. F., DiGiuseppe, R., & Yeager, R. J. (1988). *Rational–emotive therapy with alcoholics and substance abusers.* New York: Pergamon Press.

Eisenhandler, J., & Drucker, E. (1993). Opiate dependency among the subscribers of a New York Area private insurance plan. *Journal of the American Medical Association, 269,* 2890–2891.

Ewing, J. (1984). Detecting alcoholism: The CAGE Questionnaire. *Journal of the American Medical Association, 252,* 1905–1907.

Evans, K., & Sullivan, M. (1994). *Treating trauma and addiction.* New York: Guilford Press.

Flaherty, J. A., & Kim, K. (1997). Managed care for psychiatric and addictive disorders. In N. S. Miller (Ed.), *The principles and practice of addictions in psychiatry* (pp. 400–406). Philadelphia: Saunders.

Flores, P. (1988). *Group psychotherapy with addicted populations.* New York: Haworth Press.

Flowers, L. K., & Zweben, J. E. (1996). The dream interview method in addiction recovery: A treatment guide. *Journal of Substance Abuse Treatment, 13,* 99–105.

Frances, R., Franklin, J., & Borg, L. (1994). Psychodynamics. In M. Galanter & H. D. Kleber (Eds.), *Textbook of substance abuse treatment* (pp. 239–252). Washington, DC: American Psychiatric Press.

Frances, R. J., & Borg, L. (1993). The treatment of anxiety in patients with alcoholism. *Journal of Clinical Psychiatry, 54*(Supplement), 37–43.

Freedman, R., Adler, L. E., Bickford, P., Byerley, W., Coon, H., Cullum, C. M., Griffith, J. M., Harris, J. G., Leonard, S., Miller, C., Myles-Worsley, M., Nagamoto, H. T., Rose, G., & Waldo, M. (1994). Schizophrenia and the nicotinic response. *Harvard Review of Psychiatry, 2,* 179–192.

Galanter, M. (1993). *Network therapy for alcohol and drug abuse.* New York: Basic Books.

Galanter, M. (1994). Network therapy for the office practitioner. In M. Galanter & H. D. Kleber (Eds.), *Textbook of substance abuse treatment* (pp. 253–262). Washington, DC: American Psychiatric Press.

Galanter, M., & Jaffe, J. (1995). Rational recovery (RR). In J. Jaffe (Ed.), *Encyclopedia of drugs and alcohol* (Vol. 3, pp. 899–900). New York: Simon & Schuster Macmillan.

Gallant, D. M. (1988). Diagnosis and treatment of the depressed alcoholic patient. *Substance Abuse, 9,* 147–156.

Gartner, L., & Mee-Lee, D. (1995). *The role and current status of patient placement criteria in the treatment of substance use disorders.* (DHHS Pub. No. SMA 95-3021). Rockville, MD: U.S. Department of Health and Human Services.

Gastfriend, D. R. (1995, August–September). ASAM PPC validity study. *ASAM News,* p. 7.

Gerard, D. L., & Kornetsky, C. (1954). Adolescent opiate addiction: A case study. *Psychiatry Quarterly, 28,* 367–380.

Gerard, D. L., & Kornetsky, C. (1955). Adolescent opiate addiction: A study of control and addict subjects. *Psychiatry Quarterly, 29,* 457–486.

Gerstein, D. R. (1994). Outcome research: Drug abuse. In M. Galanter & H. D. Kleber (Eds.), *Textbook of substance abuse treatment* (pp. 45–64). Washington, DC: American Psychiatric Press.

Gerstein, D. R., & Harwood, H. J. (1990). *Treating drug problems: A study of the evolution, effectiveness, and financing of public and private drug treatment systems.* Washington, DC: National Academy Press.

Gerstein, D. R., Johnson, R. A., Harwood, H. J., Suter, N., & Malloy, K. (1994). *CALDATA: Evaluating Recovery Services—The California Drug and Alcohol Treatment Assessment.* Sacramento: California Department of Alcohol and Drug Programs.

Gerstley, L. J., Alterman, A. I., McLellan, A. T., & Woody, G. E. (1990). Antisocial personality disorder in patients with substance abuse disorders: A problematic diagnosis? *American Journal of Psychiatry, 147,* 173–178.

Glassman, A. H. (1993). Cigarette smoking: Implications for psychiatric illness. *American Journal of Psychiatry, 150,* 546–553.

Goedde, H. W., & Agarwal, D. P. (Eds.). (1989). *Alcoholism: Biomedical and genetic aspects.* Elmsford, NY: Pergamon Press.

Goff, D. C., Henderson, D. C., & Amico, E. (1992). Cigarette smoking in schizophrenia: Relationship to psychopathology and medication side effects. *American Journal of Psychiatry, 149,* 1189–1194.

Gold, M. (1992). Cocaine (and crack): Clinical aspects. In J. H. Lowinson, P. Ruiz, & R. B. Millman (Eds.), *Substance abuse: A comprehensive textbook* (2nd ed., pp. 205–221). Baltimore: Williams & Wilkins.

Goldsmith, R. J. (1997). The elements of contemporary treatment. In N. S. Miller (Ed.), *The principles and practice of addictions in psychiatry* (pp. 392–399). Philadelphia: Saunders.

Goodwin, D. W. (1992). Alcohol: Clinical aspects. In J. H. Lowinson, P. Ruiz, & R. B. Millman (Eds.), *Substance abuse: A comprehensive textbook* (2nd ed., pp. 144–151). Baltimore: Williams & Wilkins.

Goodwin, D. W., Schulsinger, F., Hermansen, L., Guze, S. B., & Winokur, G. (1973). Alcohol problems in adoptees raised apart from alcoholic biological parents. *Archives of General Psychiatry, 28,* 238–243.

Goodwin, D. W., Schulsinger, F., Knopp, J., Mednick, S., & Guze, S. B. (1977). Alcoholism and depression in adopted-out daughters of alcoholics. *Archives of General Psychiatry, 34,* 751–755.

Goodwin, D. W., Schulsinger, F., Moller, N., Hermansen, L., Winokur, G., & Guze, S. B. (1974). Drinking problems in adopted and nonadopted sons of alcoholics. *Archives of General Psychiatry, 31,* 164–169.

Gorski, T. T. (1988a). *The staying sober workbook: Exercise manual.* Independence, MO: Independence Press.

Gorski, T. T. (1988b). *The staying sober workbook: Instruction manual.* Independence, MO: Independence Press.

Gorski, T. T. (1989). *Passages through recovery: An action plan for preventing relapse.* New York: Harper & Row.

Gorski, T. T. (1990). The Cenaps model of relapse prevention: Basic principles and procedures. *Journal of Psychoactive Drugs, 22,* 125–133.

Greenstein, R. A., Fudala, P. J., & O'Brien, C. P. (1992). Alternative pharmacotherapies for opiate addiction. In J. H. Lowinson, P. Ruiz, R. B. Millman, & J. G. Langrod (Eds.), *Substance abuse: A comprehensive textbook* (2nd ed., pp. 562–573). Baltimore: Williams & Wilkins.

Griffiths, R. R., & Roache, J. D. (1985). Abuse liability of benzodiazepines: A review of human studies evaluating subjective and/or reinforcing effects. In D. E. Smith & D. R. Wesson (Eds.), *The benzodiazepines: Current standards for medical practice* (pp. 209–226). Hingham, MA: MTP Press.

Haaken, J. (1990). A critical analysis of the co-dependence concept. *Psychiatry, 53,* 396–406.

Hall, R. C. W., Popkin, M. K., Devaul, R., & Stickney, S. K. (1977). The effect of unrecognized drug abuse on diagnosis and therapeutic outcome. *American Journal of Drug and Alcohol Abuse, 4,* 455–465.

Hall, S. M., Munoz, R., & Reus, V. I. (1992). Depression and smoking treatment: A clinical trial of an affect regulation treatment. In L. Harris (Ed.), *Problems of drug dependence, 1991* (NIDA Research Monograph No. 119, DHSS No. ADM 92-1888). Rockville, MD: National Institute on Drug Abuse.

Hall, S. M., Munoz, R., & Reus, V. I. (1994). Cognitive-behavioral intervention increases abstinence rates for depressive-history smokers. *Journal of Consulting and Clinical Psychology, 62,* 141–146.

Harm Reduction Working Group & Coalition. (1995, fall). *Harm education communication,* Oakland, CA: Author.

Harper, J., & Capdevila, C. (1990). Codependency: A critique. *Journal of Psychoactive Drugs, 22,* 285–291.

Heath, A. C., & Martin, N. G. (1988). Teenage alcohol use in the Australian twin register: Genetic and social determinants of starting to drink. *Alcoholism, 12,* 735–741.

Heath, A. C., Meyer, J., Eaves, L. J., & Martin, N. G. (1991). The inheritance of alcohol consumption patterns in a general population twin sample: I. Multidimensional scaling of quantity/frequency data. *Journal of Studies on Alcohol, 52,* 345–352.

Heath, A. C., Meyer, J., Jardine, R., & Martin, N. G. (1991). The inheritance of alcohol consumption patterns in a general population twin sample: II. Determinants of consumption frequency and quantity consumed. *Journal of Studies on Alcohol, 52,* 425–433.

Hersen, M., Miller, P. M., & Eisler, R. M. (1973). Interactions between alcoholics and their wives: A descriptive analysis of verbal and nonverbal behavior. *Journal of Studies on Alcohol, 34,* 516–520.

Hesselbrock, V. M. (1995). The genetic epidemiology of alcoholism. In H. Begleiter & B. Kissin (Eds.), *The genetics of alcoholism* (pp. 17–39). New York: Oxford University Press.

Hester, R. K. (1994). Outcome research: Alcoholism. In M. Galanter & H. D. Kleber (Eds.), *Textbook of substance abuse treatment* (pp. 35–44). Washington, DC: American Psychiatric Press.

Hester, R. K. (1995). Behavioral self-control training. In R. K. Hester & W. R. Miller (Eds.), *Handbook of alcoholism treatment approaches: Effective alternatives* (2nd ed., pp. 148–159). Boston: Allyn & Bacon.

Holderness, C. C., Brooks-Gunn, J., & Warren, M. P. (1994). Co-morbidity of eating disorders and substance abuse: Review of the literature. *International Journal of Eating Disorders, 16,* 1–34.

Hoffman, N. G., Halikas, J. A., & Mee-Lee, D. (1991). *Patient placement criteria for the treatment of psychoactive substance use disorders.* Chevy Chase, MD: American Society of Addiction Medicine.

Horn, J. L., Wanberg, K. W., & Foster, F. M. (1987). *Guide to the Alcohol Use Inventory.* Minneapolis, MN: National Computer Systems.

Hubbard, R. L., Marsden, M. E., Rachal, J. B., Harwood, H. J., Cavanaugh, E. R., & Ginzburg, E. R. (1989). *Drug abuse treatment: A national study of effectiveness.* Chapel Hill: University of North Carolina Press.

Imhof, J., Hirsch, R., & Terenzi, R. E. (1983). Countertransferential and attitudinal considerations in the treatment of drug abuse and addiction. *International Journal of Addictions, 18,* 491–510.

Institute of Medicine. (1990). *Broadening the base of treatment for alcohol problems.* Washington, DC: National Academy Press.

Isenhart, C. E. (1990). Further support for the criterion validity of the Alcohol Use Inventory. *Psychology of Addictive Behaviors, 4,* 77–81.

Jacobson, G. R. (1989). A comprehensive approach to pretreatment evaluation: I. Detection, assessment, and diagnosis of alcoholism. In R. K. Hester & W. R. Miller (Eds.), *Handbook of alcoholism treatment approaches: Effective alternatives* (pp. 17–43). Boston: Allyn & Bacon.

Jaffe, J. H. (1979). The swinging pendulum: The treatment of drug users in America. In R. L. Dupont, A. Goldstein, & J. O'Donnell (Eds.), *Handbook on drug abuse* (pp. 7–16). Washington, DC: U.S. Government Printing Office.

Jarvik, M. E., & Schneider, N. G. (1992). Nicotine. In J. H. Lowinson, P. Ruiz, R. B. Millman, & J. F. Langrod (Eds.), *Substance abuse: A comprehensive textbook* (2nd ed., pp. 334–356). Baltimore: Williams & Wilkins.

Jerrell, J. M., Hu, T., & Ridgley, S. (1994). Cost-effectiveness of substance disorder interventions for people with severe mental illness. *Journal of Mental Health Administration, 21,* 283–297.

Kadden, R., Carroll, K., Donovan, D., Cooney, N., Monti, P., Abrams, D., Litt, M., & Hester, R. (1994). *Cognitive-behavioral coping skills therapy manual.* NIAAA Project MATCH Monograph Series No. 3, Rockville, MD: U.S. Department of Health and Human Services.

Kadden, R. M., Getter, H., Cooney, N. L., & Litt, M. D. (1989). Matching alcoholics to coping skills or interactional therapies: Posttreatment results. *Journal of Consulting and Clinical Psychology, 57,* 698–704.

Kaufman, E. (1994). Family therapy: Other drugs. In M. Galanter & H. D. Kleber (Eds.), *Textbook of substance abuse treatment* (pp. 331–348). Washington, DC: American Psychiatric Press.

Kendler, K., Heath, A. C., Neale, M. C., Kessler, R. C., & Eaves, L. J. (1992). A population-based twin study of alcoholism in women. *Journal of the American Medical Association, 268,* 1877–1882.

Kernberg, O. (1975). *Borderline conditions and pathological narcissism.* New York: Jason Aronson.

Kessler, R. C., McGonagle, K. A., Zhao, S., Nelson, C. B., Hughes, M., Eshleman, S., Wittchen, H., & Kendler, K. (1994). Lifetime and 12 month prevalence of DSM-III-R psychiatric disorders in the United States. *Archives of General Psychiatry, 51,* 8–19.

Khantzian, E. J. (1981). Some treatment implications of the ego and self disturbances in alcoholism. In M. H. Bean & N. E. Zinberg (Eds.), *Dynamic approaches to the understanding and treatment of alcoholism* (pp. 163–193). New York: Macmillan.

Khantzian, E. J. (1982). Psychopathology, psychodynamics, and alcoholism. In M. Pattison & E. Kaufman (Eds.), *Encyclopedic handbook of alcoholism* (pp. 581–597). New York: Gardner Press.

Khantzian, E. J. (1985a). Psychotherapeutic interventions with substance abusers: The clinical context. *Journal of Substance Abuse Treatment, 2,* 83–85.

Khantzian, E. J. (1985b). The self-medication hypothesis of addictive disorders: Focus on heroin and cocaine dependence. *American Journal of Psychiatry, 142,* 1259–1264.

Khantzian, E. J. (1997). The self-medication hypothesis of substance use disorders: A reconsideration and recent applications. *Harvard Review of Psychiatry, 4,* 231–244.

Khantzian, E. J., Halliday, K. S., & McAuliffe, W. E. (1990). *Addiction and the vulnerable self: Modified dynamic group therapy for substance abusers.* New York: Guilford Press.

Kleber, H. D. (1994). *Assessment and treatment of cocaine-abusing methadone-maintained patients* (Treatment Improvement Protocol Series No. 10, NIH Pub. No. 94-3003). Rockville, MD: U.S. Department of Health and Human Services.

Kosten, T. R., & Kleber, H. D. (1988). Differential diagnosis of psychiatric comorbidity in substance abusers. *Journal of Substance Abuse Treatment, 5,* 201–206.

Kosten, T. R., Rounsaville, B. J., & Kleber, H. D. (1982). DSM-III personality disorders in opiate addicts. *Comprehensive Psychiatry, 23,* 572–581.

Kosten, T. R., Rounsaville, B. J., & Kleber, H. D. (1983). Concurrent validity of the Addiction Severity Index. *Journal of Nervous and Mental Disease, 171,* 606–610.

Krahn, E., Kurth, C., Demitrack, M., & Drewnowski, A. (1992). The relationship of dieting severity and bulimic behaviors to alcohol and other drug use in young women. *Journal of Substance Abuse, 4,* 341–353.

Krasner, L. (1982). Behavior therapy: On roots, contents, and growth. In G. T. Wilson & C. M. Franks (Eds.), *Contemporary behavior therapy: Conceptual and empirical foundations.* New York: Guilford Press.

Krystal, H. (1988). *Integration and self healing: Affect, trauma, alexithymia.* Hillsdale, NJ: Analytic Press.

Leshner, A. I. (Speaker). (1997). *Drug abuse and addiction: Blending scientific and public interest psychology.* (Cassette Recording No. APA97–2276). Washington, DC: American Psychological Association.

Lesieur, H. R., & Blume, S. (1987). The South Oaks Gambling Screen (SOGS): A new instrument for the identification of pathological gamblers. *American Journal of Psychiatry, 144,* 1184–1188.

Lesieur, H. R., & Blume, S. (1990). Characteristics of pathological gamblers identified among patients on a psychiatric admissions service. *Hospital and Community Psychiatry, 41,* 1009–1012.

Lesieur, H. R., Blume, S. B., & Zoppa, R. M. (1986). Alcoholism, drug abuse, and gambling. *Alcoholism: Clinical and Experimental Research, 10,* 33–38.

Leukefeld, C. G., & Tims, F. M. (Eds.). (1992). *Drug abuse treatment in prisons and jails* (NIDA Research Monograph No. 118, NCADI No. M118). Rockville, MD: National Institute on Drug Abuse.

Levy, M. (1987). A change in orientation: Therapeutic strategies for the treatment of alcoholism. *Psychotherapy, 24,* 786–793.

Lewis, D. C. (1991). Comparison of alcoholism and other medical diseases: An internist's view. *Psychiatric Annals, 21,* 256–265.

Lewis, D. (1994). *The need for substance abuse treatment: A research and public health perspective.* Unpublished manuscript, Brown University Center for Alcohol and Addiction Studies, Providence, RI.

Li, T. K., Lumeng, L., McBride, W. J., & Waller, M. B. (1981). Indiana selection studies on alcohol-related behaviors. In G. E. McClearn, R. A. Dietrich, & V. G. Erwin (Eds.), *Development of animal models as pharmacogenetic tools* (NIAAA Research Monograph 6, NIH Pub. No. 81-1133). Washington, DC: U.S. Government Printing Office.

Liftik, J. (1995). Assessment. In S. Brown (Ed.), *Treating alcoholism* (pp. 57–94). San Francisco: Jossey-Bass.

Ling, W., & Wesson, D. (1984). Naltrexone treatment for addicted health-care professionals: A collaborative private practice experience. *Journal of Clinical Psychiatry, 45,* 46–48.

Litt, M. D., Babor, T. F., DelBoca, F. K., Kadden, R. M., & Cooney, N. L. (1992). Types of alcoholics: II. Application of an empirically derived typology to treatment matching. *Archives of General Psychiatry, 49,* 609–614.

Lubin, B., Brady, K., Woodward, L., & Thames, E. A. (1986). Graduate professional psychology training in alcoholism and substance abuse: 1984. *Professional Psychology: Research and Practice, 17,* 151–154.

Luborsky, L., McLellan, A. T., Woody, G. E., O'Brien, C. P., & Auerbach, A. (1985). Therapist success and its determinants. *Archives of General Psychiatry, 42,* 602–611.

Lumeng, L., Murphy, J. M., McBride, W. J., & Li, T.-K. (1995). Genetic influences on alcohol preference in animals. In H. Begleiter & B. Kissin (Eds.), *The genetics of alcoholism* (pp.165–201). New York: Oxford University Press.

Marlatt, G. A. (1985). Relapse prevention: A general overview. In G. A. Marlatt & J. R. Gordon (Eds.), *Relapse prevention: Maintenance strategies in the treatment of addictive behaviors* (pp. 3–16). New York: Guilford Press.

Marlatt, G. A., & Barrett, K. (1994). Relapse prevention. In M. Galanter &

H. D. Kleber (Eds.), *The American psychiatric press textbook of substance abuse treatment*. Washington, DC: American Psychiatric Press.

Marlatt, G. A., & Gordon, J. R. (Eds.). (1985). *Relapse prevention: Maintenance strategies in the treatment of addictive behaviors*. New York: Guilford Press.

Marlatt, G. A., & Rohsenow, D. R. (1980). Cognitive processes in alcohol use: Expectancy and the balanced placebo design. *Advances in Substance Abuse: Behavioral and Biological Research, 1*, 159–199.

Marshall, E. J., & Murray, R. M. (1989). The contribution of twin studies to alcoholism research. In H. W. Goedde & D. P. Agarwal (Eds.), *Alcoholism: Biomedical and genetic aspects* (pp. 277–289). Elmsford, NY: Pergamon Press.

Matrix Center. (1995). *The Matrix intensive outpatient program: Therapist manual*. Los Angeles: Author.

McCrady, B. S. (1994). Alcoholics anonymous and behavior therapy: Can habits be treated as diseases? Can diseases be treated as habits? *Journal of Consulting and Clinical Psychology, 62*, 1159–1166.

McCrady, B. S., & Epstein, E. E. (1996). Theoretical bases of family approaches to substance abuse treatment. In F. Rotgers, D. Keller, & J. Morgenstern (Eds.), *Treating substance abuse: Theory and technique* (pp. 117–142). New York: Guilford Press.

McDougall, J. (1984). The "dis-affected patient": Reflections on affect pathology. *Psychoanalytic Quarterly, 53*, 386–409.

McElrath, E. (1997). The Minnesota model. *Journal of Psychoactive Drugs, 29*, 141–144.

McFarland, B. H., Faulkner, L. R., Bloom, J. D., Hallaux, R., & Bray, J. D. (1989). Chronic mental illness and the criminal justice system. *Hospital and Community Psychiatry, 40*, 718–723.

McGinnis, J. M. (1993). Actual causes of death in the United States. *Journal of the American Medical Association, 270*, 2207–2212.

McGue, M., Pickens, R. W., & Svikis, D. S. (1992). Sex and age effects on the inheritance of alcohol problems: A twin study. *Journal of Abnormal Psychology, 101*, 3–17.

McLellan, A. T. (1983). Patient characteristics associated with outcome. In J. Cooper, F. Altman, B. S. Brown, D. Czechowicz (Eds.), *Research on the treatment of narcotic addiction* (pp. 500–523). Rockville, MD: U.S. Department of Health and Human Services.

McLellan, A. T., & Alterman, A. I. (1991). Patient treatment matching: a conceptual and methodological review with suggestions for future research. In R. W. Pickens, C. G. Leukefeld, & C. R. Schuster (Eds.), *Improving drug abuse treatment* (NIDA Research Monograph Series No. 106, DHHS No. ADM 91-1754). Rockville, MD: National Institute on Drug Abuse.

McLellan, A. T., Alterman, A. I., Metzger, D. S., Grissom, G. R., Woody, G. E., Luborsky, L., & O'Brien, C. P. (1994). Similarity of outcome predictors across opiate, cocaine, and alcohol treatments: Role of treatment services. *Journal of Consulting and Clinical Psychology, 62,* 1141–1158.

McLellan, A. T., Alterman, A. I., Woody, G. E., & Metzger, D. A. (1992). A quantitative measure of substance abuse treatments: The Treatment Services Review. *Journal of Nervous and Mental Disease, 180,* 101–110.

McLellan, A. T., Childress, A. R., Ehrman, R. N., & O'Brien, C. P. (1986). Extinguishing conditioned responses during treatment for opiate dependence: Turning laboratory findings into clinical procedure. *Journal of Substance Abuse Treatment, 3,* 33–40.

McLellan, A. T., Grissom, G. R., Brill, P., Durrell, J., Metzger, D. S., & O'Brien, C. P. (1993). Private substance abuse treatments: Are some programs more effective than others? *Journal of Substance Abuse Treatment, 10,* 243–254.

McLellan, A. T., Grissom, G. R., Zanis, D., Randall, M., Brill, P., & O'Brien, C. P. (1997). Problem-service "matching" in addiction treatment: A prospective study in 4 programs. *Archives of General Psychiatry, 54,* 730–735.

McLellan, A. T., Grossman, D. S., Blaine, J. D., & Haverkos, H. W. (1993). Acupuncture treatment for drug abuse: A technical review. *Journal of Substance Abuse Treatment, 10,* 569–576.

McLellan, A. T., Luborsky L., Cacciola, J., Griffith, J., Evans, F., Barr, H. L., & O'Brien, C. P. (1985). New data from the Addiction Severity Index: Reliability and validity in three centers. *Journal of Nervous and Mental Disease, 173,* 412–423.

McLellan, A. T., Luborsky L., O'Brien, C. P., & Woody, G. E. (1980). An improved evaluation instrument for substance abuse patients: The Addiction Severity Index. *Journal of Nervous and Mental Disease, 168,* 26–33.

McLellan, A. T., Woody, G. E., Luborsky, L., & Goehl, L. (1988). Is the counselor an "active ingredient" in substance abuse rehabilitation: An examination of treatment success among four counselors. *Journal of Nervous and Mental Disease, 176,* 423–430.

McLellan, A. T., Woody, G. E., Metzger, D. S., McKay, J., Durell, J., Alterman, A. I., O'Brien, C. P. (1995). Evaluating the effectiveness of addiction treatments: Reasonable expectations, appropriate comparisons. *Millbank Quarterly, 74,* 51–85.

Milkman, H., & Frosch, W. A. (1973). On the preferential abuse of heroin and amphetamine. *Journal of Nervous and Mental Disease, 156,* 242–248.

Miller, N. S. (1995). *Addiction psychiatry: Current diagnosis and treatment.* New York: Wiley-Liss.

Miller, N. S., & Chappell, J. N. (1991). History of the disease concept. *Psychiatric Annals, 21,* 196–205.

Miller, N. S., & Gold, M. S. (1991). Dependence syndrome: A critical analysis of essential features. *Psychiatric Annals, 21,* 282–290.

Miller, W. R., & Baca, L. M. (1983). Two-year followup of bibliotherapy and therapist-directed controlled drinking training for problem drinkers. *Behavior Therapy, 14,* 441–448.

Miller, W. R., & Hester, R. K. (1986). Inpatient alcoholism treatment: who benefits? *American Psychologist, 41,* 794–805.

Miller, W. R., & Hester, R. K. (1995). Treatment for alcohol problems: Toward an informed eclecticism. In R. K. Hester & W. R. Miller (Eds.), *Handbook of Alcoholism treatment approaches: Effective alternatives* (2nd ed., pp. 1–11). Boston: Allyn & Bacon.

Miller, W. R., & Page, A. (1991). Warm turkey: Other routes to abstinence. *Journal of Substance Abuse Treatment, 8,* 227–232.

Miller, W. R., & Rollnick, S. (1991). *Motivational interviewing: Preparing people to change addictive behavior.* New York: Guilford Press.

Miller, W. R., Taylor, C. A., & West, J. C. (1980). Focused versus broad-spectrum behavior therapy for problem drinkers. *Journal of Consulting and Clinical Psychology, 48,* 590–601.

Miller, W. R., Westerberg, V. S., & Waldron, H. B. (1995). Evaluating alcohol problems in adults and adolescents. In R. K. Hester & W. R. Miller (Eds.), *Handbook of alcoholism treatment approaches: Effective alternatives* (2nd ed., pp. 61–88). Boston: Allyn & Bacon.

Miller, W. R., Zweben, A., DiClemente, C. C., & Rychtarik, R. G. (1994). *Motivational enhancement therapy manual* (NIAAA Project Match Monograph Series No. 2, NIH Pub. No. 94-3723). Rockville, MD: U.S. Department of Health and Human Services.

Mischke, H. D., & Venneri, R. L. (1987). Reliability and validity of the MAST, Mortimer-Filkins Questionnaire, and CAGE in DWI assessment. *Journal of Studies on Alcohol, 48,* 492–501.

Monti, P. M., Abrams, D. B., Kadden, R. M., & Cooney, N. L. (1989). *Treating alcohol dependence: A coping skills training guide.* New York: Guilford Press.

Monti, P. M., Rohsenow, D. J., Abrams, D. B., & Binkoff, J. A. (1988). Social learning approaches to alcohol relapse: Selected illustrations and implications. In B. A. Ray (Ed.), *Learning factors in substance abuse* (NIDA Research Monograph Series No. 84, NIH Pub. No. 90-1576). Rockville, MD: National Institute on Drug Abuse.

Moore, R. D., Bone, L. R., & Geller, G. (1989). Prevalence, detection, and treatment of alcoholism in hospitalized patients. *Journal of the American Medical Association, 261,* 403–407.

Murphy, S., & Irwin, J. (1992). "Living with the dirty secret": Problems of disclosure for methadone maintenance clients. *Journal of Psychoactive Drugs, 24,* 257–264.

Nagy, P. D. (1994). *Intensive outpatient treatment for alcohol and other drug abuse* (Treatment Improvement Protocol Series No. 8, NIH Pub. No. 94-2077). Rockville, MD: U.S. Department of Health and Human Services.

National Clearinghouse for Alcohol and Drug Information. (1995). *Health care costs, the deficit, and alcohol, tobacco, and other drugs* (NCADI No. ML007). Washington, DC: Author.

National Institute on Alcohol Abuse and Alcoholism. (1990). *Alcohol and health: Seventh special report to the U.S. Congress* (DHHS Publication No. ADM-281–88–0002). Rockville, MD: Author.

National Institute on Alcohol Abuse and Alcoholism. (1993). *Alcohol and health: Eighth special report to the U.S. Congress* (DHHS Publication No. ADM-281–91–0003). Rockville, MD: Author.

National Institute on Alcohol Abuse and Alcoholism Project MATCH Research Group. (1997). Matching alcoholism treatments to client heterogeneity: Project MATCH posttreatment drinking outcomes. *Journal of Studies on Alcohol, 90,* 1179–1188.

Nelson, C. E. (1985). The styles of enabling behavior. In D. E. Smith & D. R. Wesson (Eds.), *Treating the cocaine user* (pp. 49–72). Center City, MN: Hazelden.

Noel, N. E., & McCrady, B. S. (1993). Alcohol-focused spouse involvement with behavioral marital therapy. In T. J. O'Farrell (Ed.), *Treating alcohol problems: Marital and family interventions* (pp. 210–235). New York: Guilford Press.

O'Brien, C. P., & McLellan, A. T. (1996). Myths about the treatment of addiction. *Lancet, 347,* 237–240.

O'Bryant, R. G., & Peterson, N. W. (1990). Social setting detoxification. In S. Shaw & T. Borkman (Eds.), *Social model alcohol recovery: An environmental approach* (pp. 23–30). Burbank, CA: Bridge Focus.

O'Farrell, T. J. (1993). A behavioral marital therapy couples group program for alcoholics and their spouses. In T. J. O'Farrell (Ed.), *Treating alcohol problems* (pp. 170–209). New York: Guilford Press.

O'Farrell, T. J., & Cowles, K. S. (1989). Marital and family therapy. In R. K. Hester & W. R. Miller (Eds.), *Handbook of alcoholism treatment approaches: Effective alternatives* (pp. 183–205). Elmsford, NY: Pergamon Press.

O'Malley, S., Jaffe, A. J., Chang, G., Schottenfeld, R., Meyer, R., & Rounsaville, B. (1992). Naltrexone and coping skills therapy for alcohol dependence. *Archives of General Psychiatry, 49,* 881–887.

Pickens, R. W., Svikis, D. S., McGue, M., Lykken, D. T., Hesten, L. L., & Clayton, P. J. (1991). Heterogeneity in the inheritance of alcoholism. *Archives of General Psychiatry, 48,* 19–28.

Pokorny, A. D., Miller, B. A., & Kaplan, H. B. (1972). The Brief MAST: A shortened version of the Michigan Alcoholism Screening Test. *American Journal of Psychiatry, 129,* 342–345.

Porjesz, B., & Begleiter, H. (1983). Brain dysfunction and alcohol. In B. Kissin & H. Begleiter (Eds.), *The pathogenesis of alcoholism* (pp. 415–483). New York: Plenum.

Portnoy, R. K., & Payne, R. (1992). Acute and chronic pain. In J. H. Lowinson, P. Ruiz, R. B. Millman, & J. G. Langrod (Eds.), *Substance abuse:*

A comprehensive textbook (2nd ed., pp. 691–721). Baltimore: Williams & Wilkins.

Primm, B. (1990). *Office for treatment improvement: Mission, goals, and program summary.* Rockville, MD: U.S. Department of Health and Human Services.

Prochaska, J. O., & DiClemente, C. C. (1986). Toward a comprehensive model of change. In W. R. Miller & N. Heather (Eds.), *Treating addictive behaviors: Processes of change* (pp. 3–27). New York: Plenum.

Prochascka, J. O., DiClemente, C. C., & Norcross, J. C. (1992). In search of how people change: Applications to addictive behaviors. *American Psychologist, 47,* 1102–1114.

Rawson, R. (1990–1991). Chemical dependency treatment: The integration of the alcoholism and drug addiction/use treatment systems. *International Journal of the Addictions, 25,* 1515–1536.

Rawson, R. (1994, April). Relapse prevention models. In J. E. Zweben & R. Rawson (Co-Chairs), *Psychological models of outpatient substance abuse treatment: Recovery oriented psychotherapy and relapse prevention models.* Workshop conducted at the 25th Annual Medical-Scientific Conference of the American Society of Addiction Medicine, New York, NY.

Rawson, R. A. (1995, April). *Psychological models of outpatient treatment: Relapse prevention models.* Workshop conducted at the 26th Annual Medical-Scientific Conference of the American Society of Addiction Medicine, Chicago.

Rawson, R. A., Obert, J. L., McCann, M. J., Smith, D. P., & Ling, W. (1990). Neurobehavioral treatment for cocaine dependency. *Journal of Psychoactive Drugs, 22,* 159–172.

Regier, D. A., Farmer, M. E., Rae, D. S., Locke, B. Z., Keith, S. J., Judd, L. L., & Goodwin, F. K. (1990). Comorbidity of mental disorders with alcohol and other drug abuse. *Journal of the American Medical Association, 264,* 2511–2518.

Reich, T., Cloninger, C. R., van Eerdewegh, P., Rice, J. P., & Mullaney, J. (1988). Secular trends in the familial transmission of alcoholism. *Alcoholism: Clinical and Experimental Research, 12,* 458–464.

Rettig, R. A., & Yarmolinsky, A. (Eds.). (1995). *Federal regulation of methadone treatment.* Washington, DC: National Academy Press.

Reynolds, R. L., & Ryan, B. E. (1990). Policy implications of social model alcohol recovery services. In S. Shaw & T. Borkman (Eds.), *Social model alcohol recovery: An environmental approach* (pp. 31–38). Burbank, CA: Bridge Focus.

Rhodes, F. (1993). *The behavioral counseling model for injection drug users: Intervention model.* Rockville, MD: U.S. Department of Health and Human Services, National Institute on Drug Abuse.

Ries, R. (1993). Clinical treatment matching models for dually diagnosed patients. *Psychiatric Clinics of North America, 16,* 167–175.

Ries, R. (1994). *Assessment and treatment of patients with coexisting mental illness and alcohol and other drug abuse.* (Treatment Improvement Protocol Series No. 9, DHHS No. SMA 94-2078). Rockville, MD: Substance Abuse and Mental Health Services Administration.

Ries, R. (1996, March). *Group therapy interventions.* Paper presented at the Second Annual Conference on Dual Disorders, Division of Mental Health and Substance Abuse Services, San Francisco.

Rimmele, C. T., Miller, R. W., & Dougher, M. J. (1989). Aversion therapies. In R. K. Hester & W. P. Miller (Eds.), *Handbook of alcoholism treatment approaches: Effective alternatives* (pp. 128–140). Elmsford, NY: Pergamon Press.

Rohsenow, D. J. (1982). The Alcohol Use Inventory as a predictor of drinking by male heavy social drinkers. *Addictive Behaviors, 7,* 387–395.

Rotgers, F. (1996). Behavioral theory of substance abuse treatment: Bringing science to bear on practice. In F. Rotgers, D. Keller, & J. Morgenstern (Eds.), *Treating substance abuse: Theory and technique* (pp. 174–201). New York: Guilford Press.

Rounsaville, B. J., & Kranzler, H. R. (1989). *The DSM-III-R diagnosis of alcoholism, psychiatric update* (pp. 323–340). Washington, DC: American Psychiatric Press.

Schlesinger, S. E. (1984). Substance misuse training in graduate psychology programs. *Journal of Studies on Alcohol, 45,* 131–137.

Schottenfeld, R. S. (1994). Assessment of the patient. In M. Galanter & H. D. Kleber (Eds.), *Textbook of substance abuse treatment* (pp. 25–33). Washington, DC: American Psychiatric Press.

Schuckit, M. A. (1985a). Trait (and state) markers of a predisposition to psychopathology. In R. Michael (Ed.), *Psychiatry* (Vol. 3, pp. 1–19). New York: Basic Books.

Schuckit, M. A. (1985b). The clinical implications of primary diagnostic groups among alcoholics. *Archives of General Psychiatry, 42,* 1043–1049.

Schuckit, M. A. (1985c). Ethanol induced changes in body sway in men at high alcoholism risk. *Archives of General Psychiatry, 42,* 375–379.

Schuckit, M. A. (1986). Genetic and clinical implications of alcoholism and affective disorder. *American Journal of Psychiatry, 143,* 140–147.

Schuckit, M. A. (1989a). Biomedical and genetic markers of alcoholism. In H. W. Goedde & D. P. Agarwal (Eds.), *Alcoholism: Biomedical and genetic aspects* (pp. 290–302). Elmsford, NY: Pergamon Press.

Schuckit, M. A. (1989b). *Drugs and alcohol abuse: A clinical guide to diagnosis and treatment* (3rd ed.). New York: Plenum.

Schuckit, M. A. (1994). Goals of treatment. In M. Galanter & H. D. Kleber (Eds.), *Textbook of substance abuse treatment* (pp. 3–10). Washington, DC: American Psychiatric Press.

Schuckit, M. A. (1995). *Drug and alcohol abuse: A clinical guide to diagnosis and treatment* (4th ed.). New York: Plenum Medical.

Selen, J., & Svanum, S. (1981). Alcoholism and substance abuse training: A survey of graduate programs in clinical psychology. *Professional Psychology, 12,* 717–721.

Selwyn, P. A., & Batki, S. L. (1995). *Treatment for HIV-infected alcohol and other drug abusers* (Treatment Improvement Protocol Series No. 15, DHHS Pub. 95-3038). Rockville, MD: U.S. Department of Health and Human Services.

Selzer, M. L. (1971). The Michigan Alcoholism Screening Test: The quest for a new diagnostic instrument. *American Journal of Psychiatry, 127,* 1653–1658.

Selzer, M. L., Vinokur, A., & van Rooijen, L. (1975). A self-administered Short Michigan Alcoholism Screening Test (SMAST). *Journal of Studies on Alcohol, 36,* 117–126.

Sherin, K. M., & Mahoney, B. (1996). *Treatment drug courts: Integrating substance abuse treatment with legal case processing* (Treatment Improvement Protocol Series, No. 23, NIH Pub. No. 96-3113). Rockville, MD: U.S. Department of Health and Human Services.

Sigvardsson, S., Bohman, M., & Cloninger, C. R. (1996). Replication of the Stockholm adoption study of alcoholism. *Archives of General Psychiatry, 53,* 681–687.

Sisson, R. W., & Azrin, N. H. (1993). Community reinforcement training for families: A method to get alcoholics into treatment. In T. J. O'Farrell (Ed.), *Treating alcohol problems* (pp. 34–53). New York: Guilford Press.

Skinner, H. A., & Allen, B. A. (1983). Differential assessment of alcoholism: Evaluation of the Alcohol Use Inventory. *Journal of Studies on Alcohol, 44,* 852–862.

Smith, D. E., Buxton, M. E., Bilal, R., & Seymour, R. A. (1993). Cultural points of resistance to the 12-step recovery process. *Journal of Psychoactive Drugs, 25,* 97–108.

Smith, J. E., & Meyers, R. J. (1995). The community reinforcement approach. In R. K. Hester & W. R. Miller (Eds.), *Handbook of alcoholism treatment approaches: Effective alternatives* (2nd ed., pp. 251–266). Boston: Allyn & Bacon.

Smith, J. W. (1983). Diagnosing alcoholism. *Hospital and Community Psychiatry, 34,* 1017–1021.

Smoking Cessation Clinical Practice Guideline Panel and Staff. (1996). The agency for health care policy and research smoking cessation clinical practice guidelines. *Journal of the American Medical Association, 275,* 1270–1280.

Sobell, M. B., & Sobell, L. C. (1978). *Behavioral treatment of alcohol problems.* New York: Plenum.

Sobell, M. B., & Sobell, L. C. (1993). *Problem drinkers: Guided self-change treatment.* New York: Guilford Press.

Steinglass, P. (1979). The alcoholic family in the interaction laboratory. *Journal of Nervous and Mental Disease, 167,* 428–436.

Steinglass, P. (1981). The alcoholic family at home: Patterns of interaction in dry, wet, and transitional stages of alcoholism. *Archives of General Psychiatry, 38,* 578–584.

Steinglass, P. (1994). Family therapy: Alcohol. In M. Galanter & H. D. Kleber (Eds.), *Textbook of substance abuse treatment* (pp. 315–329). Washington, DC: American Psychiatric Press.

Steinglass, P., Bennett, L. A., Wolin, S. J., & Reiss, D. (1987). *The alcoholic family*. New York: Basic Books.

Substance Abuse and Mental Health Services Office of Applied Statistics. (1997). *National admissions to substance abuse treatment services: The treatment episode data set (TEDS) for 1992–1995* (Advance Rep. No. 12). Washington, DC: Author.

Sullivan, M., & Evans, K. (1994). Integrated treatment for the addicted survivor of childhood trauma. *Journal of Psychoactive Drugs, 26*, 369–378.

Swift, R. M. (1995). Effect of naltrexone on human alcohol consumption. *Journal of Clinical Psychiatry, 56*(Suppl. 7), 24–29.

Tarter, R. E., Arria, A. M., Moss, H., Edwards, N. J., & Van Thiel, D. H. (1987). DSM-III criteria for alcohol abuse: Associations with alcohol consumption behavior. *Alcoholism: Clinical and Experimental Research, 11*, 541–543.

Thombs, D. L. (1994). *Introduction to addictive behaviors*. New York: Guilford Press.

Travin, S. (1995). Compulsive sexual behaviors. *Psychiatric Clinics of North America, 18*, 155–169.

Travin, S., & Protter, B. (1982). Mad or bad? Some clinical considerations in the misdiagnosis of schizophrenia as antisocial personality disorder. *American Journal of Psychiatry, 139*, 1335–1338.

Trimpey, J. (1988). *Rational recovery from alcoholism: The small book*. Lotus, CA: Lotus Press.

Vaillant, G. E. (1981). Dangers of psychotherapy in the treatment of alcoholism. In M. H. Bean & N. E. Zinberg (Eds.), *Dynamic approaches to the understanding and treatment of alcoholism* (pp. 36–54). New York: Free Press.

Vaillant, G. E. (1983). *The natural history of alcoholism*. Cambridge, MA: Harvard University.

Valle, S. K. (1981). Interpersonal functioning of alcoholism counselors and treatment outcome. *Journal of Studies on Alcohol, 42*, 783–790.

Vannicelli, M. (1992). *Removing the roadblocks: Group psychotherapy with substance abusers and family members*. New York: Guilford Press.

Verebey, K. (1992). Diagnostic laboratory: Screening for drug abuse. In J. H. Lowinson, P. Ruiz, & R. B. Millman (Eds.), *Substance abuse: A comprehensive textbook* (2nd ed., pp. 425–436). Baltimore: Williams & Wilkins.

Vigdal, G. L. (1995). *Planning for alcohol and other drug abuse treatment for adults in the criminal justice system* (Treatment Improvement Protocol Series No. 17, NIH Pub. No. 95-3039). Rockville, MD: U.S. Department of Health and Human Services.

Volberg, R. A., & Steadman, H. J. (1988). Refining prevalence estimates of pathological gambling. *American Journal of Psychiatry, 145,* 502–505.

Volpicelli, J. R., Alterman, A. I., Hayashida, M., & O'Brien, C. P. (1992). Naltrexone in the treatment of alcohol dependence. *Archives of General Psychiatry, 49,* 876–880.

Volpicelli, J. R., Clay, K. L., Watson, N. T., & O'Brien, C. P. (1995). Naltrexone in the treatment of alcoholism: Predicting response to naltrexone. *Journal of Clinical Psychiatry, 56*(Suppl. 7), 39–44.

Wallace, J. (1986). Smoke gets in our eyes: Professional denial of smoking. *Journal of Substance Abuse Treatment, 3,* 67–68.

Wallace, J. (1989). *Writings: The alcoholism papers.* Newport, RI: Edgehill Publications.

Wallace, J. (1996). Theory of 12-step-oriented treatment. In F. Rotgers, D. Keller, & J. Morgenstern (Eds.), *Treating substance abuse: Theory and technique* (pp. 117–137). New York: Guilford Press.

Washton, A. M. (1989). *Cocaine addiction: Treatment, recovery and relapse prevention.* New York: Norton.

Washton, A. M. (1992). Structured outpatient group therapy with alcohol and substance abusers. In J. H. Lowinson, P. Ruiz, R. B. Millman, & J. G. Langrod (Eds.), *Substance abuse: A comprehensive textbook* (2nd ed., pp. 508–519). Baltimore: Williams & Wilkins.

Washton, A. M. (Ed.). (1995a). *Psychotherapy and substance abuse: A practitioner's handbook.* New York: Guilford Press.

Washton, A. M. (1995b, April). *Dealing with patient resistance: Clinical, staff and program issues in a managed care environment* (Infomedix Cassette Recording No. Q149–38). Washington, DC: American Society of Addiction Medicine.

Washton, A. M., Pottash, A. C., & Gold, M. S. (1984). Naltrexone in addictive business executives and physicians. *Journal of Clinical Psychiatry, 45,* 39–41.

Washton, A. M., & Stone-Washton, N. (1990). Abstinence and relapse in outpatient cocaine addicts. *Journal of Psychoactive Drugs, 22,* 135–147.

Washton, A. M., & Stone-Washton, N. (1991). *Step zero: Getting to recovery.* Center City, MN: Hazelden.

Weibel, W. (1993). *The indigenous leader outreach model: Intervention model* (NIDA Publication No. 93-3581). Rockville, MD: National Institute on Drug Abuse.

Weider, H., & Kaplan, E. H. (1969). Drug use in adolescents: Psychodynamic meaning and pharmacogenic effect. *Psychoanalytic Studies of Children, 24,* 399–431.

Wesson, D. (1995). *Detoxification from alcohol and other drugs* (Treatment Improvement Protocol Series No. 19, NIH Pub. No. 95-3046). Rockville, MD: U.S. Department of Health and Human Services.

Wesson, D., Smith, D. E., & Seymour, R. B. (1992). Sedative-hypnotics and tricyclics. In J. H. Lowinson, P. Ruiz, R. B. Millman, & J. G. Langrod

(Eds.), *Substance abuse: A comprehensive textbook* (2nd ed., pp. 271–279). Baltimore: Williams & Wilkins.

Wiederman, M. W., & Pryor, T. (1996). Substance use and impulsive behaviors among adolescents with eating disorders. *Addictive Behaviors, 21,* 269–272.

Williams, C. (1992). *No hiding place: Empowerment and recovery for our troubled communities.* San Francisco: HarperCollins.

Winters, K. C. (1992). Development of an adolescent alcohol and other drug abuse screening scale: Personal Experience Screening Questionnaire. *Addictive Behaviors, 17,* 479–490.

Winters, K. C., & Henly, G. A. (1987). Advances in the assessment of adolescent chemical dependency: Development of a chemical use problem severity scale. *Psychology of Addictive Behaviors, 1,* 146–153.

Winters, K. C., & Henly, G. A. (1989). *Personal Experience Inventory test and manual.* Los Angeles: Western Psychological Services.

Wise, R. A. (1988). Psychomotor stimulant properties of addictive drugs. *Annals of the New York Academy of Science, 537,* 228–234.

Woititz, J. G. (1983). *Adult children of alcoholics.* Hollywood, FL: Heath Communications.

Wolfe, I., Chafetz, M. E., & Blane, H. T. (1965). Social factors in the diagnosis of alcoholism: Attitudes of physicians. *Quarterly Journal of Studies on Alcohol, 26,* 72–79.

Wright, A. (1990). What is social model? In S. Shaw & T. Borkman (Eds.), *Social model alcohol recovery: An environmental approach* (pp. 7–10). Burbank, CA: Bridge Focus.

Wright, A., Clay, T., & Weir, G. (1990). Description of the Los Angeles County "community model" alcohol recovery program: The community recovery center. In S. Shaw & T. Borkman (Eds.), *Social model alcohol recovery: An environmental approach* (pp. 75–86). Burbank, CA: Bridge Focus.

Wurmser, L. (1974). Psychoanalytic considerations of the etiology of compulsive drug use. *Journal of the American Psychoanalytic Association, 22,* 820–843.

Yalom, I. (1995). *The theory and practice of group psychotherapy* (4th ed.). New York: Basic Books.

Zweben, J. E. (1987). Eating disorders and substance abuse. *Journal of Psychoactive Drugs, 19,* 171–180.

Zweben, J. E. (1989). Recovery oriented psychotherapy: Patient resistances and therapist dilemmas. *Journal of Substance Abuse Treatment, 6,* 123–132.

Zweben, J. E. (1993). Recovery-oriented psychotherapy: A model for addiction treatment. *Psychotherapy, 30,* 259–268.

Zweben, J. E. (1995). Integrating psychotherapy and 12-step approaches. In A. M. Washton (Ed.), *Psychotherapy and substance abuse: A practitioner's handbook* (pp. 124–140). New York: Guilford Press.

Zweben, J. E., & Clark, H. W. (1991). Unrecognized substance misuse:

Clinical hazards and legal vulnerabilities. *International Journal of the Addictions, 25,* 1431–1451.

Zweben, J. E., & Payte, J. T. (1990). Methadone maintenance in the treatment of opioid dependence: A current perspective. *Western Journal of Medicine, 152,* 588–599.

Zweben, J. E., & Smith, D. E. (1989). Considerations in using psychotropic medication with dual diagnosis patients in recovery. *Journal of Psychoactive Drugs, 21,* 221–229.

Appendix A

Adult Admission Criteria

Adult Admission Criteria: Crosswalk of Levels 0.5 Through IV

Criteria Dimension	Levels of service				
	Level 0.5 Early intervention	OMT	Level I Outpatient services	Level II.1 Intensive outpatient	Level II.5 Partial hospitalization
Dimension 1: Alcohol intoxication or withdrawal potential	No withdrawal risk.	Patient is physiologically dependent on opiates and requires OMT to prevent withdrawal.	I-D, Ambulatory detoxification without extended on-site monitoring. Minimal risk of severe withdrawal.	Minimal risk of severe withdrawal.	II-D, Ambulatory detoxification with extended on-site monitoring. Moderate risk of severe withdrawal.
Dimension 2: Biomedical conditions and complications	None or very stable.	None or manageable with outpatient medical monitoring.	None or very stable.	None or not a distraction from treatment and manageable in Level II.1.	None or not sufficient to distract from treatment and manageable in Level II.5.
Dimension 3: Emotional and behavioral conditions and complications	None or very stable.	None or manageable in outpatient structured environment.	None or very stable.	Mild severity, with potential to distract from recovery; needs monitoring.	Mild-to-moderate severity, with potential to distract from recovery; needs stabilization.

Dimension 4: Treatment acceptance and resistance	Willing to understand how current use may affect personal goals.	Resistance high enough to require structured therapy to promote treatment progress but will not render outpatient treatment ineffective.	Willing to cooperate but needs motivating and monitoring strategies.	Resistance high enough to require structured program but not so high as to render outpatient treatment ineffective.	Resistance high enough to require structured program but not so high as to render outpatient treatment ineffective.
Dimension 5: Relapse and continued use potential	Needs understanding of, or skills to change, current use patterns.	High risk of relapse or continued use without OMT and structured therapy to promote treatment progress.	Able to maintain abstinence or control use and pursue recovery goals with minimal support.	Intensification of addiction symptoms, despite active participation in Level I, and high likelihood of relapse or continued use without close monitoring and support.	Intensification of addiction symptoms, despite active participation in Level I or II.1; high likelihood of relapse or continued use without monitoring and support.
Dimension 6: Recovery environment	Social support system or significant others increase risk for personal conflict about alcohol or drug use.	Supportive recovery environment and patient has skills to cope with outpatient treatment.	Supportive recovery environment and patient has skills to cope.	Environment unsupportive, but with structure and support, the patient can cope.	Environment is not supportive, but with structure and support and relief from the home environment, the patient can cope.

Note. From the American Society of Addiction Medicine's *Patient Placement Criteria for the Treatment of Substance-Related Disorders* (2nd ed., 1996). Reprinted with permission. Copies may be ordered at 800-844-8948. OMT = opioid maintenance therapy.

Appendix B

Handouts From the Matrix Center

Matrix Center, Inc., was founded in 1984 to provide empirically based treatment services and conduct research in the field of substance abuse. More than 10,000 alcohol and drug users have received treatment at the network of six Matrix Center clinics in the Los Angeles area, providing a diverse population with which to refine the manuals. The four original manuals were funded by the National Institute on Drug Abuse and the National Institute on Alcoholism and Alcohol Abuse and were subsequently modified for specialized situations. The following handouts represent some examples of the materials integrated into the training package and can be obtained from the Matrix Center, 10350 Santa Monica Boulevard, Suite 330, Los Angeles, CA 90025.

Recovery Checklist
(Use in Second Individual Session)

Outpatient treatment requires a lot of motivation and a great deal of commitment. To get the most from treatment, it is necessary to change many old habits and replace them with new behaviors.

Check all the things that you do (or have done) since entering treatment:

_____ Schedule on a daily basis

_____ Visit physician for checkup

_____ Eliminate all paraphernalia

_____ Avoid alcohol users

_____ Avoid drug users

_____ Avoid bars and clubs

_____ Stop using alcohol

_____ Stop using all drugs

_____ Pay financial obligations promptly

_____ Identify "addict" behaviors

_____ Avoid triggers (when possible)

_____ Use thought-stopping for cravings

_____ Attend individual sessions

_____ Attend educational lectures

_____ Attend early recovery and relapse prevention groups

_____ Attend 12-step meetings

_____ Get a sponsor

_____ Exercise on a daily basis

_____ Discuss your thoughts, feelings, and behaviors honestly with your counselor

Which of the above are easiest for you to do?

_____

_____

Which of the above take the most effort for you to do?

_____

_____

Which have you not done yet? Why not?

_____

_____

_____

Triggers

Triggers are people, places, objects, feelings, and times that cause cravings. For example, if every Friday night someone cashes a paycheck, goes out with friends, and uses cocaine, the triggers would be

- Friday night
- After work
- Money
- Friends who use
- The bar or club.

Your addicted brain associates the triggers with alcohol or drug use. As a result of constant triggering and using, one trigger can cause you to move toward alcohol or drug use. The trigger–thought–craving–use cycle feels overwhelming.

An important part of treatment involves stopping the craving process. The first and easiest way to do that is

1. Identify triggers.
2. Prevent exposure to triggers whenever possible (e.g., do not handle large amounts of cash).
3. Deal with triggers in a different way (e.g., scheduling exercise and a 12-step meeting for Friday nights).

Remember, triggers will affect your brain and cause cravings even though you have decided to stop alcohol or drug use. Your intentions to stop must therefore translate into behavior changes that steer you clear of possible triggers.

THE GUN IS LOADED.

TAKE YOUR FINGER OFF THE TRIGGER

---

1) What are some of the strongest triggers for you?

_____   _____

_____   _____

2) What particular triggers might be a problem in the near future?

_____   _____

_____   _____

Trigger–Thought–Craving–Use

The Losing Argument

If you decide to stop drinking or using and end up moving toward alcohol or drugs, your brain gives you permission by using a process we call *relapse justification*. Using and drinking thoughts start an argument inside your head: your rational self versus your addiction. You feel as though you are in a fight and you must come up with many reasons to stay clean. Your addiction is really just looking for the excuse, a relapse justification. The argument inside you is part of a series of events leading to drug or alcohol use. How often in the past has your addiction lost this argument?

Thoughts Become Cravings

Craving does not always occur in a straightforward, easily recognized form. Often, the thought of drinking or using passes through your head with little or no effect. It takes effort to identify and stop a thought. However, allowing yourself to continue thinking about drug or alcohol use is choosing to begin a relapse. The further the thoughts are allowed to go, the more likely you are to relapse.

The "Automatic" Process

During addiction, triggers, thoughts, cravings, and use all seem to run together. However, the usual sequence goes like this:

$$\text{Trigger} \rightarrow \text{Thought} \rightarrow \text{Craving} \rightarrow \text{Use}$$

Thought-Stopping

The key to success in dealing with this process is to not let it get started. Stopping the thought when it first begins prevents it from building into an overpowering craving. It is important to do it as soon as you recognize the thoughts occurring.

Thought-Stopping Techniques

A New Sequence

To get recovery started, it is necessary to change the trigger–use sequence. Thought-stopping provides a tool for breaking the process. The choice is

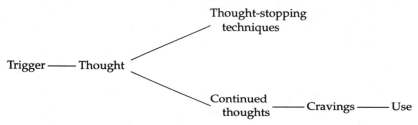

You make a choice. It is not automatic.

Thought-Stopping Techniques

Try the techniques described and use those that work best for you.

Visualization: Picture a switch or a lever in your mind. Imagine yourself actually moving it from on to off to stop the alcohol or drug thoughts. Have another picture ready to think about in place of those thoughts. You may have to change what you are doing to make this switch.

Snapping: Wear a rubber band on your wrist loosely. Each time you become aware of alcohol or drug thoughts, snap the band and say "no!" to the thoughts as you make yourself think about another subject. Have a subject ready that is something meaningful and interesting to you.

Relaxation: Feelings of hollowness, heaviness, and cramping in the stomach are cravings. These can often be relieved by breathing in deeply (filling lungs with air) and breathing out very slowly Do this three times. You should be able to feel the tightness leaving your body. Repeat this whenever the feeling returns.

Call someone: Talking to another person provides an outlet for your feelings and allows you to hear your own thinking process. Have phone numbers of supportive, available people with you always so you can use them when you need them.

> **ALLOWING THE THOUGHTS TO DEVELOP INTO CRAVINGS IS MAKING A CHOICE TO REMAIN AN ADDICT OR ALCOHOLIC**

External Trigger Questionnaire

1. Place a check mark next to activities or situations that go with drug or alcohol use for you. Place a zero (0) next to activities or situations during which you would never drink or use.

_____ Home alone

_____ Home with friends

_____ Friend's home

_____ Parties

_____ Sporting events

_____ Movies

_____ Bars or clubs

_____ Beach

_____ Concerts

_____ Driving

_____ Before a date

_____ During a date

_____ Before sexual activities

_____ During sexual activities

_____ After sexual activities

_____ Before work

_____ When carrying money

_____ After going past dealer's residence

_____ With particular people

_____ After payday

_____ Before going out to dinner

_____ Before breakfast

_____ At lunch break

_____ While at dinner

_____ After work

_____ After passing a particular freeway exit

_____ School

2. List any other settings or activities where you frequently use alcohol or drugs.

_____

3. List activities during which you would not drink or use drugs.

_____

4. List people you could be with and not drink or use drugs.

_____

5. Enter your triggers on the chart that follows.

_____

Trigger Chart

Name: _____   Date: _____

Instructions: List triggering people, places, objects, or situations in the columns below with the strongest triggers in the far right column. Put "safe" people, places, and things in the far left column and milder triggers in between.

Never Use	Almost never use	Almost always use	Always use
0% Chance of using or drinking			100% Chance of using or drinking
_____	_____	_____	_____
_____	_____	_____	_____
_____	_____	_____	_____
_____	_____	_____	_____
_____	_____	_____	_____
_____	_____	_____	_____
These are "safe" situations.	These are low risk, but caution is needed.	These situations are high risk. Staying in these is extremely dangerous.	Involvement in these situations is deciding to stay addicted. Avoid totally.

STAYING SOBER IS A CHOICE

Internal Trigger Questionnaire

During recovery there are often certain feelings or emotions that trigger the brain to think about drinking or using drugs. Read the following list of emotions and indicate which of them might trigger (or used to trigger) thoughts of using for you:

____ Afraid	____ Frustrated	____ Neglected
____ Angry	____ Guilty	____ Nervous
____ Confident	____ Happy	____ Passionate
____ Criticized	____ Inadequate	____ Pressured
____ Depressed	____ Insecure	____ Relaxed
____ Embarrassed	____ Irritated	____ Sad
____ Excited	____ Jealous	
____ Exhausted	____ Lonely	

A. I thought about drinking or using when I felt:

_____

_____

B. Circle the above emotional states or feelings that have triggered your use of drugs or alcohol recently.

C. Has your use in recent weeks or months been

____ 1. Primarily tied to emotional conditions

____ 2. Routine and automatic without much emotional triggering.

D. Are there any times in the recent past in which you were attempting to not use and a specific change in your mood clearly resulted in your taking a drink or using chemicals? (For example, you got in a fight with someone and used or drank in response to getting angry.) Yes ____ No ____

If yes, describe: _____

E. Go back to the trigger chart and enter these triggers.

Five Common Problems in Early Recovery: New Solutions

Everyone who attempts to stop alcohol and drug use runs into situations that make it very difficult to maintain sobriety. Listed below are five of the most common situations that are encountered during the first few weeks of treatment. Next to these problems are some suggested alternatives for dealing with these situations.

Problem	New Alternative
Happy-Hour Syndrome	*During These Time Periods*:
An automatic feeling at specific times of day that a drink would be very satisfying.	Schedule attendance at Matrix or a 12-step meeting. Schedule exercises. Plan an activity with a sober friend or family member.
Anger and Irritability	*Tell Yourself that*:
Small events can create feelings of anger that seem to preoccupy the thinking process.	Recovery involves a healing of brain chemistry. Moods will be affected; it's a natural part of recovery. Exercise helps. Talking to a therapist or supportive friend helps.
Alcohol in the Home	
Because you decide to stop drinking, it doesn't mean everyone else in your house decides to stop.	Get rid of all drugs and alcohol, if possible. Ask others if they would refrain from drinking and using at home for a while. If you continue to have a problem, consider moving for a while.
Boredom and Loneliness	
Stopping drug and alcohol use often means that many normal activities and people must be avoided.	Put new activities in your schedule. Go back to activities you enjoyed before your addiction took over. Develop new friends at AA, exchange telephone numbers.

Special Occasions

Parties, dinners, business meetings, weddings, holidays, etc. without alcohol and drugs can be difficult.

Have a plan for answering questions about not drinking.
Have your own transportation to and from events.
Leave if you get uncomfortable or start feeling deprived.

Are any of these issues likely to be a problem for you in the next few weeks? Which one?

_____

_____

_____

How will you deal with it? _____

_____

_____

Avoiding Relapse Drift

How It Happens

Relapse does not suddenly occur. It does not happen without warning and it does not happen quickly. The gradual movement, however, can be so subtle and so easily explained away (denied) that often a relapse feels like it happened suddenly. This slow movement away from sobriety can be compared to a ship gradually drifting away from where it was moored. The drifting movement can be so slow that you don't even notice it.

Interrupting the Process

During recovery each person does specific things that work to keep him or her sober. These "mooring lines" need to be clearly stated and listed in a very specific way so that they are clear and measurable. These are the ropes that hold the recovery in place and prevent the relapse drift from happening without being noticed.

Maintaining Recovery

Use the Mooring Lines Recovery Chart to list and track the things that are holding your recovery in place. Follow these guidelines when filling out the form:

1. Identify 4 or 5 *specific* things that are now helping you stay sober (e.g., working out for 20 min 3 times per week).
2. Include items such as exercise, therapist and group appointments, scheduling, 12-step meetings, eating patterns, etc.
3. Do not list attitudes. They are not as easy to measure as behaviors.
4. Note specific people or places that are known triggers and need to be avoided during the recovery.

The checklist should be completed regularly (probably weekly). When two or more items cannot be checked, it means that relapse drift is happening. Sometimes things interrupt your mooring lines. Vacation, illnesses, and holidays sometimes cannot be controlled. The mooring lines disappear. Many people relapse during these times. Use the chart to recognize when you are more likely to relapse and decide what to do to keep this from happening.

Mooring Lines Recovery Chart

In becoming sober you have had to learn to do certain new behaviors, behaviors that work for you in keeping you sober. It is too easy to accidently drop one or more of these mooring lines. That allows your recovery to drift toward relapse. Charting the new behaviors and checking occasionally to make sure the lines are secure can be very useful.

Use the chart below to list those activities that are very important to your continuing recovery. If there are specific people or things you need to avoid, list those. Look back at your list regularly to check yourself and make sure you are continuing to stay anchored in your recovery.

Mooring line behaviors	Date (✔)	Date (✔)	Date (✔)	Date (✔)	Date (✔)
1.					
2.					
3.					
4.					
5.					
I am avoiding	Date (✔)	Date (✔)	Date (✔)	Date (✔)	Date (✔)
1.					
2.					
3.					

Appendix C

Resources

Addiction Research Foundation. Treatment planning tools for and assessment of relapse hazards and relapse prevention, by Helen Annis, PhD (Inventory of Drinking Situations and the Situational Confidence Questionnaire) can be ordered in paper and pencil or client computer interactive software. 33 Russell Street, Toronto, Ontario, Canada M5S 2S1. Telephone: 1-800-661-1111.

Addiction Severity Index. Manual and tapes; Order No. AVA Delta Metrics TRI 19615VNB2, National Technical Information Services. Telephone: (703)487-4650 or 1(800)238-2433.

Alcoholics Anonymous (AA) General Services Office. Literature and audiovisual materials on alcoholism and AA. Box 459, Grand Central Station, New York, NY 10163. Telephone: (212) 870-3400.

Alcohol Use Inventory. Alcohol assessment tool available from National Computer Systems, 11000 Prairie Lakes Drive, Eden Prairie, MN 55344. Telephone: 1(800)431-1421.

Brown University Center for Alcohol and Addiction Studies. Curriculum and training materials for physicians and other health care professionals. Brown University, Box G-BH, Providence, RI 02912. Telephone: (401)863-1000.

Center for Substance Abuse Prevention (CSAP) Hotline. Helps employers, unions, and community-based substance abuse prevention organizations in the development and implementation of workplace prevention programs. Telephone: 1(800) WORKPLACE.

Center for Substance Abuse Treatment (CSAT) Hotline. Aids individuals in linking them to treatment in their communities. Telephone: 1(800)662-HELP.

Center on Addiction and Substance Abuse (CASA) at Columbia University. This organization is a multidisciplinary group that works to study and combat all forms of substance abuse. Publication Catalog. 152 W. 57th St., New York, NY 10019. Telephone: (212)841-5200.

Center on Alcoholism, Substance Abuse, and Addictions (CASAA). Motivational interviewing articles and tapes by W. R. Miller, PhD. Research Division, Department of Psychology, University of New Mexico, Albuquerque, NM 87131-1161.

Chemical Dependency Adolescent Assessment Project (CDAAP). Assessment tool for adolescent alcohol and other drug abuse. Available from Western Psychological Services, 12031 Wilshire Blvd., Los Angeles, CA 90025. Telephone: (310)478-2061.

Drug Abuse and Alcoholism Newsletter. Currently edited by Marc Schuckit, MD, this four-page newsletter covers a wide range of topics in Schuckit's highly readable style. It is distributed 10 times a year on a complimentary basis as part of the foundation's continuing education program. Vista Hill Foundation, 3420 Camino del Rio North, Suite 100, San Diego, CA 92108. Telephone: (619)563-1770.

Hazelden Foundation. Training and publications on alcohol and drug problems. Publication catalog and newsletter. 15251 Pleasant Valley Road, P.O. Box 176, Center City, MN 55012-0176. Telephone: 1(800)328-9000.

Johnson Institute. Training programs, literature, and audiovisual materials. 7205 Ohms Lane, Minneapolis, MN 55439. Telephone: 1(800)231-5165.

Matrix Institute on Addictions (Rick Rawson, PhD, and colleagues). Neurobehavioral model of outpatient stimulant addiction treatment. Manuals, slides, client worksheets. 10350 Santa Monica Boulevard, #340, Los Angeles, CA 90025. Telephone: (310)785-9666.

Narcotics Anonymous (NA) World Service Organization. 12-step program similar to AA for those involved with drugs other than alcohol. Newsletter and publications. P.O. Box 9999, Van Nuys, CA 91409. Telephone: (818)780-3951.

National Association of Alcoholism and Drug Abuse Counselors (NAADAC). Certification program for counselors. Newsletter and study guide for certification examination is available. 3717 Columbia Pike, Suite 300, Arlington, VA 22204. Telephone: (703)741-7686.

National Clearinghouse for Alcohol and Drug Information (NCADI). The information service of the Center for Substance Abuse Prevention of the U.S. Department of Health and Human Services. It serves as the central point in the federal government for information materials about alcohol and other drug problems. The Treatment Improvement Protocol Series by the Center for Substance Abuse Treatment, the Project Match Monograph Series, and National Institute of Drug Abuse Research Monographs as well as a Publications Catalog may be ordered from this source. P.O. Box 2345, Rockville, MD 20852. Telephone: (301)468-2600 or 1(800)729-6686.

Parents Resource Institute for Drug Free Education (PRIDE). Youth alcohol and drug abuse prevention programs and literature. Free catalog. 3610 Dekalb Technology Parkway, Suite 105, Atlanta, GA 30340. Telephone: (770)458-9900.

Personal Experience Screening Questionnaire (PESQ). Adolescent screening tool for alcohol and other drug use. Available from Western Psychological Services, 12031 Wilshire Blvd., Los Angeles, CA 90025.

Rutgers University Center of Alcohol Studies. Large collection of alcohol information. Free catalog. Smithers Hall, Busch Campus, Piscataway, NJ 08855-0969.

To Locate a Physician Familiar With Addiction

American Society for Addiction Medicine (ASAM). 4601 North Park Avenue, Chevy Chase, MD 20815. Telephone: (301)656-3920 or 1(800)844-8948.

American Academy of Psychiatrists in Alcoholism and Addictions. P.O. Box 376, Greenbelt, MD 20768. Telephone: (301)220-0951.

Note. Each of the above organizations can provide membership lists, but they cannot and will not recommend individuals.

Author Index

Subject Index

About the Authors

Robert D. Margolis, PhD, is a psychologist in private practice in Atlanta, Georgia. For the past 20 years he has specialized in the treatment of addictive disorders, mostly with adolescent patients, but also with adults. For the past 10 years he has served as Director of Psychological Services at Ridgeview Institute and as Program Director for the Action Program, an intensive outpatient program for adolescents with substance abuse or emotional problems, also at Ridgeview Institute.

Dr. Margolis founded and now serves as chairperson of the Colleague Assistance Committee for the Georgia Psychological Association. He has served as consultant to the American Psychological Association on professional impairment and substance abuse issues. In addition, Dr. Margolis has presented numerous training seminars and continuing education workshops and has written articles and book chapters on alcohol and other drug problems.

Joan E. Zweben, PhD, is the founder and executive director of the 14th Street Clinic and Medical Group and the East Bay Community Recovery Project in Oakland, California. These affiliated organizations have been providing medical and psychosocial services to alcohol and other drug dependent patients and their families since 1979, and are training sites for graduate students and interns in the San Francisco Bay Area. Dr. Zweben received her undergraduate degree from Brandeis University and her doctorate in psychology (clinical) from the University of Michigan. She is licensed in California, holds the American Psychological Association (APA) College Certificate of Proficiency in the Treatment of Alcohol and Other Psychoactive Substance Use Disorders, and is a Fellow of Division 50 of APA. Dr. Zweben is the author of over 40 articles and book chapters and editor of 10 monographs on treating addiction. She is active in training professionals from a variety of disciplines who work in mental health or addiction treatment settings. She is also Clinical Professor of Psychiatry in the School of Medicine, University of California, San Francisco.